Timewatch

*To the people who have talked to me about time
and specifically to Mary and Brian who have since
died of cancer*

Timewatch

The Social Analysis of Time

Barbara Adam

Polity Press

First published in 1995 by Polity Press in association with Blackwell Publishers.

Editorial office:
Polity Press
65 Bridge Street
Cambridge CB2 1UR, UK

Marketing and production:
Blackwell Publishers
108 Cowley Road
Oxford OX4 1JF, UK

238 Main Street
Cambridge, MA 02142, USA

ISBN 0 7456 1020 X
ISBN 0 7456 1461 2 (pbk)

A CIP catalogue record for this book is available from the British Library and the Library of Congress.

Typeset in 10 on 12 pt Times by Best-set Typesetter Ltd., Hong Kong

Printed and bound in Great Britain by Marston Lindsay Ross International Ltd, Oxfordshire

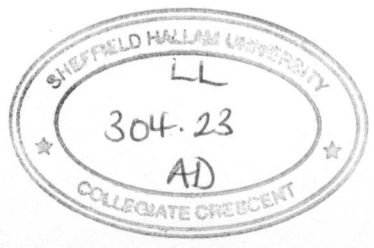

Contents

Acknowledgements

Many people have contributed to the creation of this book, most notably the people who have talked to me about how time enters their lives and what time means to them. I would like to acknowledge here their invaluable contribution. I would further like to thank Stuart Allan, Jane Lones and Fiona Mackie for reading the entire script as well as Colin Hay and Alessandra Tanesini for comments on single chapters; their constructive criticisms were invaluable and very much appreciated. My special thanks, however, go to my husband and colleague Jan Adam whose critical comment and unflinching support underpin all I have written. Moreover, none of my work would be possible if he had not taken on more than his fair share of work in our labour-intensive household. Thanks also to my family as a whole for being so tolerant and to my daughter Miriam in particular not only for stepping in when I got home late on the days when it was my turn to cook or shop but also for checking my references to such a high degree of perfection.

This book has arisen from research conducted over the past eight years and consequently draws to varying degrees on the following papers: (1988) 'Social Versus Natural Time: A Traditional Distinction Re-examined', pp. 198–226 in M. Young and T. Schuller (eds.), *The Rhythms of Society*, Routledge & Kegan Paul; (1989) 'Feminist Social Theory Needs Time. Reflections on the Relation between Feminist Thought, Social Theory and Time as an Important Parameter in Social Analysis', *Sociological Review*, 37: 458–73; (1992a) 'Modern Times: The Technology Connection and its Implications for Social Theory', *Time and Society*, 1: 175–92; (1992b) 'Time, Health Implicated: A Conceptual Critique', pp. 153–64 in R. Frankenberg (ed.), *Time and Health and Medicine*, Sage; (1992c) 'There is More to Time in Education than Calendars and Clocks', pp. 18–34 in M. Morrison, (ed.), *Managing Time for Education*, University of Warwick; (1993a) 'Within and Beyond the Time Economy of Employment Relations', *Social Science Information*, 32: 163–84; (1993b) 'Time and Environmental Crisis: An Exploration with Special Reference to Pollution', *Innovation in Social Science Research*, 6: 399–413; (1994a) 'Perceptions of Time', pp. 503–26 in T. Ingold (ed.), *Companion Encyclopedia of Anthropology, Humanity, Culture and Social Life*, Routledge; (1994b) 'Re-Vision: The Centrality of Time for an Ecological Social Science Perspective', in S. Lash, R. Grove-White, and B. Wynn (eds.), *Risk, Environment and Modernity: Towards a New Ecology*, Sage, in press; (1994c) 'Running Out of Time: Environmental Crisis and the Need for Active Engagement' in T. Benton and M. Redclift (eds.), *Social Theory and the Environment*, Routledge, in press. I would like to thank the publishers for giving permission to use some of that material and to express my appreciation to the following colleagues, students and editors who have commented on drafts of the papers: Jan Adam, Stuart Allan, Paul Atkinson, Ted Benton, Dawn Clarke, Tia DeNora, Marco Diani, Ronald Frankenberg, J. T. Fraser, Judith Green, Tim Ingold, Tom Keenoy, Alwyn Jones, George Newell, Martin Read, Michael Redclift, Teresa Rees, Tom Schuller, Ginger Weade, Brian Wynn and Michael Young.

A passage from Penelope Lively's (1991) *City of the Mind* has been reproduced by Permission of Penguin Books Ltd and Harper Collins, USA.

Finally, I would like to acknowledge a few very special books that have given me intense pleasure and provided invaluable food for thought, inspiration and, above all, a context within which to think, argue and develop: (in chronological order) Pirsig's *Zen and the Art of Motorcycle Maintenance*; Capra's *The Tao of Physics*; Sheldrake's *A New Science of Life*; Giddens's *Central Problems in Social Theory*; Kern's *The Culture of Time and Space, 1880–1918*; Stanley and Wise's *Breaking Out*; Harvey's *The Condition of Postmodernity*; Romanyshyn's *Technology as Symptom and Dream*; Hayles's *Chaos Bound*; Giddens's *Modernity and Self-Identity*; Beck's *The Risk Society*; and Ermath's *Sequel to History*.

Barbara Adam

Introduction

Conversations about time

'When I think about time I think that it won't be long before I am old and die. We have only so much time to live and that is not very long at all. Well, take my mum, for example, she is old now and she will die. (*His mother is thirty-five, suffers from multiple sclerosis and has been tied to a wheelchair for the last five years.*) When you think a lot about time it goes by that much quicker which means I grow older that much faster. On school days I just think whether it is nine o'clock yet because school starts then and I must not be late. Next I think about time at three o'clock when it is time to go home. My worst thing of thinking about time is on the days when I come home from school before my parents have returned from shopping or from the hospital which means that I have to go to a neighbour's house. This is really an awful time because I don't know how long I'll be there and when my parents will come home.'

(*David, ten years old, pupil in a village primary school*)

***

'How time enters my life? I was born and now I am fifteen years old. We use the word when we ask what time it is. We talk about closing time, lunch-time, getting-up time, and that time is up. What time is, that is more difficult to say. It is not a person, not a thing, not a vegetable. It's a period and units, the day chopped up into hours, minutes and seconds. But it also divides the past from the future. We can see the past in pictures and writing but we can't be

there – that is *a* time. *The* time is *now*, this very second. But I do not know what it is we are chopping up into units. I think it's an illusion since there isn't anything to be chopped up.'
(*Miriam, fifteen years old, pupil in a British comprehensive school*)

***

'Time is about those things that happen to you and around you, those things over which we have no control. People die, accidents happen. I have no control over when the sun or the moon come up, when the pub opens, or when my friend is going to turn up today. I could get to be 105 years old or die tomorrow. Time has to do with movement. If everything stood still there would be no time, only matter. It's a mystery which we don't think and talk about. Only in programmes like *Dr Who* does time become important with 'time lords', 'time travel' and the 'time machine'. Today everything goes by the clock but, if this hadn't been started, we might organize our lives only by the sun or something else. Time then would be something quite different.'

(*Tobias, eighteen years old, car mechanic*)

***

'Time is a scarce resource. I associate it with pressure and with the desire to use it in a meaningful way. I try to keep a very strict separation between my private and my working time; but the association with pressure and a shortage of available time is equally relevant for my private life and my working life: there is always too much to do, more than is possible. Family, friends, the house and the garden, elderly parents and making music all require time, and far more of it than I have available during my private time.

'For me time is a dimension within which everything moves and happens. In conjunction with space it is a universal framework. We can't move through space without time and vice versa which means that we can't pass, spend, or allocate time without occupying space. Nothing exists and happens without time and space.

'I think that the chronic shortage of time is linked to a steady increase of options and to growth in the potential for choice and action. Cities in particular provide us with far more possibilities than we can ever realize. At the same time, however, this widening discrepancy between the potential and that which can be realized enforces greater concentration and more focused plans and actions. It is also connected to our attitude to speed: if something can be done more quickly, then something else can be fitted into that freed-up period of time. This positive evaluation of tempo and speed – the faster the better – which permeates our contemporary life, derives from a purely economic approach to time: the bigger the quantity and the shorter the production time the better for business. This artificial, economic creation of speed as a positive value has been unquestioningly incorporated into our everyday lives. It has become a taken-for-granted fact.'

(Christoph, fifty years old, Ph.D. in philosophy, publisher,
father of three daughters)

***

'Time enters my life in two significant ways. One has to do with ageing and the life-span and the other with time passing and coping with things to be done in a day. The decades seem important – like watersheds – important points in one's life where one is so aware in terms of what one would like to *be* and *be doing* and that in turn to the *social standards* and to *expectancy*. For a mother, the daily pattern seems so predetermined and there is always this pressure to be productive and not to be wasteful. Routines are terribly important because then there is no need for thinking about it and weighing things off. This all takes time and brings with it the danger that one ends up achieving nothing. A routine is essential for security because it represents the *possible*. I can't operate without an overall scheme because this represents the frame within which things are possible – the real potential. Plans which are far into the future or for which I can see no potential just get me frustrated. It is the little plans which are achievable that lead to satisfaction, not the thoughts about big major issues. At eighteen you think about solving the world's problems but you don't get beyond it. I need to see myself being effective in my actions rather than wasting time with great schemes and plans for the distant future.

'On reflection I relate time to the day and night and the sense of the year. Whatever you do, time passes – goes on outside our control. We can't stop that process. We can't make more hours in a day. We could in terms of a convention but we would not be changing anything in terms of this ongoing process. Hours are only a particular division we have imposed on this ongoing change of night and day. It makes me think of people in places such as Iceland where they have such different daylight and darkness patterns. They must not just be living different lives but also have a different perception of themselves and differ in terms of what they expect of themselves.

'Now, my husband likes to work at night because there is less pressure. It must have to do with the feeling that he *could* go on all night and because he is not distracted by what is awaiting him afterwards. All that is expected of him at night is sleep – not so if he wants to do an hour or two of work in the morning as part of a full programme of work and meetings during a day. Night-time seems to be a different sort of time from day-time even in a physical sort of way. The homoeopath has said in relation to my son's asthma that it makes sense that he coughs most between 3 and 5 a.m. It seems research has revealed that the earth's energy field is different then – even machines have a minute change in their motion and slow down.

'Birth and death make up our life-span and yet, when people die they are not gone but leave behind a presence and so did the people before them and those before. It's a spiritual experience of presence of persons and peoples past. Anything outside the time-span of our own experience is difficult to comprehend. An oak which we know to be 400 years old, a castle or events in history – we can't really know what they experienced, what it was like then. We can only get rare insightful feelings. We value old things and try to preserve them for the future so that they may serve as records for our present and what then will be the past. We are deeply interested in finds which connect us to the distant past, be they archeological finds of preserved people or of things made by people. We value old buildings, paintings and antique furniture. It somehow connects us to past peoples and gives us an insight into their lives, their existence, which would otherwise be beyond our reach due to the passage of time.

'That passage can be so variable. I once had my car parked on a slope outside a hotel and my baby was in a cot in the back. As I turned, standing in front of the hotel, I saw my car rolling down gathering speed and aiming for another car. I knew what I had to do. I had to run to the car, open the door, get inside and pull the handbrake. Between my seeing the car rolling and my achieving to stop it not more than a second could have passed and yet, time was suddenly stretched out to become eternal – everything seemed possible.'

[After that we entered an interesting dialogue about the many devices we have to stop, slow down, or speed up time, in other words, how we try to gain control over, or cheat, that which seems so firmly located outside our influence: time. We talked about trying to stay young, about preventing decay and making plans

for the future, about insurance, LSD, hypnosis, meditation, religion, art, architecture, writing, printing, language, technology,
tradition . . .]
(Mary, forty-two years, Joint Honours student of psychology and
sociology, ex-teacher and art administrator, mother of three boys.
Four years after this interview Mary died of cancer.)

***

Time forms such an integral part of our lives that it is rarely thought
about. There is no need, it seems, to reflect on the matter since daily life,
the chores, routines and decisions, the coordination of actions, the deadlines and schedules, the learning, plans and hopes for the future can be
achieved without worrying about what time might be. It is, in fact,
extraordinarily difficult to think and talk about time. Only very special
circumstances such as these long, interactive, conversation-interviews
seem to allow for the necessary reflective attitude to probe beyond the
most superficial single associations – clocks and calendars, opening
times, timetables, seasons – and for bringing to the surface what we
normally take for granted. Such conversations invariably evoke total
surprise at the degree of difficulty encountered in attempts to talk about
the role and nature of time. It was something none of my interlocutors
had ever been asked to think or talk about. When they did engage with
the topic, death emerged as an unexpected feature of their reflections.
This tended to be the case irrespective of the respondents' age and
personal situation. While they were taken aback by the complexity of the
task, I was amazed at the variation and uniqueness of the answers.
Everyone, it seems, holds a very exclusive, personal meaning-cluster of
time, a distinct but not fixed composition, one open to changes and
linked to shifts in personal circumstances, emotional states, health, age
and context. That which is rarely thought about thus constitutes a central
component in our tacit knowledge-base. Multiple, composite, simultaneous, open-ended and changing, those personal meanings are at variance
with the majority of social studies of time and their respective theoretical
bases. This book is an attempt to take seriously the complexity of social
time as it arises from personal accounts, academic research, and to a very
limited extent from fiction, and to explore its implications for social
science theory and practice.

If one-to-one conversations about time show us the multiplicity and
breadth of conceptualizations of time in sequence, workshops on the role
and nature of time in everyday life allow us to observe that complexity all
at once: the network of meanings becomes visible as it is assembled from

the variety of brief and rather restricted reflections of individual group members. It takes on form as one thought triggers off others in the various members of a workshop. In such collective thinking situations, the association of time with clocks and calendars combines with that of deadlines, chores, routines, milestones, stress and ageing. Feelings that time presents constraint, discipline, control and structure are shared with the experience of time in terms of opportunity, points of reference and order or of celestial motion, the rhythms of the body and social organization. A sense of pressure and shortage or the need to prioritize and wait are complemented by an appreciation of time as a process of learning and healing or as luxury and relativity. The past, present and future get joined up with life-stages, activity and the commodity. Weekends, working days and the educational calendar are linked to time as organization, coordination, experience, memories and fears. Thus, once we bring the taken-for-granted to the forefront of our attention, the spell of clock time is broken. The invisible is given form.

In this book I want to continue this process, to move beyond the time of clocks and calendars and to make explicit what constitutes a largely unreflected aspect of contemporary social science: time embedded in social interactions, structures, practices and knowledge, in artefacts, in the mindful body, and in the environment. I do not aim to familiarize the reader with existing studies and theories of social time. I have written about these extensively in other work (Adam 1988, and 1990 especially Chapter 1) and, moreover, since then excellent reviews (Bergmann 1992, Nowotny 1992) and a journal (*Time and Society*) have been published which can provide that information. Instead, I want to bring time in its multiple expressions to the forefront of our social-science understanding and introduce its central role in and for our subject matter, methods and theories. In all of these domains it is the multiplicity, simultaneity and mutual implication that pose the biggest challenge to established traditions: the rational approach of abstraction, reduction and objective observation falsifies temporal experience and misses the central characteristics of the phenomena under investigation. The chapters that follow set out some of those constantly shifting, transient complexities and explore ways of keeping together what social science traditions have taken apart, namely, time with reference to the personal–public, local–global, natural–cultural dimensions of social life and in relation to the subjective–objective, synchronic–diachronic, linear–cyclical and contextual–general parameters of social theory.

In '"My" Time, "Our" Time, "Other" Time' I focus on one personal moment and from there I let the social times unfold. I move from the 'I' to the 'We' to the 'Other', from the personal via the collective to the distant stranger, and establish simultaneously both a stronger collective temporal base and sharper differentiating features than are generally allowed for in traditional anthropological and historical studies. I demonstrate the coexistence of multiple times, reveal how language provides us with clues about this multiplicity and show how the resultant complexity cannot be contained within the classical dualisms of social science analyses. I thus pay serious attention to everyday experience and make the personal central to my work. I give a detailed account of clock time and offer a first analysis that serves as broad basis for all the other themes to which clock time is central. This allows me to home in on specific aspects of clock time in later chapters and avoid unnecessary repetition. Finally, I argue for the importance of getting to know the unreflected backcloth of 'own' time upon which 'other' times are constructed. Concern with the disattended temporalities of the social sciences' subject matters as well as the researchers' own methods and theories is central to this work and guides the approach to each of the subjects that follow.

Focus on the taken-for-granted and emphasis on the everyday and personal experience are continued in Chapter 2, 'Of Time and Health, Life and Death'. Here I stress the mutual implication of time and health, life and death and demonstrate how the times of 'nature' and the mindful body are inseparable from human being, well-being and processes of everyday life. I then address once more a theme opened up in the previous chapter: the complex relationship between clock time which foregrounds chronology, finitude and death and the life-generating times of the procreative body embedded in the rhythms of its 'natural' environment. Through the example of birthing I explicate how encounters with life and death take those involved beyond the realm of everyday time and how they bring to the fore times that are normally disattended, even submerged in subconscious being. Most importantly, I argue that the times of the mindful body and the physical environment cannot be excluded from social science analysis and that we need to bring together mutual implications and contextual–personal differences of times in analyses of specific events. Finally, I show how the way time is conceptualized makes a difference, how it affects not merely social science practice but our daily lives, our health and our relationship to birth and death.

The dominant approach to time, the way time is conceptualized, related to and used, tends to be established during childhood. Thus, in Chapter 3, 'Education: Learning the Habits of Clock-time' I show how the institutional structures and practices of Western-style education work to socialize, habituate and train young people into the clock-time approach to time which, in turn, has the effect of pushing into oblivion the myriad of times that make up the temporal complexity of everyday life. I provide some historical background to the tightly choreographed routines of school life and reveal the roots of the prevalent time discipline in the triad of the monastic rules of St Benedict, the rise of science and the development of clock time for the mediation of natural and cultural processes. I suggest that social scientists in general and educational researchers in particular have to penetrate beyond the dominant times of clocks and calendars, timetables and schedules to the complexity of times – lived, experienced, generated, known, reckoned, allocated, controlled and used as an abstract exchange value – if they are fully to grasp time in educational practice and if such research is to bring about change not only in contemporary education but also in the children's later lives. I explain how existing approaches to social time mirror perspectives in education and educational research and suggest that the tradition is inadequate for the comprehensive mapping of educational time. I argue the need to take account of time-based invisibles such as aspects of the multiple life-worlds and the past–future extension; and, on the basis of my analysis, I caution against generalizations across time and the belief in an objectively observable reality uncontaminated by observation and unaffected by time. Finally, I analyse the relevance of Marx's, Durkheim's, Mead's and Schutz's writings on time for contemporary analyses of social life in general and educational practice in particular, before I consider some of the implications for social science of taking the complexity of times seriously.

In Chapter 4, 'The Time Economy of Work Relations' I examine contemporary work rhythms, their sources and their implications for participants. I demonstrate the connection between clock time, money, speed and efficiency and indicate how the market economy depends on a standardized, decontextualized, commodified time. Closely associated are both my exploration of 'free time' and a discussion of the high value of speed and flexibility. I show 'free time' to be not free but *produced time* which renders it inapplicable to all those outside paid employment, and I propose that the valorization of speed and flexibility has to be appreciated in relation to the economic principles of profit, efficiency and competition. In the context of work I consider women's ambiguous relationship to time and argue that a time that is generated and given cannot be encompassed within the time economy of employment relations. I demonstrate, in other words, that many women's times as well as the times of all those outside the time of markets and paid employment are not translatable into an abstract exchange value, that such time, therefore, is constituted in the shadow of the market economy. In addition, I suggest that the important feminist deconstructions of social time are in danger of being reabsorbed into the very framework of analysis they make problematic as long as women's time is conceptualized dualistically, that is, in contradistinction to men's time and the commodified time of the market. This means that neither contemporary Marxian, Weberian and Functionalist analyses of work time nor feminist deconstructions are adequate to embrace the temporal complexity of contemporary work relations. I insist, instead, on the need to take account of personal experience and a wide range of other sources of information, sources which are normally not admissible as social science evidence, and on the value of establishing these as bases for more appropriate conceptualizations of the complexity of contemporary working times.

In Chapter 5, 'Global Times and the Electronic Embrace', I focus on phenomena and practices that entail or bring about globalized times and I speculate on some global futures. I explore the influence of technology on the global present, global time zones, standard time and world time, all of which constitute the framework for a global perspective. I examine the technologies of clocks, heat-engines and electronic communication for their suitability as metaphors for the social times of contemporary social life and argue the need for social scientists to reconceptualize some of their basic premises such as the exclusion of technological principles, the evasion of ontological questions and the dependence on nation states as a primary unit of analysis. The traditional conceptual tools need to be supplemented and to some extent displaced by simultaneity, instantaneity, uncertainty and implication, all key features of global time, if social science is to become adequate to its contemporary subject matter.

In Chapter 6, 'The Times of Global Environmental Change' I explore substantive issues of pollution and identify their temporal character before investigating some of the conceptual issues relevant for effective action. I show how the time characteristics of pollution – out-of-sync time-frames, time-lags, vastly expanded time-horizons, uncertainty and longevity of materials – are handled with political 'short-termism', economic production for obsolescence, and positivist science. I demonstrate further how in the face of global environmental hazards the construction of nature as 'other' is losing its meaning and natural status. The focus on environmental time thus aids the re-vision of social science, its assumptions about the nature–culture relation and the role of nature for and in the social sciences. Like Chapter 2, this chapter on environmental time highlights the fundamental implication and interpenetration of nature and culture. Beyond this corrective, it stresses the need for active engagement and concern with the uncertainty of a science-based im/ material future. The circle then closes with a demonstration of the importance of everyday life as a source for theoretical inspiration: we are back at ' "My" Time, "Our" Time "Other" Time' with a densely woven net of inseparable connections and nodal points, each one implicating the rest and vice versa.

In the last chapter I draw out the consequences for social science of both the findings and the approach. This involves drawing on contemporary theories of the complexity of life and identifying common bases, points of departure, and potential directions for a time-sensitive social science. That is to say, in 'The "Temporal Turn": Mapping the Challenge' I step back from the material presented in Chapters 1–6 and locate the implications of my time-based approach with reference to issues raised in postmodernist thought and chaos theory. I discuss the importance of the re-visionary concept of implication and show its relevance for as well as its relation to postmodernist critiques of a 'metaphysics of presence', 'logocentrism', objectivity and truth. I make visible the in/visibilities and im/materialities of contemporary existence and explore the tensions that arise from taking seriously what remains disattended in traditional approaches. Finally, I demonstrate the inescapability of responsibility. I argue the need for engagement once we appreciate that not only is the personal political but the political personal, not only the scientific subjective but the subjective scientific, not only the local global but the global local. Recognition of this changes personal responsibility from an option to a moral imperative and from a scientific taboo to a necessity.

This book is not conceived as a story with a beginning and end. With the exception of the first and last chapters, which ought to be read first and last respectively, readers may enter anywhere, start from any point, and begin to weave the web until the point is reached where the connections of each to all are established. Each chapter tells a different part of the story, focuses on different aspects of the complexity of time, and brings to the fore different theoretical and methodological considerations. Thus, the first chapter provides a very detailed account of clock time which is then presupposed in the other chapters which, in turn, highlight different aspects and implications of the dominant clock-time view of time. Chapter 2 uses focus on the body to give a detailed account of 'natural time' which is then taken as given in other chapters, particularly in Chapter 6 on environmental time. Chapter 3 on education is utilized to show the importance and relevance for contemporary social science of the classical approaches to time of theorists such as Heidegger, Mead and Schutz and to draw out methodological considerations that apply equally to all the other chapters. Chapter 4 elaborates the link between Weber's writings on the protestant ethic and economic approaches to time, taking as given the discussion in Chapter 1 on clock time and Marx's theory of the commodification of time. This chapter also details feminist responses to theories of time, as do the accounts of body and environmental time. Finally, the chapters on globalization and the environment focus on the impact of technology on everyday life and theory. Thus, while able to stand on their own, the chapters tell a networked story. Each single chapter implicates the others, presupposes them for an adequate grasp of the complexities of times at the level of everyday life, social theory and social science practice. With this book I put into practice Derrida's (1982: 6) insight that 'there is nowhere to *begin* the sheaf or the graphics of *différance*. For what is put into question is precisely the quest for a rightful beginning, an absolute point of departure.'

Insofar as there has to be a sequence and a rationale for the order of the issues raised, I move from the personal to the global and from the substantive to the theoretical. These divisions and 'progressions', however, are merely ones of emphasis in a book where focus on any one sphere implicates the others and where attempts at linear, cumulative exposition are continuously foiled by multiple connections, relations and permeations. Multiplicity, simultaneity and implication are therefore key features of this work, while the struggle to 'tell a story' that can have no beginning and no end determines its particular style. For inspiration and for 'evidence' I draw on a multitude of sources ranging from personal experiences and fiction to research findings and media coverage. I am particularly committed to giving an authoritative voice to the many people who have talked to me about time and to foregrounding the everyday and the personal. This embodying and contextualizing of understanding is to be achieved, however, without losing sight of the equally important universal and global features of social life. With respect to style, I have resorted to using a more literary mode of expression wherever the linear, rational method of social science discourse failed me in my endeavour to convey the complexity, simultaneity and mutual implication of social times.

Finally, it is important to note that the explicit focus on time forces us to question established traditions, deprives us of old certainties and presents us instead with potential. It puts us under pressure to *make* theory rather than reinterpret existing thought, to *become* theorists rather than historians of classical and contemporary ideas. Even more importantly, it suggests ways not merely to deconstruct but to reconstruct both common-sense and social science understanding. It offers openings for important reconceptualizations which will be necessary if we as social scientists, as citizens, as educators and as parents are to be active participants in the creation of a viable twenty-first century.

1

'My' Time, 'Our' Time, 'Other' Time

There is no single time, only a multitude of times which interpenetrate and permeate our daily lives. Most of these times are implicit, taken for granted, and seldom brought into relation with each other: the times of consciousness, memory and anticipation are rarely discussed with reference to situations dominated by schedules and deadlines. The times expressed through everyday language tend to remain isolated from the various parameters and boundaries through which we live *in* time. Matters of timing, sequencing and prioritizing stay disconnected from collective time structures, and these in turn from the rhythms, the transience and the recursiveness of daily existence. It is a central argument of this book that this complexity needs to be understood and conceptualized, that it must not remain an untheorized backdrop to contemporary social science analyses. I begin this process of explication by focusing on just one moment of my time, a point in time that illustrates the mutual implication of own, collective and other time.

Just one moment of 'my' time

She points to the exits, shows us how to breathe through an oxygen mask and demonstrates how to put on and inflate a life-jacket. The early morning sunshine is blazing through the tiny windows. The newspaper gives detail and background to yesterday's news and to the ongoing war in the former Yugoslavia.

No other form of transport separates my life so remorselessly into distinct before-and-after sections. A flight interrupts the flow of living. Everything about it contributes towards a watershed between what I had been doing so far and what I was going to do: the necessary trust in a technology far removed from my daily interactions, the distances, heights and speeds involved, the emergency procedure, the performance of getting on and off a plane, the crossing of time zones and the attendant gaining or losing time depending on whether we move west or east respectively. And yet, there is continuity. It extends backwards from concern about the safety of my car in the long-term car park, to the smooth journey to the airport and the correctly estimated travel time from home, to worries about whether the house has been left in a safe condition, decisions about packing, via reflections on unfinished work in college right back to my childhood. Equally, it extends forward to the impending meeting, hospital visits, friends and relatives, work in progress, immanent and long-term plans for the future.

My ears are popping. I change the time of my watch and despair about the (all-too-customary) incurred delay at take-off. I think of my brother. When I rang last night he had not regained consciousness. They said in the hospital that even though this was an unusually long delay it was still within the range of the normal for open-heart surgery – not yet cause for concern. When we left this morning it was too early to inquire. There will be no more news until I meet my sister at the airport. The lack of information places him and our relationship in limbo. Images of injuries and pain in instances where I had been with him merge with visions of him now: in hospital on a life-support machine, a severed ear on a skiing holiday, a bad tooth extraction, a fall from a tree.

He was showing off in the school garden. He had climbed higher and more daringly than ever before that summer and now he was showing off. I don't know what I was more worried about, that one of the teachers would find him or that he might fall down. I went back to the class-room so that I could not be implicated. As the older sister I was always held responsible for his bad behaviour.

I did not see him fall. I only heard the kids give a subdued scream in unison and I remember that the school yard went unnaturally quiet after that. It took a while for the realization that something was wrong to sink in. I can still feel the crisp air, the bright blue sky and the warm September sun, the clothes I was wearing, the argument I had had with my father about wearing knee-socks.

Almost as soon as I had turned to leave the class-room I knew that something was wrong and I wished, I wished so hard, that it was not true. They were all clustered around the tree at the end of the school garden. No teachers stood out in the crowd. As I got closer the tight knot of kids had already begun to loosen. I think some of my friends told me that he was all right but I don't think I heard that. All I remember is the deep panic, the laming feeling that engulfed my whole being while I was trying to get there.

And then I saw him standing – he looked very pale – in almost unflustered cockiness, investigating his limbs.

As the years went by, the height from which he fell increased with every telling of the story and so did the magnitude of the miracle of his unscathed survival. I had no means of putting my usual dampener on his story. I was not there. Mine is a memory of worry and terror.

My father died because they had not developed open-heart surgery when he needed it thirty years ago . They say it is a routine operation by now. My brother assured everyone, including himself, that he would be all right; all the same, he said goodbye and put all his affairs in order. Unlike the routine confrontation with the potentiality of death during a flight, this encounter is more unique, more direct, goes deeper and re-sulted in action: I regularly plan to see the notary – he made a will. There is, however, a similarity in the trust we both had to extend: to the pilot, the design of this plane and its maintenance on one hand and to the surgeon, the anaesthetist, the medical technology and drug companies on the other. There is a personal dimension in the case of my brother's open-heart surgery that is lacking in a flight situation, but the degree of distance from the respective expert systems seems quite compatible. 'I put myself in thy hands' used to be an integral part of the dialogue with God. Today it is an irreducible part of secular existence: we live it on a daily basis each time we interact with the products of science and with expert systems.

While the one stewardess is still busy taking off her demonstration life-jacket, another offers me a drink and asks me to put down my tray. Securely rooted in my past and extended towards my future, I have no choice but to embrace uncertainty.

***

The last few pages describe a moment which lasted no longer than it took for the stewardess to point to the exits and demonstrate the use of the oxygen mask and the life-jacket. This brief moment, though unique in my life, is not exceptional with respect to time. Memories – sudden sharp ones and generalized amorphous ones – are integral to every moment of our being. The simultaneity of mundane, extraordinary and global events, of past, present and future, of being at home, in hospital, in college, in an Eastern European region ravaged by war, in a different time zone and in a school garden of an earlier historical period, all this constitutes part of contemporary temporal existence. Contents differ but the principle remains the same: we are temporally extended in time and space. We transcend not just our present but our historical, socio-cultural and geographical location. Moreover, our temporal being expands beyond our personal boundaries to significant others and even to strangers. Our relationship to them constitutes part of who we are.

If we reflect on that moment we find that time enters into every tiniest aspect of it. Time is implicated in the attention to instructions and the headlines in the newspaper, in the expectations, images and reflections, in the memories, worries and enforced trust. It is central to the considerations and calculations, the weighing off and the decisions. It is fundamental to the sequences, durations and simultaneities of thoughts and actions, to knowledge of traffic rhythms and to routines on aeroplanes, in colleges and hospitals. It is part of seasons and our relationship to them. It permeates the multiple systems of communication from language to telephones and radio as well as the knowledge that there are good and bad, right and wrong times for doing and saying things. Moreover, the time inherent in that moment is multifaceted: time has something to do not only with clocks or timing but also with sequential ordering according to priorities. It further relates to irreversible changes, records and identity, to both cyclical and linear processes and, last but not least, it is used and controlled as a resource. Time is simultaneously experienced and constituted, abstracted and reified. All these aspects of time are equally important. None can be excluded when one seeks to understand that moment in its temporal entirety. To isolate one aspect for study without having all the others implicated is to falsify the experience. Moreover, those thoughts, feelings, memories, awarenesses, the working knowledge and the states of consciousness did not happen in sequence. They were present simultaneously. The order in which I recounted them seems irrelevant. Other sequences would have been equally valid since nothing was causally related. There was an instruction about actions to be taken in the event of an emergency. What followed coexisted in that moment of consciousness. The awareness of the engine noise, the renewed resolve to make a will, the knowledge of my brother's suspension between life and death, all were coeval with the memory of my brother's fall and seeing the headline about the war, with the uncertainty and the anxiety tinged with hope, with the irritation about the delayed take-off and my contemplating the possibility of dying in an airline crash. The multiplicity of awarenesses, choices, memories, considerations as well as the trust in technology and expert systems were all present at the same time. Yet, despite this simultaneity, there was sequential order. Nothing was jumbled. Nothing happened backwards. The coexistence was coherent.

Focus on just one moment, therefore, allows us to see what tends to be obscured in studies of longer events and research on, for example, work,

education, city rhythms, hospital routines or daily time use. It brings to
the forefront the multiplicity, simultaneity, boundedness and extension
of times without masking their direction and order. It makes our tacit
knowledge visible and shows that the time of clocks and calendars is but
one aspect of the many times that bear on our lives simultaneously. It
demonstrates that the time which marks minutes and hours, the days of
the week and months of the year, the time that fixes decades and centuries as well as time zones, is only one, if a central, part of contemporary
Western time.

Calendar and clock time are important but they take no priority
within that brief moment. As multiple parameters and frames within
which life is conducted and organized they are an integral component of
this fraction of life. There can be no doubt that they matter. The time of
the day, for example, makes a difference. There is little traffic between
four and six o'clock in the morning so this was a good time for a smooth
journey to the airport. But, it was the wrong time to ring up the hospital.
We had a one-hour delay at take-off because seven o'clock is one of
the busiest departure times at London's Heathrow airport, with planes
taking people to early-morning meetings all over Europe. Travelling
times on the road and in the air can be predicted on the basis of past
experience and the common knowledge that traffic follows a daily
rhythm of peaks and troughs. Equally relevant is the time of the year: the
peak travelling period is just coming to an end. School has started back
after the long summer holidays. In (British) universities preparations are
well on their way for the Michaelmas term and a new intake of students.
The days are getting shorter and the periods of darkness expanding. The
glorious autumn sunshine has an uplifting effect on everybody and keeps
at bay the expectation of winter, the spectre of darkness and gloom.
Those examples are some of the more accessible aspects of the importance of the time of day and of the season. As clock and calendar
time they constitute the most social dimension of temporal influences
which span from the cosmic to the atomic level of our being, all equally
important if not equally visible.

Hidden from everyday understanding and social science concerns are
the effects on our being to the very last cell in our body of our environmental rhythms: day and night, moons and seasons (see also Chapter 2
on time and health). They underpin our development as humans and as
living organisms. They mark us as creatures of this earth. Those environmental changes from dark to light, warm to cold, wet to dry set the
developmental pattern for all living forms on this planet, to be internalized and adapted for specific evolutionary and environmental niches.
From cells to organs and even brain activity, our physiology is tied to

those periodicities. Women's reproductive cycles are tuned to it and so are our collective activity and rest patterns, all superbly timed and orchestrated into a symphony of rhythms. Sickness and even death tend to cluster around specific times of the day, synchronized with the temporal patterning of our earth: asthma attacks shortly after midnight, heart attacks and strokes around nine o'clock in the morning, onset of fever from bacterial infection between early morning and midday, from viral infections between early afternoon and evening (Rose 1989: 87–90). The multitude of coordinated environmental and internal rhythms give a dynamic structure to our lives that permeates every level of our existence. They constitute temporal frameworks within which activities are not only organized and planned but also timed and synchronized at varying speeds and intensity.

Thinking about time, therefore, involves rhythm with variation, a dynamic structure of framing, timing, synchronization, duration, sequence, tempo and intensity. This cluster of time characteristics is implicated at all levels of being from the most physical of planetary movements via physiological rhythms to patterns of social organization, from the taken-for-granted via the invisible to the obvious, from the imposed via the lived to the culturally constructed. All interpenetrate and have a bearing on each other. All coexist and are lived simultaneously. All are known on an everyday level with varying degrees of clarity, from the most tacit to the theorized. Social scientists, of course, tend to delimit forms of time to the social level only and within that to some very select areas. In contrast to this tradition, I want to show the advantages for social science of a closer alignment with the knowledge embedded in everyday living, of shifting the emphasis from single-perspective visions and discipline-governed concerns to the less bounded, less certain complexity we interact with on a daily basis. This necessitates that we take seriously the transitory dimension of social life. It means embracing the entropic and the creative with a commitment and resolve thus far largely evaded by social scientists, avoided for fear of the spectre of relativism.

The account of that moment on the plane is imbued with temporality, with the transient aspects of social life: the prospect of death, the awareness of the fragility of life, the continuity and ephemerality of news, the ageing of people, the technology and the machines into which they place their trust, cooling cups of coffee, disintegrating sweets, used-up fuel and energy to keep the aircraft flying. We relate tacitly knowing to all these expressions of temporality. Temporality, however, is only an aspect of the complexity of times; it is always accompanied, in addition to those already mentioned above, by aspects such as time-spans, continuities and identities. Humans, like all other beings, have a typical, if continually expanding, life-span of existence which influences actions today as well as plans for the future. When people die before that expected life-span has been reached we consider them to have died 'early' or 'before their time'. When an aeroplane crashes due to metal fatigue its age always plays an important part in the ensuing investigation. It should not have happened, it is consequently argued, since the aircraft was only three, five or however many years old. Within their life-span machines decay and people age. In living beings the temporality of decay is balanced by that of growth and renewal, with the decaying part of that inter-play increasingly gaining the upper hand as we get older. The cycle of birth and death, finally, constitutes the ultimate form of renewal and regeneration.

The temporality of life unto death and the parameter created by the cycle of birth and death are not merely endured; as humans, we have a relationship to that central dimension of existence: religions are based on questions about origin and destiny. Social customs such as the burial of the dead, the marking of birthdays and the recording of births and deaths are developed around that relationship. Even our identity is formed within its remit. Despite the fact that nothing in our body, our physical appearance or our knowledge has remained unchanged, we think of ourselves as the same person now as the one that was born many years ago, hated particular teachers, had measles on holiday in Italy, fell in love, married, had children and studied sociology. Furthermore, we re-late to each other as selves with an identity whose past has left a record, whether this be an objective biography of significant dates, a record of socially noted achievements and/or failures, or whether it be in the form of our own and other people's memory. Some of these traces remain after our death, some fade out with our extinction, others are mere flickers known to but a few. The leaving of records is one of the material ex-pressions of temporality, the census being the social equivalent to the rings in a tree trunk or geological strata.

Entailed within those processes is an irreversible unidirectionality, an arrow of time. There can be no rejuvenation, no unknowing, no reconsti-tution of pollution back into aeroplane fuel. But it is within the power of the human mind to visit past events, to re-invent them, create alternative versions and plan a multitude of futures. We are able to imagine the world in a projected future-present upon which we can reflect and make our choices. On the basis of this capacity I can be simultaneously in hospital, in college, in an aeroplane and places distant in both geography and history. It is not within our gift, however, to reverse processes. The arrow of time reigns supreme. Humans may slow down the processes of decay and ageing, fix the transient world in concepts and theories, art and artefacts, but they cannot undo their actions. Reversibility has eluded them: ageing and entropy are facts of life and material existence. People get older not younger. Cars rust; they do not get newer and shinier. In any spontaneous interaction energy is dissipated. This energy is not lost to the totality but exists in a form no longer usable for the same work. In the case of technological processes this dissipated energy constitutes pollution. Organic processes, in contrast, create time. Their arrow points not merely towards decay and death but to growth and life. The interconnectedness and interdependence between systems mean that dissipated energy of one system is utilized as a source of energy by another. We are only just beginning consciously to partake in time-creating processes, to recognize the centrality and significance of mutual implication and to apply the ecological principle to efforts to cope with pollution.

Thus, a most private moment of consciousness, a moment of 'my' time, is never just that. It is inseparable from 'our' times, the times of the environment and the social collectivity. The converse, of course, is equally the case: social knowledge, even the physical environment, is constituted through my and others' experiences, interactions and personal times. This means that 'my' time is not only irrevocably implicated in my everyday life but also in my professional activities as a sociologist: what I see, understand and write is mediated through it. Two central sources of the shared nature of 'my' time are language and the organization of collective life to the rhythm of the clock. From the moment we acquire it, language frames our temporal experiences, whilst the clock seems to mediate a large proportion of our social interactions. Focus on the way we employ the concept in everyday usage, therefore, provides a rich source of data on the breadth and diversity of times shared by people speaking the same language; focus on clock time allows us to see the backcloth upon which experiences of 'our' and 'other' times are drawn and constructed.

Cultural expressions of 'our' time: language and clocks

Words, phrases, meanings

Time is the most widely used noun in the English language. It is not surprising, therefore, that our everyday communications are full of references to it: we speak of clock time and winter time, of opening times and bad times, of the right time for action and the timing of an interaction. We refer to the time of things and processes, to a time that flies and a time that takes its toll. We move freely between all these senses of time and know them intimately without giving much thought to their differences. I want to disrupt this natural attitude by giving some attention to those differences and extracting from them clusters of characteristics that allow us to *see* the complexity. In other words, I want to make the taken-for-granted visible.

The different uses of the concept entail diverse qualities and meanings of the common term. Time is multifaceted: it is involved in physical processes and social conventions, in the abstract relations of mathematics and concrete relations between people. We measure it in clock-time units and by celestial motion, with the aid of recurrent events and through changes in our bodies. We utilize it as a medium of exchange for goods, services, or payment. We use it as a resource of nature, of society, of people, and of institutions; each in turn constituting a boundary within which choices and selections for action have to be made. Time for us is clearly not exhausted by the clock-time measure. The minute, the hour, the week, the day, the phase of the moon, the year, Christmas and Easter, production and growth cycles, generations and the lifetime of a person all form time-frames within which we plan and regulate our daily lives. The birth–death parameter, rhythms of nature, and social structures of recurring events constitute a time that allows us to live *in* time.

Looking at these different times more closely, we can identify a 'time *when*': when the fields and mountains were covered in snow, when the banks open, when traffic is at its worst, when Yugoslavia was torn apart by civil war, when BA flight 573 leaves for Munich, when my brother had a heart operation, when we were young, when the children are expected to go to bed, when school starts. In Western societies this 'when time' is likely to be based on a time grid provided by the calendar, the clock, or both, but it is unlikely that clocks and calendars will be the only sources for the timing and temporal location of these social activities and natural phenomena. Whilst airline timetables and bank opening times, for example, are unimaginable without the aid of clocks and calendars, the latter are not the sole regulators of those particular conventions. The scheduling of flights, for example, is governed equally by seasonal variation in demand, by airspace, competition and financial considerations, to name just a few additional influencing factors. Similarly, bank opening times are coordinated with the day-time working activities of those likely to use the bank's services. They are also guided by the law of the land that regulates other opening times and by reasons relating to internal work schedules and tradition. Children, in contrast, may be told that it is bed-time because it is getting dark outside or because a specific television programme has finished. For children these are far more persuasive arguments than the fact that it is eight o'clock in the evening. Furthermore, the existence of clock and calendar time does not prevent us from locating the past, present and future with reference to events, processes and social relations. I do not know the date of my brother's fall but I remember that it was autumn and the beginning of his first and my final year in primary school. When we remember our childhood, dates and clock time become irrelevant. This means that since clock and calendar time are not our only sources of reference it makes little sense to polarize 'other time', the times of earlier historical periods or those of contemporary pre-industrial societies, with the clock time of Western societies. We need to recognize that considerations relating to social interactions and the physical environment have not been replaced by the rationalization of time. Rather, they still play an important part in remembering and in deciding when it is time for certain events to take place. All we can meaningfully state is first, that our social actions can, if necessary, be internationally organized and coordinated through a standardized network of time that spans the globe, and second, that this time is deeply embedded in the fabric of Western, industrial societies. That is to say, the existence of clock time, no matter how dominant, does not obliterate the rich sources of local, idiosyncratic and context-dependent time awareness which are rooted in the social and organic rhythms of everyday life. The abstract, quantified, spatialized time of clocks and calendars forms only one aspect of the complexity of meanings associated with the time 'when', the time that forms a parameter of our existence and locates us *in* time.

This becomes even more obvious when we are dealing with 'good' and 'bad' times for action. If Western time really were characterized exclusively, or even predominantly, by the linear quantity of clock and calendar time, then any reference to 'good' and 'bad times' would be meaningless. As Gioscia (1972: 83) points out, 'in assuming that time is two-dimensional (i.e. linear), we make it impossible for phrases like "a hard time", "an easy time", a "high time," and/or "a low time" to be anything other than euphemism'. Clock and calendar time which could be dominant factors concerning the time 'when . . .' recede into the background in decisions about the 'right' time to make a will, to ring the hospital, to end a friendship or to apply for a job.

Questions about 'good' or 'bad' times for action, moreover, are primarily about *timing*, and this in turn may be dependent on a wide variety of factors. The day of the week and the hour of the day might be one consideration but other things will play an equal if not more impor-

tant role in such decisions. Issues relating to the past and future of that
particular relation or event become pertinent. The participants' information, their well-being and strengths, their skills, anxieties and weaknesses as well as the state of the relationship itself must be allowed for.
Furthermore, the socio-historical, economic and political context may
play a crucial role in decisions on what constitutes the 'right' time for
action, as will the norms, practices and values of those involved. Even the
weather and the seasons may make an important difference and might
therefore be taken into consideration.

All types of 'when time', then, could entail considerations relating to
clock and calendar time but these are never the only ones. The rhythms
of nature and the seasons, social norms, traditions and habits, physiological changes and 'social timers', knowledge of the past and anticipations
of its consequences, all are brought to bear on calculations about the
future. They all come together to be inextricably interwoven in judgements about what constitutes the 'right' time to engage in certain activities. Whilst the existence of clock time facilitates context independence
and global standardization, decisions about the timing of even the most
habitual of actions are made on a unique basis and with reference to a
particular context. 'When time', we can conclude, exists in all societies.
In their particular expressions, however, we find that some clusters of
sources are shared whilst others are culturally unique. Neither quantity
nor quality, neither society nor nature, neither the clock nor tasks seem
to form single sources to specific cultural expressions.

In addition to *timing* and the location *in* time, *temporality* forms a
central component of time in everyday English communication. Time
taking its toll, springtime and the coming alive of nature, growing old and
feeling old, these times could also be about a time 'when' – when the
apple tree blossoms, when I was born, when I am old, when my time
comes to die – but contained in these ideas is the fundamental knowledge
of irreversible change fused with cycles of return. Whereas timing and
time-frames are dominant aspects of 'when time', temporality comes to
the fore when we focus on processes. Plants grow, produce seeds and die.
People and animals are born, live and die. We speak of the cycle of life
and death. Within each cycle, however, the changes are unidirectional.
As I have already mentioned above, there can be no un-ageing, no un-
dying, no un-birth. We can re-live past moments in our minds but we
cannot reverse the processes of the living and material world. We know
the unidirectionality of time from geological and historical records, from
physical processes involving energy exchange, from the irreversible accumulation of knowledge, and from the fact that people and things get
older and never younger and newer. We know that the sequence of the
diurnal cycle goes from dawn to midday to dusk to night and not back-

wards from dusk to midday to morning. These examples demonstrate that cyclicality and irreversible linearity are not, as so frequently asserted, the dominant time perceptions of traditional and modern societies respectively. Rather, they are integral to all rhythmically structured phenomena (Adam 1990: 70–6, 87–90).

Yet, when we say that time takes its toll and that people, animals and things get older, we imply additional aspects of time to those of cycles of return and of linear directionality. Each directional cycle simultaneously constitutes a *time-frame* within which we organize, plan and regulate our daily existence: night and day, the seasons, birth and death. Moreover, *our lives are lived unto death*, to use Heidegger's (1927/1980, 1969/1972) terminology, and during each present the past we have already lived and the future we still expect to live play a central role in the way we experience, plan and act. Not only that, we have a relationship to our past, present and future; we take an attitude to our origin and destiny. Collectively these aspects of time affect the way we see ourselves, our families, our society and our fellow human beings. They influence the timing of our interactions, the way we relate to others, and how we interpret daily and extra-ordinary events. Timing and the time-frame aspect of time are thus implicated in temporality in the same way as temporality is implicated in the former. This triple implication, however, does not yet exhaust the complexity of the concept as it is used in everyday communication: *tempo* and *intensity* make up further 'components' of the meaning-complex of Western time.

Within the boundaries set by the multitude of physical, biological and cultural time-frames, the timing and temporality of processes advance at various speeds. We speak of time passing slowly or going by too quickly. Time flies when we are having fun: it drags when we are waiting. There never seems to be enough of it when we are busy and too much of it during periods of enforced idleness. Tempo and intensity surround us at every level: we know that a birthday tomorrow can feel like an eternity to a little child whilst a birthday one year ago can seem like only yesterday to an old person. The dormant period of winter is followed by a burst of growth in spring. One job needs to be rushed to completion, whilst another has to be slowed down to stay in phase not only with other production processes but also with demand. Rates of action and reaction, be they metabolic or social, are fundamentally implicated in how much can be achieved within any given time-frame, in the timing of actions, and in the temporality of existence. All, in turn, are involved in our experience of the speed of time passing.

This demonstrates the mutual implication of time (as frames and parameters), timing, temporality and tempo whenever the concept is used in everyday communication. It shows that cyclical time is neither the opposite of linear time nor separable from moments passing and recurring; that it is neither the opposite of the unidirectional temporality of physical and living things nor of the social processes of Western societies, but rather fundamentally entailed therein. 'Our' social time as it emerges from common usage is inseparable from the rhythms of our earth. Complexity reigns supreme. My identification of some key concepts which mutually implicate each other is therefore not intended as a new delimiting device. Rather, the four *t*'s of *t*ime, *t*emporality, *t*iming and *t*empo should be used as crutches only, to be cast away when they have served their purpose.

Clock time

The second social expression of 'our' time I want to focus on is clock time. In contrast to the variable parameters created by the birth–death cycle, by night and day and by seasons, the time-frames generated by seconds, minutes, hours and days are characterized by invariance, context independence and precision. The twenty-four-hour clock measures the 'same' twenty-four hours in Iceland during the winter as in Britain during the summer. Since time has been standardized across the globe, one hour of clock time is one hour wherever we are: it replaces variable 'hours' that change with the seasons and the continuum of 'local times' that preceded world time. From the late eighteenth century onwards, time has been divided into equal sections of one-hour differences, increasing as we move east and decreasing as we move west, with the strange result that we can gain or lose a day by crossing the international date-line. Moving among the Aleutian Islands in the Pacific, for example, we can celebrate a birthday twice or miss it altogether. In conjunction with the clock, this rationalization of time exerts a key influence on social life in industrial societies and permeates even those aspects of time we share with other societies across the world. Moreover, it is deeply implicated in the taken-for-granted understanding of time that forms the basis from which contemporary Western social scientists construct their images of 'other' time. It is therefore important to explore it more fully.

Both calendars and clocks incorporate time as measure and they measure time. It is important to appreciate the creation of this double role since it resulted in a fundamental paradox: the measure is designed to the principle of invariance, whilst the natural time it measures is characterized by fundamental variance. In other words, the hours of daylight change minimally every day, the constellations of the stars do not recur in exactly the same position, not every year has 365 days. This makes the measure qualitatively different from that which it measures. (Clocks may be designed to the principle of invariance, but the measure of the hour, the minute and the second is in fact variable. It is subject to environmental influences such as gravity, but we tend to disregard that variability and focus on the invariable abstraction: the idea of the second, the minute and the hour. The invariability of the measure is in fact an artefact of universal scaling.) Unlike the variable rhythms of nature, the invariant, precise measurement is a human invention and in our society it is this created time which has become dominant to the extent that it is related to as time *per se*, as if there were no other times.

Furthermore, the clock is a machine designed to the laws of classical mechanics. Like all other machines, it is a material embodiment of classical mechanics, designed to the principles of idealized invariance, simplification, motion without change, and reversibility (Adam 1990: 50–55; Shallis 1983 esp. Chapters 2 and 4). As a mechanical model of the universe the clock expresses time as distance travelled in space. But it also creates a time that is no longer dependent on its source. The development of the pendulum played a central role in the creation of this first artificial, independent time standard. The pendulum's regular oscillations are counted and translated into a directional succession, yet, as I indicate elsewhere (Adam 1988: 209), the direction is an artefact of the numbering system. It is not an integral aspect of machine time since the counting of the oscillations is irrelevant to the working of the machine, and their directional succession is given only by the mathematical convention by which the number three follows the number two and not vice versa. The meaning of time, on the other hand, is not encapsulated in either the oscillations or the number system. We cannot tell by looking at a clock whether it is eight o'clock in the morning or the evening, summer or winter, in the northern or southern hemisphere since this knowledge fundamentally depends on the rhythms of nature. Context-independence and rationalization have been traded off against meaning, qualitative difference and harmony with natural and social rhythms. Despite this shift in emphasis, however, clock time has not replaced the multiple social, biological and physical sources of time; rather, it has changed the meaning of the variable times, temporalities, timings and tempos of bio-cultural origin.

The overarching meaning of the artefactual time, as I show in the chapters that follow, constitutes our most taken-for-granted reality, which means that we find it difficult to raise it to an explicit level of understanding. Its distinctiveness does, however, become visible in the realm of industrial work where employers buy the time of their workers (see Chapter 4 on time and work for detailed analysis). In this context time is the medium through which labour is translated into an abstract exchange value: it is fundamental to the exchange between work and money (Giddens 1981: 130–4). Furthermore, time is contested in industrial disputes. Conflicts over time-control can be observed throughout the history of strikes where the duration of the working day, week, year and working life, the pace of work and break-times, overtime and time off, holidays and paid leisure time are at the centre of the disagreements (Blyton 1989; Hassard 1989a and 1989b; Keenoy 1985; Rinderspacher 1985: 217–227; Starkey 1988; Thompson 1967). Labour time as quantity and abstract exchange value is no longer merely used, passed or filled: it is an integral component of production; a quantity that helps to mediate exchange. It has become a commodity. Here the control is no longer over the time-structuring of the activity but over the commodity itself. With this commodification, the control of time has become an ineradicable, integral aspect of industrial social life and as such it affects the timing, the tempo and even the temporality of that life. The commodification and the control of time thus need to be recognized as specific phenomena of industrial and industrializing societies. This dual characteristic of control and commodification is conventionally associated with clocks and the measurement of time. The relation, however, is a complex one. Chronological calendar and clock time, related to as an independent, objective reality and understood as being time *per se*, forms the king-pin of industrial time without being the sole cause. Since all societies reckon time in some way, the mere existence of 'our' time-reckoning devices should not be understood as the cause of the reification and subsequent commodification and control of time.

To reckon time entails that we know the times proper to things, processes and events and that we can recognize the time of each as consistent in relation to others that are both faster and slower. It is therefore not necessarily their regular, rhythmic occurrence but our knowledge of their consistency in relation to other events and processes, that matters (Elias 1992). Cooking rice or the burning of a particular stick, for example, are processes that are consistent with reference to other processes. As such they can be used as measures for short time-spans similar to a multitude of other consistent processes that have been used since earliest human history for time-reckoning purposes all over the world. Like the definition of short periods by external means, the capacity to reckon long time-spans is by no means limited to modern civilizations either. Many ancient societies arrived at complicated calendar systems without relating to that time as a resource or a commodity. Archaeological evidence of notations of lunar cycles shows that lunar time-reckoning goes back some 30,000 years (Marshack 1972 in Fraser 1987: 46). Stonehenge, which is widely believed to have served a calendrical function, is dated between 1800 and 1400 BC, and the earliest water-clocks, discovered in Egypt, were in existence since the fifteenth century BC. Early civilizations such as the Maya had established complex calendrical systems, and the Chinese had invented a mechanical clock which predated that of the Western world by many centuries. Therefore, neither the reckoning of time nor its measurement with the aid of a clock constitutes the specific nature of industrial time. Rather, industrial time is a time that is abstracted from its natural source; an independent, decontextualized, rationalized time. It is a time that is almost infinitely divisible into equal spatial units, used as such in daily interactions, and related to as time *per se*.

It is not the measurement of time, then, that is the prime source of the qualitative difference between clock time and the multitude of other times. Rather, machine time has been reified to a point where we have lost touch with other rhythms and with the multiple times of our exist- ence. Most importantly, with the dominance of this reified time we seem to have forgotten that the entirety of our reality needs constantly to be re-activated and re-created in the present; that all of our past needs to be gathered up in the present and reconstructed in the light of new knowl- edge (see Adam 1990, Chapter 6). It appears that we can recognize time- constituting processes only when we encounter them in societies whose perceptions of time differ markedly from our own. Such societies, we consequently argue, construct time in the present through traditional practices, myths and rituals, while we live in a time that is a 'smooth flowing continuum in which everything in the universe proceeds at an equal rate' (Whorf 1956: 57). In the world of years, days, hours and seconds, of time-budgeting, deadlines and time pressure, in contrast, it is argued that time is no longer primarily associated with the creation of reality. Science, philosophy and history have replaced myth and sacred traditions. Yet the process has remained the same; through it we preserve and transmit not only our knowledge but also our existence. Like the members of 'traditional' societies, we construct and constitute time in the present. We have merely lost our awareness of it: our reification of the artefactual time as time *per se* has crowded out that knowledge from our conscious perception. Ingold (1986: 202) suggests that we can recog- nize the time-constituting process only after we have transcended dualis- tic thinking in which we oppose change and persistence, synchrony and diachrony. Thus, the chapters in this book shift the emphasis from dualisms to multiplicity and bring to the forefront of our attention the construction of times past, present and future.

The artefactual time of decontextualized, abstract hours, minutes and seconds is implicated where time is controlled and where it is used as a medium for the translation of labour power into a monetary value. Unlike the time transcendence which is characteristic of human culture generally, this homogenized, quantitative time which we use, allocate, control and sell on the labour market is not a human universal. It belongs firmly to the history of Western economic life and paid employment. (Adam 1990: 104–26; Giddens 1981, 1990; Hohn 1984; Thompson 1967; Thrift 1981, 1988). The aim and the capacity to transcend our species-specific time, in contrast, seems to be a general human trait. It is evident in the existence of religions, myths and theories, art and architecture, agriculture and technology: asking metaphysical questions, having a relationship to our own finitude, accommodating a temporal world to the principles of permanence, all contribute to the process of time transcendence. This means that the societies studied by anthropologists, archeologists and historians are not exempt from that capacity simply because they have not objectified and abstracted time; they merely differ in the way they practise this time transcendence. Humanity shares an effort to control the environment, the timing and synchronization of collective action, the entropic processes of decay and the decline of our bodies. Imposing their control over the time embedded in their living conditions, humans have consistently transcended the times of their existence. Hägerstrand (1985: 10) accentuates this point when he argues that 'culture can be viewed as a system of major modifications of naturally embedded time in the material world'. It is the control over this embedded time, common to humanity, which needs to be differentiated from the control over time *per se*, over the reified, artefactual time associated with economic social relations and the rationalization of social life. The differentiation, however, cannot be achieved in dualistic terms.

Only the externalized, material time can be used as resource, related to as if it were real, controlled in its own right, and exchanged for money. Due to the prominence of commodification and control, industrial time seems best conceptualized with reference to power. Furthermore, we need to recognize that those relations of power are not restricted to situations in which time is exchanged for money: they permeate the most private times of consciousness, the moments 'when', the right time to act, the timing of interaction, the tempo embedded in natural and social processes, and the time-frames within which we organize social life. The multiplicity of times all implicate each other, which means that new 'additions' are not merely grafted on to existing ones, they change their nature in the process. Once created, clock time has become an integral, ineradicable aspect of social life and as such it affects the control, the timing, the tempo and even the temporality of that life. 'Western time' is thus very clearly not to be charted in dualistic terms. It is neither to be contrasted with a cyclical time of 'traditional', 'cold', pre-industrial societies nor to be defined in contradistinction to the times of nature. Clock time, which alters the meaning and the constitution of the complexity of time in practice, pervades humanity to varying degrees: few societies are completely untouched by it, many live a compromise between the artefactual time and their local times, but no society has completely replaced the multiplicity of time(s) with clock time. In other words, particular clusters are expressed in specific contexts but there exists no society for which machine time constitutes the only source of social time: absolute distinctions and dichotomies are rendered obsolete for social science analyses of historically and culturally specific times. 'Other' time, therefore, needs to be constructed on new terms.

Social constructions of 'other' time

Them and us

The experience of time is integral to human existence. The way we perceive and conceptualize that experience, however, varies with cultures and historical periods. That is to say, the meanings and values attributed to time are fundamentally context-dependent. This recognition underpins all studies of 'other' time, be they anthropological, historical or sociological. These studies, which have tended to concentrate on systems of time-reckoning in different societies and on how time is perceived, organized and structured, are characterized by a common feature: they dichotomize societies into traditional and modern ones in which the time perception of the former is constructed through its opposition to the dominant images of 'our Western time'. Thus it is proposed that 'their' time is cyclical rather than linear, encapsulated in tradition rather than constituting the motor of history. The most common antinomies are as follows:

'Our' times	*'Other' times*
historical	traditional
linear	cyclical
irreversible	reversible
changing	stable
quantitative	qualitative
clock-based	task/event-based

calendar-based	nature-based
decontextualized	embedded
abstract measure	ecological measure
'hot' society	'cold' society
organic solidarity	mechanical solidarity
diachronic study	synchronic study

If, however such dichotomization is unwarranted for 'our' time, for reasons I have outlined above, it is unlikely to be appropriate for cultures past and present that are markedly different from our own. Irrespective of their respective disciplines, studies of social time seem to share two interrelated problems: first, time is implicated not only in the subject matter of anthropology, history and sociology but also in the lives, understandings and methods of those who conduct the studies. Second, in spite of its omnipresence, time is curiously invisible and constitutes one of the most taken-for-granted features of our lives. As such it forms the largely implicit base from which studies are conducted and from which the time of 'the other' is explicated. For these reasons I want to suggest that studies of 'other time' are not merely dealing with difficulties of translation between cultures. Rather, the problem extends far deeper to the *unquestioned* understanding of Western time; it reaches the very base from which researchers construct the time of 'the other'. (I am concentrating on anthropology in this final part of the first chapter but these issues will be readdressed in the final chapter of the book where I broaden the argument to social theory and social science more generally.)

The dichotomization into 'traditional' and 'modern' time has been extensively criticized and more recently a number of additional problems have been identified with approaches that construct differences along too simplistic lines. In anthropology, for example, there has been criticism of the portrayal of a 'uniformity across the population and of cultural forms unchanged for decades and centuries' (Cottle and Klineberg 1974: 164) as well as condemnation of the practice of locking interlocutors into the frozen present of anthropological discourse. 'Functionalism, in its fervour to explore the mechanisms of living societies,' Fabian (1983: 20) contends, 'simply put on ice the problem of time.' With Fabian's seminal work on *Time and the Other*, the pendulum has swung from an emphasis on difference to a recognition of coevalness; and with the writings of Adam (1988, 1990, 1992a) and Ingold (1986) the Newtonian/Cartesian premises of our Western theories have been exposed. Closely associated with these critiques is a rising awareness of both the constitutive nature of knowledge (Harris-Jones 1985) and the need for reflexivity (Cohen 1990a, 1990b; Ortner 1984). Harris-Jones (1985: 238) thus proposes a necessary shift from an 'archaeology of knowledge' to an activist approach to culture, and Cohen (1990a: 22) states boldly that 'selfless anthropology is out of date'. The self, Cohen continues, needs to be accommodated 'as a matter of scholarly principle and practice'.

The positivist belief in an uncontaminated, objective reality is, however, so deeply ingrained in social science praxis that researchers tend to view their own assumptions as immaterial and resist considering them as subjects for reflection. Few go further than paying lip-service to Habermas's (1973: 161) insistence that 'the terms that we bring from within ourselves to the process of inquiry – in any and every domain, including science – are amenable to a reflection that is rational for the very reason that it carries the potential for a more inclusive conceptualization that is better attuned to the common interest of the human condition'. Emphasis on reflexivity is, of course, not new. In *The Critique of Pure Reason* Kant (1781/1966: 16) pointed out that we are like judges who compel their witnesses to answer questions that they themselves have posed. Over 200 years ago Kant was arguing that *observers bring their own faculties of reason to the constitution of the objects of their observation and thus to the formative moment of knowledge*. With respect to our topic this implies that we cannot understand other cultures' approaches to time without drawing on our own understanding. Reflexivity is thus necessary not only because knowledge is constitutive but also because we construct others to the templates of our own theoretical models. With the long-standing acceptance of Kant's insights and the recent emphasis on reflexivity it seems surprising that the backcloth upon which our descriptions are drawn remains unattended, that the nature and models of our own time are left unexamined, and that we fail to acknowledge that any analysis of 'other time' is a simultaneous commentary on 'our time'. An explicitly reflexive approach to time becomes imperative, however, once we recognize first, that the 'alien' time is commonly explicated in terms of what it is *not*, and second, that the existing dualistic models of 'own' and 'other time' are fundamentally flawed.

The assumed backcloth

For this reason I want to bring to the forefront the backcloth upon which descriptions are drawn. I want to make visible the assumptions that inform the Western understanding of time. Not the explicated 'other time' but the implicit time of the 'invisible observer' is therefore going to be the primary focus of my attention. The point is *not* to provide detailed critiques of particular authors' work but to establish the general principle of a pervasive and persistently problematic tradition in social science. I have deliberately chosen for examination classical studies and models that have since been widely criticized, rather than contemporary exponents of such approaches, in the hope that the conceptual distance will entice not the usual unproductive defensive reactions but an openness to consider the problem and potential responses to it.

The studies of Evans-Pritchard (1940/1969) and Whorf (1956) and the conceptual models of Lévi-Strauss (1963/1972) provide excellent exemplars of classical analyses of 'other time'. It is, however, neither their respective analyses of the differences between 'our' and 'other time' nor, as I have already mentioned, the many critiques offered in response to these studies which are of interest here. Rather, it is the stereotypical backdrop of unquestioned 'Western time' against which the respective time perception of the 'traditional' cultures are delineated which needs to become the centre of our attention.

From Whorf's (1956) linguistic study of Hopi Amerindian cosmology the experience of Western time emerges as a unidirectional, continuous flow, with sequences of events 'strung up' on a line, which extends from the past into the future. The Western conceptualization of time is portrayed as abstract, linear, and associated with motion. It arises when Whorf describes the Hopi view of time in terms of what it is *not*. He writes of a world in which experiences are *not* sequentially stretched out on a line but simultaneous, cumulative and amalgamated in an organic complex. He depicts a time that is *not* an objectified spatial quantity, a time that is *not* made up of discrete instants that follow each other but is characterized by a cumulative getting later. 'For the Hopi, for whom time is not a motion but a "getting later" of everything that has ever been done,' Whorf (1956: 151) writes, 'unvarying repetition is not wasted but accumulated.' The Hopi's linguistic thought background, he suggests further (1956: 57), is *without* our abstract, linear, sequential concept of time and *lacks* a notion of time as a 'smooth flowing continuum in which everything in the universe proceeds at an equal rate, out of a future, through a present, into a past'.

The same approach to the analysis of 'other time' can be detected in Evans-Pritchard's (1940/1969) study of the Nuer, a Nilotic tribe of Sudan in East Africa. Evans-Pritchard constructs the tribal time of oecological cycles and structural relations against a backcloth of spatial calendar and clock time. With respect to the oecological cycles he argues that 'a twelve-month system does *not* incommode Nuer' (p. 100), that they 'do *not* to any great extent use the names of months to indicate the time of an event' (p. 100), that there are '*no* units of time between the month and day and night' (p. 100), that 'time has *not* the same value throughout the year' (p. 102), that their time words are '*not* pure units of time reckoning' (p. 99), and finally, that they 'have *no* expression equivalent to "time" in our language, and they *cannot*, therefore, as we can, speak of time as though it were something actual, which passes, can be wasted, can be saved, and so forth' (p. 103). (My emphasis in quotes pp. 99–103.) With respect to Nuer structural time Evans-Pritchard proposes that *unlike* our time which passes and progresses, the movement of their time must be recognized as an illusion since the tribal time structure stays constant. This means that their 'perception of time is no more than the movement of persons, often as groups, through the structure' (p. 107). He then contrasts this time with our historical one in which each event is accorded a unique position in the time grid of dates and clock-time units. He proposes that our time stretches over far greater distances than tradition, and that mythological events, unlike their historical counterparts, do 'not precede another, for myths explain customs of general social significance rather than the interrelations of particular segments and are, therefore, not structurally stratified' (p. 108). The backcloth of 'our time' emerges from these two studies in association with a number of clustered characteristics: as an abstract, spatial quantity that is divisible into single units; as a two-dimensional, linear, directional flow or succession of equal rate that extends from the past to the future (or vice versa); and as something that passes or can be saved, sold or wasted. All these aspects appear in the analyses as isolated single units, untheorized in relation to each other, and for the sole purpose of providing the contrast to the alien time which is portrayed as simultaneous, qualitative, cumulative, amalgamated and complex in the case of Whorf's analysis, and as cyclical, structural time in events, processes and social relations in Evans-Pritchard's account.

These classical studies can serve as (Weberian) 'ideal types' for research on time where detailed observation and interviews with informants constitute the raw data from which researchers seek to 'uncover' implicit assumptions and the world-views of their interlocutors, and upon which they build models and construct explanations. In such traditional research the assumptions upon which the questions, observations and models are based remain invariably unquestioned. The poverty of 'own time', however, as I have shown, centrally influences the construction of 'other time'. It is this poverty of the assumed time that is at issue here. Before I move on to Lévi-Strauss's dichotic models I want to look briefly at an analysis of 'other time' that deviates from this problematic tradition.

As an African who has been subject to missionary influence, Mbiti learned to see his familiar world through the eyes of a stranger. Furthermore, in order to become part of another world Mbiti had to make the

strange familiar: he had to get to know the Western time of the mission-
aries before he could participate in that life. It is not surprising, therefore, that Mbiti's backdrop of Western time, against which he explains
African time, far surpasses that of his Western colleagues. In Mbiti's
(1969/1985) work on African religions and philosophy the image of
Western time emerges once more as linear and subject to the threefold
division into past, present and future. But, unlike the Western time of the
previous analyses, Mbiti's backdrop time is complex and it is theorized in
relation to abstraction, objectification, spatialization, context-independence and commodification. Mbiti contrasts the 'produced time' of
African peoples with the Western commodity which is exchanged on the
labour market as an objective quantity. Similarly, he distinguishes between the need of members of traditional African societies to experience
and constitute time and the objectified quantity expressed in the time
grids of dates, hours and minutes of Western and Westernized societies.
Unlike Evans-Pritchard and Whorf's shadowy image of linearity, succession and motion, Mbiti identifies the Western time characteristics of
linearity and an equal past and future extension in relation to numerical,
context-independent calendars. Furthermore, he implies a connection
between the mathematical, abstracted time of calendars and time as a
commodity; between days, months and years and a time that can be used,
sold, exchanged and controlled.

     From the difference in the two approaches we can see that it matters
whether the backdrop time is assumed or given equal status in the
analysis. For Western social scientists and historians to treat their taken-
for-granted time as an object of reflection requires that they bring everyday knowledge and the sources of their metaphors into high relief and
focus on that which remains disattended in studies of 'other time'. It
necessitates that they investigate the complexity of their personal time in
relation to the times of their collectivity and that they give detailed
attention to the technologies and artefacts that centrally influence their
understanding of that time. Such focus will put a swift end to the models
that force us to choose between time and temporality, clocks and natural
rhythms, linearity and cyclicality, change and order, history and myth,
quantity and quality, events in time and time in events, since life in
Western societies, as I have shown above, does not take place exclusively
on the two-dimensional plane of linear, chronological time.

Dichotic models

We build models in order to render our subject matter intelligible. We
construct representations so that Nuer time reckoning and Hopi cos-

mology, for example, become meaningful in the context of our own understanding. It is inevitable, therefore, that descriptions and explanations are simplifications of that which they represent. It could not be otherwise, for even the smallest aspect of social reality is infinite in its complexity. Not the practice of model building, then, but the nature of the models and the assumptions underpinning them are at issue here, for the latter are rarely questioned or held up for scrutiny and the former seem invariably built on dichotomies that construct the time of other cultures in contradistinction to our own. Cyclical time and emphasis on repetition are contrasted with linear time and historical being, and, as we have seen earlier, 'a smooth flowing continuum in which everything proceeds at an equal rate' (Whorf 1956: 57) is differentiated from a 'shallow' past and future extension (Evans-Pritchard 1940/1969: 108). Lévi-Strauss, the 'most notable model architect' (Barnes 1971: 538), has provided an additional host of time-based dichotomies that are all too readily adopted as templates for models with which to contrast 'traditional' and 'modern' societies (anthropologists Barnes 1971, Fabian 1983 and Ingold 1986 being notable exceptions).

Lévi-Strauss distinguishes Western time, dominated by history, irreversibility and succession, from the times of societies among whom simultaneity and non-cumulative, cyclical and even reversible processes prevail. Accordingly, Lévi-Strauss argues, the social sciences have to deal with two different categories of time.

Anthropology uses a 'mechanical' time, reversible and non-cumulative . . . [in contrast] historical time is 'statistical'; it always appears as an oriented and non-reversible process. An evolution which would take contemporary Italian society back to that of the Roman Republic is as impossible to conceive of as the reversibility of the process belonging to the second law of thermodynamics. (Lévi-Strauss 1963/1972: 286)

This quote epitomizes the extraordinary claims that are being made by Lévi-Strauss with reference to time. An 'evolution' that would take a small scale agricultural society 'back' to its hunter–gatherer past is surely no less absurd than the suggestion that contemporary Italian society could return to the Roman Republic. We may speak of societies 'reverting back' to historically earlier forms of socio-economic organization but this can never be more than a figure of speech since social reversibility is no more possible than growing younger, ashes turning back into logs, or the progression of a day moving from evening to midday to morning. If this is the case, what possible basis could there be for characterizing traditional peoples' time as reversible, non-cumulative, non-directional, simultaneous and circular rather than irreversible, cumulative, directional, successive and linear? What possible grounds could there be for Lévi-Strauss to use a mechanical model of 'reversible time', given his requirement that the model has to be adequate to its subject matter and given that he insists that the 'best model will always be that which is true' (1963/1972: 281)? The questions take on a further significance when we recognize that even by Lévi-Strauss's own admission such dichotomies cannot be upheld as mutually exclusive, since 'even the most elementary kinship structure exists both synchronically and diachronically' (1963/1972: 47). If, as Lévi-Strauss advocates, anthropology as an academic discipline is to be characterized by a structural analysis built on mechanical, non-cumulative models and the idea of 'reversible time', then, according to my analysis of 'our time', this approach would be most suitable to the study not of traditional but of contemporary Western societies, since only the latter are organized to a mechanical machine time based on the Newtonian principle of reversibility. This reversal too, however, would be flawed since, even for industrial societies, machine time forms only part of the complexity of social times. On the basis of the evidence provided so far we could let the case rest. Since, however, those dualisms of cyclical/linear, reversible/irreversible time and repetition/ change orientation in 'cold' and 'hot' societies in conjunction with synchronic and diachronic analyses still hold such powerful sway in social science and historical analyses, they merit some further deconstructive attention. My purpose, in this last section of the chapter, is neither to trace the many mutations and adaptations these dualisms have undergone nor to render new and better interpretations of the way authors have employed them. Rather, I want to show their potential, or lack of it, for explaining social time in its culturally specific complexity and make explicit the assumptions that underpin the structuralist model which are derived, as Lévi-Strauss (1963/1972: 314) freely admits, straight from classical mechanics.

Cyclical time is the time mode conventionally imposed on traditional, small-scale societies, and this is posited in contradistinction to an assumed linear time of contemporary industrial societies. It entails the idea of an impoverished or 'shallow' past extension (as Evans-Pritchard 1940/ 1969: 108 defined it), a barely existent future orientation, even life in a 'timeless present' (Kluckhohn and Strodbeck 1961). It conjures up a world of 'eternal return', a world where the difference between the past and future can be dispensed with since what has been recurs and what is to come has already been, a world where destiny is synonymous with origin. Some historians and social scientists, however, have presented evidence to the contrary and argued that no human society could be said to live in such a cyclical time (Adam 1990: 127–48; Aguessy 1977; Bergmann 1992; Bourdieu 1979; Dunne 1973; Eliade 1954/1989; Fabian 1983; Kinget 1975; McElwain 1988: 267–78; Nowotny 1985). This is neither to deny that for some societies the heading towards the future is simultaneously a regaining of the past nor to argue against findings that some societies put greater efforts than others into the active creation of permanence. Rather, it is to suggest that these are variable features of all human cultures in the same way that time-frames, temporality, timing, tempo, a relation to the past, present and future and, to a limited extent, even clock and calendar time, form integral parts of contemporary human existence. It is to insist that this complexity of times cannot be expressed through the dualisms of cyclical and linear time. In other words, the antinomies become meaningless with respect to the direction, form and the process of time when we recognize that the times of even the most archaic societies are constituted on the basis of general cultural characteristics that defy classification in terms of cyclicality and invariability. The presence of myths and religious beliefs, the relationship to birth and death, and the creation of tools, artefacts, art and architecture suggest a past and future extension and a time transcendence that vastly exceed the cycle of seasons or even a person's lifetime. This applies irrespective of whether or not time has been developed as a separate concept, whether or not the language is tensed like ours, and whether or not time has been objectified in some way. To ask metaphysical questions, to not merely live one's life but to have a relationship to one's existence, and to reconstruct a temporal world to the principles of permanence, as I have argued earlier, are universal marks of culture and evidence for a time extension that cannot be encompassed by the concept of cyclical time.

To have a relationship to death, for example, extends human beings beyond the cycles of nature, even when their daily lives are dominated by concerns that do not reach beyond the growth cycle of seasons or when their explicit aim is to join the realm of their ancestors (see Adam 1990, Chapter 6). Furthermore, to take an attitude to the realm of the caused, the actual and the potential transforms the problem of existence into a conscious act of living unto the future, into an achievement of preemptiveness, anticipation and creativity. 'The human thing is not merely to live, to act, to love', writes Dunne (1973: 20). 'It is to have a relationship to one's life, one's action, one's love, even if the relationship is simply one of consent, simply a "Yes".' To relate to birth and death, origin and destiny is an existential condition of human cultural life. What makes our lives worthy of being preserved in memory and story, worthy of being kept alive after our death, Dunne (1973: 23) argues, is the transcendence of life and death in our lives. Not a thing of life, this transcendence is always an immortality of the spirit which is constituted by our relationship to the temporality of life. To conceptualize archaic or traditional societies with reference to cyclical time thus constitutes a denial not only of culture but also of the spiritual dimension of their lives. It even denies them a symbolic capacity since knowledge of a past and future entails representational, symbolically-based imagination. Endowed with it, human beings do not merely undergo their presents and pasts, they shape and reshape them. With objectified meaning they cannot only look back, reflect and contemplate but can also reinterpret, represent, restructure and modify the past. They can gather up all the collective past and re-create it as present in the present. They can plan alternative futures, imagine past futures, and dread future pasts. Thus, the idea of any society living in a cyclical time of endlessly recurring sameness is as untenable as the contrast to contemporary Western society being characterized by linear time.

It is essential to appreciate that all social processes display aspects of linearity and cyclicality, that we recognize a cyclical structure when we focus on events that repeat themselves and unidirectional linearity when our attention is on the process of the repeating action. Whether we 'see' linearity or cyclicality depends fundamentally on the framework of observation and interpretation. Furthermore, to conceptualize traditional societies as cyclical and therefore 'timeless' demonstrates that the person making that statement implicitly identifies time with historical, chronological dating. Whilst there is no doubt that the time-creating, time-eliminating and time-transcending practices, expressed through ritual, myth and worship, are qualitatively different from their equivalents in our society, it is highly inappropriate to call them 'cyclical', 'timeless' or 'out of time and space' since these meanings are fundamentally tied to a clock time-based meaning of time. It is therefore not the concept of cyclicality itself that is at issue here, since cyclical processes by definition involve repetition with variation, linearity and progression. The problem is with the meaning associated with cyclical time in studies of 'other time' and with the fictitious contrast to an untheorized 'Western linear time'. We can thus resolve the unsatisfactory dichotomy between cyclical and linear aspects of time by demonstrating both their fundamental mutual implication and their relativity to the perspective of the observer. No such resolution, however, is available in the case of the opposition between reversible and irreversible time.

The idea of reversibility is to be located in Newtonian physics where abstract motion is postulated as symmetrical with respect to the past and future. It is applied in classical physics to such phenomena as the swinging of the pendulum, or the elastic collision of billiard balls where, if a film were taken of the events, we could not tell whether it was running forward or backward. As I have outlined above, the Newtonian concept of reversibility is based on the assumption that everything is given and, irrespective of the number of transformations a system undergoes, it could, in principle, retrace all the changes and return to its original state. It is a general mathematical property of dynamic equations, explain Prigogine and Stengers (1984: 61), 'that if the velocities of all points of a system are reversed, the system will go "backward in time". . . . What one dynamic change has achieved, another change defined by velocity inversion, can undo, and this way exactly restore the original condition.' Reversibility signifies the possibility of un-acting, un-relating and un-associating, un-knowing and un-structuring. It means that ashes igniting themselves and turning back into logs, leaves picking themselves off the ground and attaching themselves to the branches they came from, old rusty cars turning back into gleaming limousines, all have to be considered as possible, in principle, as the irreversible world of our experiences. Applied to social life, this idea is clearly an absurdity. Not only that, it even poses major problems within the natural sciences. It not only contradicts common-sense knowledge but also some of the most recent theories in theoretical physics (Hawking 1988; Prigogine 1980) where temporality is now established as a law of nature.

With respect to human social life we can state that events may recur at regular intervals and in a seemingly unchanging way without being reversible. Rather, cultural life constitutes time, entails time and is enacted in time: it creates a new past and a new future and involves time as sequence, duration, intensity, passage and irreversible direction. In other words, time is fundamentally implicated in even the most repetitive of social phenomena. Furthermore, it is not time but events and tasks that are endlessly repeated. Consciousness, experience, knowledge and the execution of the tasks, in contrast, are irreversible: they constitute time. Going to work every morning, tending the animals, organizing the food for the family and washing the dishes could classify as recurring, repetitive, habit-infused activities, but this makes neither them, nor the time in which they occur, reversible since there can be no un-going to work, no un-tending the animals, no un-washing up. Nothing can be undone and restored to its 'original condition': time neither stands still nor goes backwards.

Having shown reversibility to be an abstraction, a Newtonian idealization inapplicable to human social life, we now need briefly to look at the idea of sameness. We need to examine the proposition that we can dispense with the distinction between past and future because that which has been recurs, and that which is to come has already been. 'Repetition of the same' is considered a particularly apt description of very slow-changing societies, 'cold' societies in Lévi-Strauss's terminology. It entails the belief that the conscious and deliberate efforts of the members of those societies to annul, as much as possible, the effects of the temporality of social life is best characterized by our concept of sameness, an assumption that is highly problematic when even in physics the likelihood for just one cubic centimetre of air to recur in exactly the same composition has been calculated as a chance of 10 to the power of 10 trillion (Eigen 1983: 37–41), which is a mathematical expression for 'as good as never'. If 'repetition of the same' is that unlikely for a mere cubic centimetre of air, we can safely consider it beyond the bounds of the possible for any human social event exactly to repeat itself so that we might classify it to be 'the same'.

The effort to fix the transient world into knowable stability and permanence, moreover, is a general human endeavour, not merely a characteristic of traditional and archaic societies. Writing music, or making films and compact discs are contemporary efforts to reproduce originals in unchanging form. But neither a myth being told nor a record being played can be considered to be 'the same' in repetition. The story-tellers and their stories, the listeners, their records and their equipment, have all grown older. They constitute a different past and present and anticipate an altered future irrespective of the explicit efforts towards an unaltered re-enactment of some original state. 'Repetition', as Stegmüller (1969: 175) explains with reference to Heidegger's work on time, 'is no empty bringing back of the past; not a mere binding of the present to that which has irrevocably gone, but a deep response to that which has been whilst simultaneously being a decisive revocation of the effects of the past in the present' (my translation). Repetition can be the 'same' only in abstraction, by artificially excluding contexts and effects.

We need to recognize that repetition and irreversibility are not separate or even separable concepts. They are both linked to the becoming of the possible. By conflating repetition, cyclicality and sameness with reversibility, the opportunity to theorize the creation of reality and the relation between cycles of return and directional change have been missed (see Adam 1990: 28–31). Furthermore, what is generally conceptualized as 'timeless' refers mostly to rates of change that are very much slower than those of the observers' frames of reference: traditional societies are only extremely slow-changing in comparison with contemporary Western standards but not, for example, in relation to geological change. Once more we find the implicit framework of the observer centrally implicated in the definition and classification of the objects of anthropological observation. We thus need to allow for the constitutive nature of our framework of reference and to free ourselves from the positivist belief in an objective reality untouched by our observations.

We need further to apply this awareness to the concern to define the subject matter of anthropology in distinction and relation to history. This delineation of synchronic and diachronic analyses for anthropology and history respectively has to be recognized as an anthropological quest for scientific status since the synchronic method of anthropology is considered to meet the requirement of analyses that are 'uncontaminated by time'. This, of course, is an illusion since, as Fabian (1983: 24) correctly points out, 'no matter whether one chooses to stress "diachronic" or "synchronic", historical or systematic approaches, they all are chronic, unthinkable without reference to time'. Both are based on the abstract time of clocks and calendars. Both offer a description of their subject matter either as it exists at one moment, or 'over time'. Moreover, as synchronic and diachronic analyses are fundamentally tied to clock and calendar time only, both may well be inappropriate tools for analyses of societies that do not share our abstracted, objectified time-frame. Furthermore, neither is sufficient on its own to grasp social life. As Giddens (1981: 17) notes, 'a stable order is one in which there is close similarity between how things are, and how they used to be'. Therefore, it is misleading to suppose, he continues, 'that one can take a "timeless snapshot" of a social system as one can, say, take a real snapshot of the architecture of a building. For social systems exist as systems only in and through their "functioning" (reproduction) over time.' Not only is it erroneous that time becomes identified with change in analyses that utilize the synchronic–diachronic division, but also that the nature of change becomes fundamentally tied to the reversible time of Newtonian physics. This, as I have shown above, excludes the embedded time of things and processes, life and knowledge; and it leaves us no basis from which to conceptualize creativity, novelty or time constituted in the present.

The contrast of routine and sameness with progressive change and creativity directs our understanding toward an either-or mode where we end up dichotomizing what are integral aspects of all human life. In Western social life, emphasis on the linear seems to crowd out recognition of the cyclical and we lose sight of the vital part that repetition plays in the constitution of our own social structure. Having lost touch with our own cyclicality, we project it on to our objects of investigation: we construct it as 'other time'. 'We' and 'our time' must therefore not be presupposed or left implicit. To make explicit what we know intimately at the non-discursive level requires a phenomenological attitude. It demands that we extricate ourselves from the natural attitude and take the position of the stranger; that we look at our own time through the eyes of those who are conventionally the object of social science attention. That is to say, we must get to know that invisible time and recognize its fundamental role in the constitution of the lives and institutions of those we study.

Key points

At the substantive level I have shown
- that a multitude of times coexist
- that our everyday language provides clues about the complexity of social times
- that all human beings are temporally extended beyond their own life time.

With reference to methodology I have argued
- for a complexity that cannot be contained within the classical dualisms of social science analysis
- for the need to pay attention to everyday experience
- for the importance of getting to know the unreflected backcloth of 'own' time upon which 'other' times are constructed.

2

Of Time and Health, Life and Death

In the first chapter I look at the bases of 'my times' and 'our times' as they arise from consciousness, language and the organization of everyday life to clock time and I focus on the untheorized backcloth of 'other times' that underpins their construction. In the course of that investigation it became clear that an explicit focus on time renders traditional dualisms highly problematic: cyclical and linear time, reversibility and irreversibility, synchronic and diachronic analyses of cold and hot, traditional and modern societies; central dichotomies of classical social science discourse disintegrate when the multiplicity of times is allowed to come to the fore. In this chapter I want to highlight the complexity of body times and its uneasy relationship to the invariable, finite time of the clock. Such analysis is important because, traditionally, the social nature of time is asserted or assumed from the outset. Ever since Durkheim's (1915) writing on the social nature of time, and Sorokin and Merton's (1937) seminal paper on that topic, social scientists have contrasted social with natural time. These dualistic analyses exclude as irrelevant the times of the body and the natural environment and they avoid an involvement with ontological issues. The traditional approaches are tied to two underlying beliefs: that science has no base from which to deal with questions of ontology and that the 'times of nature' and the physical environment lie outside the boundaries of social science inquiry. Existential issues, it is reasoned, belong to the realm of philosophy and metaphysics, 'natural' and artefactual time to biology and physics. Both these assumptions, as I show and argue throughout this book, are in need of reassessment.

Luhmann (1982) notes how social scientists evade questions about the nature of time. He pin-points the ontological dilemma when he writes:

If this question is posed directly and framed as one about essences, it cannot be adequately answered. On the other hand, there is a substantial danger that, if we leave this question unaddressed, we shall think about social history in crude and inadequate ways. (Luhmann 1982: 299)

For Luhmann, an explicit understanding of time is a necessary precondition for an adequate social theory. Temporality, he insists, is a constitutive dimension of the subject matter of social science which means that 'time can no longer be treated merely as a category underlying our knowledge of social life' (1982: 290). More recently, feminist analyses have refocused our attention on time and its constitutive role in consciousness, language, history and the construction of social life (Brodribb 1992; Ermarth 1992; Forman and Sowton (eds.) 1989; Kristeva 1981). In that work time has become a political issue. 'To deny its centrality', writes Forman (1989: 9), 'is to disregard a fundamental truth about women and to make invisible an aspect of our reality which is not only philosophically "authentic" but is critical to our political activity.'

Equally important has been the recent move to reintegrate 'natural times' into social science analyses (Adam 1988, 1990; Graham 1990; Held and Geissler (eds.) 1993; Shallis 1983; Young 1988) since this too has wider implications. The need for social scientists to take account of 'nature' and the physical environment has become particularly pertinent with the rise of environmental problems. 'A consideration of the environment', argues Newby (1991: 6), 'raises precisely the same kind of fundamental questions about the organization of society that faced the early founders of the discipline when they encountered the rise of industrialism, capitalism and liberal democracy.' Despite the urgency of the subject, the environment poses a problematic focus for social science in general and sociology in particular since, as Newby (1991: 7) points out, 'the very *raison d'être* of sociology has rested upon identifying and demarcating a disciplinary paradigm quite distinct from, and irreducible to, the natural and the biological'. Questions about the environment cannot be dealt with appropriately, in other words, while the environment and nature are theorized exclusively in symbolic terms, without cognizance of their materiality, and while engagement with questions about humans in nature and as nature is omitted from social scientist analyses (Benton 1993; Harris-Jones 1992; Midgley 1979).

In this chapter I use the focus on time as a first step towards addressing the nature–culture interpenetration, a move that will be continued in later chapters, most specifically so in Chapter 6. In the following account I show how the times of the mindful body and the environment are integral to social time and I demonstrate the need for understanding the multiple times of existence in relation to each other. Body time, an area of study I have merely touched on in the first chapter, becomes important when considering the connections and intersections between time and health, life and death. If I elevate here the times of the body over social times it is not to promulgate some natural determinism but merely to redress this long-established imbalance in the social sciences. Research on the rhythmicity of the mindful body works the seam of intersection between nature and culture, body and mind, life and death, while an explicit focus on both time and health makes visible what tend to be unquestioned conceptual givens in studies on that topic (Frankenberg (ed.) 1992; Roth 1976). My task here is to bring the taken-for-granted into high relief, to demonstrate connections and intersections, and to identify the implications of such a re-vision for social theory and practice.

Body time and well-being

The rhythms of the environment and the body are inseparable from human being, from well-being and from everyday social life. As I have already shown in the previous chapter, those rhythms underpin our evolution and development as human beings. Day and night, the tide, moons and seasons mark us as dwellers on the planet earth and specific regions therein. Studies collated by Luce (1973) and Rose (1989), for example, demonstrate how rhythmicity, timing, temporality and tempo are fundamental to our being and how their particular interplay signifies health, ill-health or even death. As living beings we are permeated by rhythmic cycles which range from very fast chemical and neuronal oscillations, via the slower rhythms of heartbeat, respiration and circadian rhythms, to menstrual and reproductive cycles, and to the very long-range recurrences of seasonal and even climatic changes. What is important to appreciate, as Fraser (1982: 145) points out, is that 'the cyclic behaviour of all organisms involves the collective, orchestrated temporal programs of all these processes together'. Activity and rest alternations, cyclical exchanges and transformations, seasonal and diurnal sensitivity, all form the silent pulse of our being. They seem to constitute those aspects of life we take most for granted.

> Though we can neither see nor feel them, we are nevertheless surrounded by rhythms of gravity, electromagnetic fields, light waves, air pressure, and sound. Each day, as the earth turns on its axis, we experience the alternation of light and darkness. The moon's revolution also pulls our atmosphere into a cycle of change. Night follows day. Seasons change. The tides ebb and flow. (Luce 1973: 16)

These rhythms affect plants, animals and human beings alike. Not just everything we do, but all of our body's physiological processes are *temporally organized and orchestrated*. We eat, sleep, breathe, use energy, digest, perceive, think, concentrate, communicate, interact and work in a rhythmic way. All processes of our body are accurately timed and paced so that our organs, tissues and hormones are produced at mutually related rates. The food we eat would poison us were it not for a surge of activity of kidney and liver enzymes which, in turn, had to be produced ready for accelerated action.

Daylight and darkness act as cues to keep us synchronized with our environment and this circadian cycle (circadian = circa one day) is an important organizing principle of our physiology. Desynchronization, on the other hand, expresses itself through loss of health (Aschoff 1965 (ed.), 1981 (ed.) and 1983; Brown et al. 1970; Cloudsley-Thompson 1980; Conroy and Mills 1971; Fraser 1987; Rose 1989; Young 1988). Our body temperature, blood pressure, respiration and pulse, our haemoglobin and amino-acid levels, our hormone production, our liver and kidney function, our cell divisions, even our strengths and weaknesses rise and fall within this circadian cycle (Aschoff 1983; Luce 1973: 112–36). Importantly, each of the processes takes a different 'length of time' to complete one cycle. We breathe, for example, 15 = 20 times per minute, but our heart beats 60 = 80 times during the same period. While we are awake we show observable cycles of activity and rest of about 90 = 100 minutes and our digestive system takes on average three hours to complete a cycle before we begin to be hungry again. Moreover, the duration of these cycles may vary with age, body size, and between individuals.

Day and night, furthermore, are not the only environmental rhythms to which we respond. This is demonstrated by menstrual cycles, seasonal growth, the cyclical variation in hormone levels and certain illnesses (Luce 1973: 217–31). Even the occurrences of births and deaths, as I have shown in the previous chapter, indicate seasonal variation (Rose 1989: 87–90), and the influence of seasons on our health is acknowledged through lay expressions such as winter gloom and spring fever, the winter cold, hay fever, and the summer flu. Our body rhythms, we can clearly state, are not only orchestrated into a coherent whole but are also synchronized with the rhythms of the environment: they resonate with the multiple pulses of our earth.

The contemporary environment of industrial and industrializing countries, however, is permeated by *Zeitgeber* (providers of time) and rhythms that are superimposed on those nested body and planetary times. Clock time and artificial light are two such examples. Over the centuries, as I show throughout this book, the clock clearly has had a dramatic influence on the organization of social life by shifting the emphasis of everyday living and working patterns *from variable rhythms to invariant ones* which, in turn, created a tension that has been widely commented on, most notably by industrial and medical anthropologists and sociologists (Bellaby 1992; Clark 1982; Frankenberg 1992; Helman 1992; Pizzini 1992; Rinderspacher 1985; Thomas 1992; Young 1988). With electrification, in contrast, the hours of 'day'light have been artificially extended to a point where the distinction between day and night could be eliminated in countless production and service sectors of work. While sunlight as radiant energy seems to be one of the most important forces which tunes us, along with most other living creatures, to the cycles of our earth, our lives today are influenced by this other, new source of light. With the aid of electricity we have begun to 'colonize the night' to use Melbin's (1987) phrase. Yet those 100 years of being able to light the natural hours of darkness have to be seen in relation to our circadian evolutionary history. Whilst humans may be the most flexible beings in terms of the range within which they can vary their body rhythms, electricity has not existed for long enough for us to accomplish physiological changes that would allow us to treat night and day interchangeably.

Aschoff's (1965 (ed.), 1981 (ed.) and 1983) experiments in lightproof conditions show that human body rhythms which evolved in conjunction with the dark–light cycle of the earth have clear limits to their adaptiveness. Moreover, it is generally recognized that inverting day and night, keeping long, erratic hours and working rotating shifts predispose us towards ill-health. It is less well known that this is predominantly due to the desynchronization of those evolutionary, finely tuned and orchestrated rhythms. Thus, research on shift-work, for example, shows that lack of concentration, tiredness and fatigue, even accidents and illness may be the outcome. (Dirken 1966; Folkard and Monk (eds.) 1985; Luce 1973; Reinberg and Ghata 1965; Reinberg et al. 1984; Rinderspacher 1985; Rose 1989). Collectively those studies demonstrate that the invariability of clock-time rhythms, sudden changes in established rhythms, and the superimposition of alien rhythms stress our capacity to synchronize and calibrate the multitude of physiological and social rhythms; in other words, they affect our well-being.

So far I have stressed the need to appreciate body times in their embeddedness in planetary motion and the rhythms of our earthly environment. Before I relate these times more explicitly to clock-time structures, however, I want to focus on endogenous body time, that is, time which is largely governed from within the body. It will suffice here to use just one example. The process of giving birth constitutes one such temporality and is particularly well suited to theorizing the relation to the surrounding environment of clock time.

Tracking the archetypal time of birthing

Birthing (without clinical intervention) is governed by internally organized rhythms that link hormone with muscle activity, synchronizing the needs of the unborn child with those of the mother's body. While unique to the experience of each mother–foetus unity, it simultaneously shows time characteristics common to that particular event irrespective of a woman's culture, race and class. To identify the special time of women giving birth, let me quote Fox since her writing on the matter most closely parallels my own and documented experience of the temporality of that event.

> The woman in labour, forced by the intensity of the contractions to turn all her attention to them, loses her ordinary, intimate contact with clock time. (Fox 1989: 127)

> For her, time stands still, moments flow together, the past and the future do not lie still behind and before her. In place of sequence, and linear relation, there is an overwhelming richness of sensation, which pulls her attention from the outer world. She is immersed in the immediacy of her experience. Her body is no longer a neutral background for her consciousness. (Fox 1989: 132)

A woman giving birth encounters all of time and no time, the centre of being and oneness with the universe, the unity of life and death. The experience is simultaneously temporal, timeful, timeless and extended in time. As this experience becomes embodied in the woman's being, constituting an integral part of her mindful body, her memory and her consciousness, it forms part of her identity. It fuses her physiological, conscious and unconscious Self with an event in which the everyday times of clocks, calendars, schedules and deadlines have no place. And yet, of course, for women in industrial and many industrializing countries this archetypal time of the birthing process tends to take place in a context where clock time reigns supreme.

In the labour wards of hospitals everything is measured against the calendar and the clock: the timing of labour and the length of each stage, the baby's heartbeat and the progress in cervical dilation, the lengths of the contractions and their spacing. The more intrusive the obstetric assistance, the more the woman is forced to oscillate between the all-encompassing body time of her labour and the rational framework of her clock-time environment. She has to answer questions, report on her sensations, and listen to instructions. Her out-of-rational-time state is clearly at odds with the abstract, ordered world of time measurement. Taking charge over her time, the attendants transform their exclusion from the centre into a situation of clear purpose and control and translate an unmanageable process of archetypal time into one more closely akin to the manageable chronology of industrial production: first this, then that, at the right time, for preset periods, and for the appropriate duration. It seems clear that a woman's entry into the time of her labouring body disrupts the attendants' sense of time, their dependence on the predictability and reliability of clock time, and that it raises for them the spectre of uncertainty, separation and death. Thus, like anthropologists constructing their subjects to the templates of their own untheorized assumptions, obstetricians project their time onto the birthing event. This reformulates an archetypal time event into a chronology. A feminist activist committed to home births tells the following anecdote:

'A couple of weeks ago I was involved in a radio programme (Radio Wales) with a consultant obstetrician about Sheila Kitzinger's book *Home Birth* which had just been published. During our chat "off the air" he was at pains to say that he thought that women like me were being a little unfair about obstetricians and that we were attacking a stereotype. I had said that one of the reasons I insisted on a home birth was that I couldn't bear to be timed in labour by doctors anxiously consulting their watches and expecting me to perform to a standard curve. The obstetrician defended himself and said that they did not do that any more – why, for example, only last week he had allowed a woman to go four hours and three minutes in the second stage of labour. I raised my eyes to heaven and said that this was exactly the kind of thing I meant and was trying to avoid. He couldn't understand that I wanted to give birth in a space where time seemed unimportant.'

(*Gill Boden, private communication 1993*)

This very brief sketch of the body time of birthing in the context of Western-style obstetrics demonstrates clearly that we have to conceive of the complexity of such a time in terms other than the traditional separation of natural from social times and the exclusion of the former from social science analyses. Even the idea of oscillating between two times – the archetypal and endogenous temporality of the birthing process and the rational clock time of obstetrics – is misleading since those times interpenetrate and mutually inform each other's meanings. For the attendants, for example, the purity of clock time becomes contaminated as they are drawn into, respond, and draw back from the archetypal time of birthing. For the woman in labour the different times blend into each other and interpenetrate to constitute a cohesive, mostly unproblematic, whole. This is particularly so for women giving birth for the first time.

> 'During the course of my labour I lost track of time; I stopped caring about what time of day it was. I was unable to focus on anything outside the labour process.
>
> 'When the contractions started I was still very aware of time: I was noting the lengths of the contractions and the time between them. But as the pain became more intense I lost that kind of awareness, lost track of time, I let go and got absorbed in my body even though I still wanted to hear what they were saying. I ceased to care about the monitor and left the monitoring job to the others. There was, however, one kind of time-consciousness I had to maintain: the appropriate timing of taking the gas-and-air mixture in relation to the contractions. I had to learn how to use it to its best effect but, after the initial conscious effort to get this right, I was able to achieve the desired result without having to concentrate on it.
>
> 'I began to regain my normal sense of time during the stitching-up process but I remember thinking how terribly long it took. With a shower, shortly after the completion of the stitching, I fully returned to my everyday sense of time.'
>
> (*Abridged interview with Cindy, thirty-three, lecturer,*
> *mother of a baby boy*)

In the work of feminist researchers such as Fox (1989), Pfeufer Kahn (1989), Pizzini (1992) and Thomas (1992) female body time has been moved to the centre of social science investigation in general and discussions on time and health in particular. Through their analyses we can appreciate how the degree of clock-time imposition changes the meaning of the birthing situation from a primordial *passage from death–birth to life* on one end of the spectrum to the passive *awaiting of being delivered* of a child on the other end. Intimately tied to an awareness of the differences along this continuum is an understanding that those variations simultaneously entail different meanings of well-being, interpretations ranging from well-being associated with the pain and creativity of *giving life* at one extreme to painless *delivery* at the other. In each single case the 'incompatible' temporalities interpenetrate with differential weighting to constitute a unique time experience. For our purposes here it is important that we begin to see together what has been separated in traditional social science analyses and that we recognize, in conjunction with the common features, the uniqueness and the complexity of each single situation and event. Most importantly, we need to appreciate that the complexity of times I discuss in Chapter 1 and in the chapters that follow is integral to and equally constitutive of the times of giving birth and associated conceptions of well-being.

This last point, of course, applies to all the body times referred to so far in this chapter. Thus, contained within the rhythmic organization of our body are speed, sequencing, timing, temporality, intensity, spacing, pacing and prioritizing of single actions and cycles. This means that these structural aspects of time apply equally to the rhythms of the body and those of social life. In the normal course of daily life, for example, we time, sequence, prioritize and pace our activities without much conscious thought; and the organization of our body rhythms certainly does not need our conscious attention. Getting up, having breakfast, catching the bus, doing homework, cooking dinner or reading a patient's notes all get done, knowing first, how long these activities take, and second, when and how fast they need to be done in relation to other activities, other demands and available time. The complexity, in other words, is deeply embedded in the taken-for-granted realm of non-discursive knowledge.

To grasp that complexity of times, it is principally important not to lose sight of the multiplicity of rhythms during the study of any particular one. In other words, all expressions of rhythmicity, periodicity, temporality, tempo, timing, orientation in time and relation to time have to be appreciated *together* if we want to get a sense of the connections between time and health, life and death. The explicit focus on any one, I suggest, must implicate all others, since the classical tradition of separating social from natural phenomena in order to eliminate the latter from the inquiry allows us neither to understand social time in its full complexity nor to conceptualize the social past in relation to the industrial present. It means further that we need to recognize that pre-industrial rhythms are not superseded by industrial ones, archetypal times not replaced by chronology. Rather, the primordial times persist and permeate our present while the imposed temporalities affect and subtly transform body and environmental time to a point where we can no longer conceptualize them in a meaningful way as separate. Just as clock time is permeated by planetary rhythms, so body times are acculturated and socialized into the metronomic beat of the clock. We are clearly not dealing with simple dichotomies or before-and-after situations: natural

and social, body and mind, female and male, life and death, traditional
and industrial time are in need of reçonceptualization.

So far in this chapter I have emphasized the structural continuity of
the time base of physiological, socio-mental and social processes without
theorizing their differences. There is, however, one discontinuity which is
of deep significance for our well-being; the structural break I have in
mind here relates to the social construction of clock time. This disjunc-
ture of times affects our health not only at a personal level but also, as I
argue in later chapters, at a collective and even global level. It thus
requires some further attention.

Clock time is finite

Clock time, the organizational time-frame and structure of industrial
production, is governed by the non-temporal principle of time, a time
that tracks and measures motion but is indifferent to change. Abstracted
from its natural source, this machine time, which I discussed in detail in
the first chapter, is created to the goal of invariant repetition and perfect
repeatability. As such it is clearly at odds with the rhythms of our body
and the 'natural' environment where variation and the principle of temporality are a source of creativity and evolution: what constitutes life for
one spells failure for the other. Furthermore, only the quantity of machine time is limited. It is finite because it excludes becoming. It does not
create time in the present but it *is* time: a time that is running on and out.
A time that constitutes the present and principally includes becoming
and repetition with variation, in contrast, is neither finite nor usable as a
quantitative measure. Equally, a time generated in time-giving activities
and reproduced through birth is ongoing, continuous and ever-renew-
able. This is a temporal time where, according to Bergson (1910) and
Mead (1932/1980), the future is *becoming* in a way that can never be a
mere repetition or rearrangement of what has been. Here, time is created
in ceaseless emergence; it is constitutive. While this time-generating
capacity is integral to all social existence, it seems that the finite resource,
the quantity which is running out, is a phenomenon that belongs *exclusively* to societies that have created an objective machine time and
relate to their creation as being time *per se*. As such, clock time forms an
integral part of contemporary Western societies' time-consciousness.
Time-efficiency, time-budgeting, time-management, they all belong to
the clock-time conceptualization of time.

What then might be the significance of that difference with respect to
well-being? Dossey (1982) and Helman (1992) write of 'hurry sickness'.

They associate a great number of diseases with the pervasive feeling of time running out, with the speeded-up pace of living, and with the pressure of getting things done in time. I want to propose that these kinds of time-based diseases are premised on a clock-time conception of finite time: a time that is a quantifiable, measurable, usable resource and a parameter for achievement. 'Dead'lines, time management and the ever-increasing pace of life, I suggest, have to be understood in relation to clock time. They are meaningless with respect to the embedded, creative and constitutive times of life and the 'life'lines of renewal created by women's being (Brodribb 1992; O'Brien 1989b). They are out of sync with the generative times of the body and as such they affect our physiological well-being. Dossey (1982) shows how an intense sense of urgency speeds up human body rhythms with the frequent outcome of heart disease, high blood pressure, a lowering of the immune function and an increase of susceptibility to infection and cancer.

> Having convinced ourselves through the aid of clocks, watches, beeps, ticks, and a myriad of other cultural props that linear time is escaping, we generate maladies in our bodies that assure us of the same thing – for the ensuing heart disease, ulcers, and high blood pressure reinforce the message of the clock: *we* are running down, eventually to be swept away in the linear current of the river of time. For us, our perceptions have become our reality. (Dossey 1982: 50)

The more severe the illness, the more the message that time is running out becomes pertinent since it enforces a confrontation with finality and the dead(end-of-the)line. Many have noted fear as the dominant contemporary response to death and have interpreted much of our social endeavours and our health care as a response to that fear (Aries 1976; Becker 1973; Mitford 1963). Fear, however, elicits physiological responses very similar to those already encountered in stress states where hurrying after unmet deadlines within ever-diminishing finite time is associated with increased heart rate and high blood pressure (Helman 1992). We can now see the cycle closing to an invariant circle going round and round: a finite quantity of time which is running down and out, stress, disease, fear of death, time running out, stress, disease, fear of death *ad infinitum*. Health, therefore, is not only identifiable by the harmonious orchestration of the rhythms of our biological and social being but also with reference to how we relate to the times of the world around us, our identity, and the past, present and future.

Medical practitioners and other healers have found that time-slowing strategies such as meditation, bio-feedback, imagery, hypnosis and autogenic training can be used to intercept that closed circle and to counteract those contemporary time diseases (Dossey 1982; Graham 1990: 108–85). If, however, we want to effect changes that pre-empt the diseases rather than attempt a cure, then, I suggest, it becomes essential that we bring time in its multiple expressions to the conscious level of our understanding. We need to begin to recognize the difference and the continuity between the times of becoming and the time of created in-variability, the times of life and the time of death. We need to lift time from the level of the taken-for-granted meaning to an understanding that knows the relation between the finite resource, birth–death and being–becoming, between chronology, the archetypal time of birthing and the seasons. We need to de-alienate time: reconnect clock time to its sources and recognize its created machine character. As such, concern with the multiple time dimensions of our lives is no mere theoretical, academic exercise; rather, it is a strategy for living. For this purpose, temporal time, the symbol of life, needs to be allowed to take a position of high visibility. Recognizing time running out as our creation, temporal time as present-creating becoming, and both as fundamental to our lives enables us to re-view the mutual implication of time and health and gives us choice for action.

Death as central to the process of life, as continuity, and as the begin-ning of new life is an understanding central not only to all the world's religions but also to the natural sciences: it is integral to human being. Clock time, day and night, the seasons, and the birth–death parameter provide us with boundaries and frameworks by which we live *in* time and all define limits to our actions. While birth–death and the rhythmic boundaries of the environment fundamentally entail becoming, clock time's invariable repetitions confront us with that which is irrevocably gone, with the relentless entropy of physical processes and with absolute finitude. Thus if we conceive of death in terms of clock time we deprive ourselves of an essentially human understanding of that event: we de-humanize death. I began this chapter with an exploration of body rhythms and the intersection of life–death at the moment of birth; I end it with thoughts on the unity of birth–death at the moment of death.

For a person facing death, time takes on a new meaning: it is no longer taken for granted. Moreover, the past, present and future become signifi-cant in very different ways for those involved: the persons preparing for death, their families, and the medical professionals engaged routinely with the prevention of death. Here I want to let a family speak of their time experiences at a point in their lives where they are facing the prospect of death. Instead of closing with the customary concluding remarks, I would like to open out the chapter, to give the reader room to reflect on the complexities and multiple incoherences brought to the surface by the broad sweep of issues raised in this exploratory investigation.

Cancer time and the prospect of death

'A cancer patient can't generalize time any more. Time becomes specific: the idea of mortality, cognizance of existence. With others you behave and react spiritually. Your interactions and statements are still spontaneous but they are immediately retracted and reflected upon in relation to so little time left.

'Time assumes a different meaning. Time is the passage of phases and interludes until it all stops. You begin to dwell more on the spirituality of life – your life in relation to the spirit world of the future. Time is no longer so important in relation to the self but in relation to the preparation about the next part of life.

'The period of maturity and old age is no longer available to you. You are in a cancer time-warp that relates only to you. With cancer you prepare for the end of life where I would normally expect to live another thirty years. Cancer is therefore a time disturber. It makes you visit places where you have never been before. The night is no longer for sleeping but for reflecting.

'What is good about it is that it allows you this time phase for growth, for cementing ideas within yourself. But it is also a time for being tested – you have everything taken away from you – your life of activity – and you are forced into a life of reflection. What do you do with all that precious time that is still given to you?

'In hospital you live on a diet of regimented time. Nothing else exists outside it. The only way to survive is to submit to it. Knowing your illness is important – you cannot compromise over it. Your acceptance of what they can offer has to be a conscious choice. Once you have made the decision to accept the treatment then you submit to it and submerge yourself in it: you welcome it as the only way to get through it and be victorious.

'Daytime is positive in its distracting quality. Night-time, in contrast, is a reaffirmation of everything that is internalized. It is a period when you surface to encompass yourself and understand yourself. Night-time enforces a one-to-one relation: you and your conscience, your consciousness, your unconscious, your reality. But this is also wearying and wearing because your body needs sleep unlike your mind which needs to reflect. Previous to the cancer I did not have much time to reflect. I reflected only during special times – time out – not on a continuous basis. I had too much to do. I was too much action-orientated. It is interesting that the right hip – the seat of my cancer – is the place where action comes from.

'Time for me used to mean action and action is excitement. Today time is awareness, comfortableness, memory. Part of it is about dying which you have to consider. The proximity of death slows everything down. You don't skip things any more; you let them come to you, dwell on them and do nothing to avoid them. With cancer there is nothing left to avoid: no mysteries, no big fears.'

(*Brian, forty-seven years, graduate, international consultant in fish farming; married, father of two children (seventeen and twenty-five) . . . Brian died two months after this interview*)

***

'I feel squashed by time: time running out and time lasting too long. There is Brian's illness and everyone around me dying: close members of my family, neighbours, my dog. There is so little time to accomplish things while simultaneously time is dragging on – waiting for death. I am cornered, squeezed between the two. I can only just cope with the routines of daily living while for me personally time is standing still. I am stuck in a period of pure survival.

'I have been living with a sense of urgency for the past six years or so. It relates to the feeling that I have been on the right track only for brief moments during my life. Now that my fiftieth birthday is approaching, I question the meaning of my life. One way to cope is to live more in the body and the present, less in the head, the past and the future.

'Work is completely in the present. The children are only interested in the now. For nine hours of the day I am living with them and this is quite good – it keeps me sane. At home, time and energy stop. School time is more hectic but it is alive and purposeful. I spend less time at home but it seems longer. between the two there is no time/space for my own life.

'Time to me is about life-span and the ageing of individuals against the background of the history of our world, the universe, eternity. I do not have much of a problem with history and eternity, more so with life-span and the present. Surrounded by so much death – just past and imminent – I feel compelled to look for more

meaningful activities, more meaningful conversations, more meaningful relationships. I lost tolerance and patience for anything trivial and mundane.'
(*Dominique, forty-nine years, teacher, married to Brian, mother of two children (seventeen and twenty-five)*)

***

'When there is more to do than I can achieve by a given deadline then time enters my life as panic. The older I get the faster time passes. Half an hour now is like a minute before. I like to take a lot of time but even large amounts seem smaller and smaller. Weeks fly by and there is never enough time to do all the things you want to do. I quite enjoy waiting because it is a period where nothing else can be done and where I can read and enjoy myself.

'I have to learn to live in the moment rather than planning and anticipating. Dad's illness changed the meaning and value of time for me. I must preserve it, spend it differently. I used to put things off to the next day; now I do it on the same day and feel good. Despite my different attitude to time, however, it still rules my life: deadlines are always pressing, I never have the feeling I get it all done. I need a regular rhythm and lots of sleep otherwise I get run down.

'Dying does not frighten me any more. My body and mind are growing together. Now that I like my life and myself, death simply means that those around me will suffer when I die. On the opposite side, time is an important factor with respect to having children, this is a major decision that cannot be postponed indefinitely.

'Time to me means seasons; everything is cyclical. My being and death is incidental to it. If the world gets blown up tomorrow there will still be time. Time is perpetual. Everything repeats itself.'
(*Marie, twenty-five years, art college graduate (sculpture), infant teacher, daughter of Brian*)

Key points

At the substantive level I have shown
- the centrality to well-being of body times and their embeddedness in and interdependence with the rhythms of the environment
- how the various conceptions of time are linked to different actions and approaches to time and health

- how encounters with birth and death take those involved beyond the realm of everyday time and bring to the fore times that are normally disattended, even submerged in subconscious being.

With reference to methodology I have argued
- that body times and the times of the physical environment cannot be excluded from social science analyses
- that we need to recognize together the mutual implication and differences of times for analyses of any specific event
- for the centrality of a social science concern with time since how time is conceptualized makes a difference; it affects not merely social science praxis but our daily lives, our health and our relationship to birth and death.

3

Education: Learning the Habits of Clock Time

The dominant conceptualizations of time detailed in this book are clearly not universals. In their particular expressions, the time of the clock, the measure and the finite quantity, all with their implied emphasis on death, constitute central characteristics of a 'Western' cultural identity. The complex relations to own and other time, life and death, work and 'natural' time, in other words, are culturally transmitted, learnt during early childhood and bedded down over the many years of schooling. Not explicitly taught but part of the hidden curriculum of education, these dominant temporal structures and norms of society are absorbed, maintained, re-created and changed in daily educational practice. It is for this reason that social scientists seeking to take seriously the temporal dimension of everyday life need to concern themselves with time in education.

From a certain age onwards both pupils and the adults who teach them have no difficulty with the question 'What is *the* time?', with learning to tell *the* time: to know *the* time is to know clock time. An answer to the question 'What is *time*?', in contrast, is likely to pose substantial problems for children and teachers alike. Ideas like 'time is money', 'time flows like a river', 'time is a natural process of day following night following day *ad infinitum*', or 'time is a resource to be sold and controlled', would jostle for prime position in any definition of what time might be. The abstract exchange value, absolute unidirectionality, diurnal and seasonal cycles, the measure and the quantity are not easily reconciled and sit uncomfortably with a question that presupposes time in the singular. Yet it is the singular clock-time conception that underpins the dominant experience of school time where bells and buzzers, clocks and calendars reign supreme.

Critical engagement with the question 'What is *time*?', therefore, requires that we move out of the natural attitude, that we make the implicit visible and turn our attention to the taken-for-granted. It necessitates further that we focus on connections, relationships and interpenetrations, and recognize the multiplicity of times: lived, experienced, known, generated, reckoned, allocated, sold, controlled and used as an abstract exchange value. Once sensitized to the complexity, we can see beyond *the* time a multiplicity of times expressed in social structures, knowledge and interactions, and in the physical, living and created environment. Thus, we need to unravel the dominant representations of time, show them to be socio-historical constructions and acknowledge their hidden role as guides to seeing and understanding. This involves not just detailing the extensive time-structuring of education by clock and calendar time but bringing to the fore aspects of time that tend to be disattended by academics and practitioners alike. Moreover, if social science is not merely to describe and explain but to offer critique and analyses for change, then the most mundane and common-place temporal dimensions of everyday life need to be explored alongside extraordinary and novel ones, education and work alongside birth and death, new technologies and globalized processes.

Critical theory for change therefore needs to show the complexity of times, the very specific impact on social life of the clock-time view of time, and the potential of alternative visions and approaches. It needs to make explicit the socialization to a clock-time reality not just with respect to the subject matter but also with reference to the backcloth of unquestioned social science assumptions: social scientists need to become reflective about their own practices. Thus, where the previous chapters created bridges between the personal and the collective and stressed the fact that we are both embodied and embedded in our environments, this chapter brings to the forefront of our attention the mismatch between the temporalities of the subject matter and those of the methodological and conceptual tools for study; and it shows how some classical social theorists have provided starting-points for more appropriate approaches to the complexity and interpenetration of times in education. In this chapter I therefore render visible the multiplicity of times in educational interactions, research and theory.

Clocks, timetables and schedules

The time of clocks and calendars, of minutes, hours, days and years, is unquestionably the dominant time experience in contemporary Western education: so many minutes set aside for the next test, so many hours for a particular topic, so many years for each stage of the children's educational career. Learning, teaching and even the payment of teachers are established and calculated on the basis of calendars and clocks. It is this universalized, decontextualized and quantitative time which underpins the physical structuring devices of Western education: bells, buzzers and preset units of lesson times, timetables and schedules, all of which function as time structures, as parameters within which pupils study and educators teach, record, review and plan. These artefactual devices thus constitute a framework for the explicit organization of educational time, they form the structural base from which to budget and spend that time effectively, make it pass faster or slower, and restructure its use for greater cost and learning efficiency. Beyond this most explicit structural expression of time as framework and parameter, time is implicated in the intricate processes of timing and synchronization, the careful sequencing and prioritizing, the speed and intensity of educational processes.

Even the most cursory examination of the way education is organized in Western-style societies shows that everything is timed. The activities and the interactions of all its participants are orchestrated to a symphony of buzzers, bells, timetables, schedules and deadlines. These time markers bind pupils and staff into a common schedule within which their respective activities are structured, paced, timed, sequenced and prioritized. They separate and section one activity from another and secure conformity to a regular, collective beat. They inform students and staff when the day's education commences and when it ends. They signal that it is time to switch attention from mathematics to history, or from the class-room to the sports field. The beginning and the end of lessons, the term, the school year, and the dates and times for tests and examinations are some of the fixed points within which subjects, teachers' activities and the students' expected progress are programmed (Ball et al. 1984; Delamont and Galton 1986). Within the overall structure of finite time resources and nested timetables, activities are scheduled for preset durations. They are arranged to follow certain sequences and to happen at a specific rate, at a particular time in the children's lives, over a fixed period, and for a set number of times.

In addition to being synchronized and coordinated into the overall organizational structure of the school, the education system and the socio-political system of the country as a whole, those school activities are allocated, prioritized and selected according to a calculation of the finite time resources of teachers and their pupils. 'School life is organized by and into complex sequences', argue Ball et al. (1984: 43). 'The daily institutional reality of the school takes its experiential form from these sequences, and it is their finite length which constrains activity and provides the basis for the setting of priorities and making allocations.' Each single timing, synchronization and allocation is in turn nested within a multiplicity of others, ranging from educational plans and curricula reforms down to the didactic detail of the time structure of individual lessons.

The timetable therefore plays a particularly important role in school life. It provides all participants with a regular routine within which the carefully scheduled learning, teaching, examining, assessing, managing, administrating, cleaning, eating and playing can proceed in an orderly and predictable manner. It ensures the choreography of the daily mass movement of pupils both to and within the school, and guarantees the correct number, sequence, duration and compatible combinations of subjects for each year group and individual choice combinations. The timetabled routine makes certain, in other words, that there are fixed points for all activities (Delamont and Galton 1986: 138). Moreover, daily rhythms of arrival, registration, lessons and breaks are nested in weekly recurrences of set combinations of lessons, fixed for the whole school year. Both in turn are embedded in larger cyclical variations governed by the social and educational calendar, the preparations for the Christmas play, sports events and examinations.

The 'when', 'how often', 'how long', 'in what order' and 'at what speed' of school activities are thus largely predefined for pupils and their educators: entry and exit points to the various stages of education are age-graded, the time for studying each subject is fixed for each level of study. Not only the dates for examinations but also the speed at which they are to be completed are fixed with reference to calendar and clock time. In other words, assessments are made not only in terms of whether or not pupils know what they have been taught; rather, judgement is passed with regard to whether they can reproduce what they have learnt within a predetermined period of time. To finish an examination 'too early' might produce a judgement of carelessness or a verdict that the questions were not given due consideration. Not to finish 'on time', to be 'slow', would generate an equally negative response: the pupil obviously did not know the material well enough, had to spend too much time thinking, and left open to speculation whether or not he or she could have answered all the questions had there been more time. How much time is to be spent on each task is meticulously preplanned for them in the name of efficiency and effectiveness without allowances being made for individual and local differences, special circumstances and personal preferences.

The structural time of education discussed so far is intimately tied to the time of the clock. As such, it is divisible into mathematically equal units. It is perceived as a quantity that can be sectioned into distinct time slots and allocated for mutually incompatible activities, manipulated as a finite resource and used as an abstract exchange value. In the educational setting, evidence of the segmenting and compartmentalizing of time is overwhelming: work time is segregated from break-time and home time. Homework time is (or should be) distinct from television and sleeping time. Holiday time separates one term from the next. Equally prevalent is the use of this quantitative time as both a measure and a resource. This facilitates the budgeting, planning and predicting of an 'ideal' time use for others: five minutes to complete the next multiplication task, fifteen minutes to run around the perimeter of the school grounds, and two months to complete the section on the economic infra-structure of the Amazon Rain Forest in a human geography course.

However, as I argued in the previous chapter, clock time as a resource is finite. This means that only so much can be done in one lesson; only so much can be packed into one year's teaching; any additional material requires rescheduling. It means further that the 'available time' has to be allocated with care, the scarce resource budgeted efficiently. Pupils may be told that they need to speed up on their essay-writing (less time for same amount of work), spend more time on their homework (more work over longer time), and take more care over their project work (more time for same work). Teachers may need to exclude sections of a course in order to be able to teach important new material in the same amount of time; and headteachers need to juggle the allocated person-hours to cover the curriculum. Finally, quantified time can be used as an abstract medium of exchange: one hour of detention for a specific misbehaviour, twenty hours' more teaching time to be purchased to cover the increase in pupil numbers. In education, as in the wider context of work and employment relations, the time of clocks and calendars is therefore not only carefully sectioned and used as a resource to be allocated, budgeted, managed and controlled, it is also a commodity. As a commodity, moreover, it is fundamentally linked to relations of power. School-children learn very subtly that some people's time is regarded as more important than others. They absorb hierarchies by getting to know who waits for whom, who controls and structures the time of others and who is subjected to such time control. (For the relation between waiting and power see also Frankenberg (ed.) 1992 and Schwartz 1979.)

The requirement in Western-style societies to produce good work fast, at the correct rate, to deadlines determined by timetable and calendars, is thus underpinned by quantitative time. It is this dominant time, so central to our adult social life, which gets habituated during childhood through the time discipline promoted in education: time has to be used effectively and budgeted with care. Every task has its own optimal time. 'Time-wasting' is considered acceptable only during specially created periods of time – official break-times, weekends and holidays – where it has been redefined for children and adults respectively as play-time and relaxation. While such time discipline forms a mostly unquestioned dimension of adult existence, for children it constitutes one of a number of hidden curricula. For them, school is the place where the puritan, utilitarian approach to time is absorbed and internalized.

The Benedictine heritage

This particular approach to time, as I show in this book, is not a human universal. It is peculiar to a Western way of life. Social scientists from Weber (1904–5/1989) to Foucault (1977) have argued that punctuated and sectioned time which provides strict guidelines for activity and rest periods was first developed in the monasteries of the West, that it has been bequeathed to us by the Benedictine monks. Through their analyses, social scientists have established a link between the secular time discipline of contemporary life and the ascetic daily rounds of monastic existence. Thus, Mumford (1934/1955) writes:

> It was [however] in the monasteries of the West that the desire for order and power, other than that expressed in the military domination of weaker men, first manifested itself after the long uncertainty and bloody confusion that attended the breakdown of the Roman Empire. Within the walls of the monastery was sanctuary: under the rule of the order surprise and doubt and caprice and irregularity were put at bay. Opposed to the erratic fluctuations and pulsations of the worldly life was the iron discipline of the rule . . . So one is not straining the facts when one suggests that the monasteries – at one time there were 40,000 under the Benedictine rule – helped to give human enterprise the regular collective beat and rhythm of the machine; for the clock is not merely a means for keeping track of the hours, but of synchronizing the actions of men. (Mumford 1934/1955: 4–5)

St Benedict required his monks to be occupied at all times so as to avoid idleness. His attitude to time can be summed up in Rule XLVIII which states that 'Idleness is the enemy of every soul' (McCann 1970: 28). Zerubavel (1981: 33–4) shows how there were annual, weekly and daily routines and timetables governing the set times for all activities from bathing, bloodletting and mattress-filling to prayer, work and sleep. Weber (1904–5/1989: 118, 154) explained how the purpose of the rationalized conduct was to overcome *status naturae* and to free people from their dependence on impulses and the world of nature. Gradually this concern for rational action and proper time-keeping spilled over into the countryside and the market-place until, by the end of the fourteenth century, time was routinely recognized as money and 'became thought of independently of what was happening in time' (Thrift 1988: 81). The negative time discipline of preventing the waste of time was fused with the more active one of intensifying efforts, with the move towards maximum speed and efficiency (Foucault 1977: 154). In Western societies we have imposed the monastic schedule on ourselves, our children and their educators. That is, we have adopted this reified, abstracted time and its rationalized control as an educational strategy. In the sixth century, when the Benedictine monks first introduced fixed and preset times for each of their activities, this was a revolutionary practice. Today it is neither questioned as a practice nor doubted as a principle: it is simply taken for granted. It has become the inescapable reality for twentieth-century Western education.

Today, bells, timetables, schedules and educational calendars, the key structuring devices of educational practice based on clock time, are hegemonic to a point of making invisible any times constituted outside the quantitative mode. This has consequences, as I show in other chapters, for how we relate to our body, health and the environment, and for the establishment of equality, equity and equal opportunity between different sexes, age-groups, races, cultures and economically classified regions of the globe, to name just a few such affected relationships. With respect to our present focus on education with its powerful socializing and habituating impact, it is important to move beyond a single definition of *the* time and recognize a multiplicity of times in each moment of interaction and learning. Such appreciation of the complexity of times in education is important not only for better social science analyses but also for changes in educational practice. In the next section of this chapter I therefore turn my attention away from the most explicit time dimension of Western education and focus on other, less obvious aspects. These range from time boundaries and durations established by implicit norms, to the synchronization of multiple time-worlds, and from the times embedded in key concepts to times as experienced by those involved in the educational enterprise. I sketch a brief outline of this complexity and argue that these aspects need to be encompassed not only if research is to better account for times in educational praxis than has been the case to date, but also if we want to facilitate change in educational practice, that is, to weaken the hegemony of the clock-time perspective on life. I suggest, in other words, that an explication of the complexity of times is important if we as social scientists, citizens and private persons want to play a part in the destabilization of the taken-for-grantedness of the clock-time approach to daily life. In Chapters 6 and 7 I extend the argument further and suggest that such an action approach to the contemporary subject matter of social science is not merely a choice but an inescapable necessity.

Norms, experiences and the joining of life-worlds

So let us begin once more to look beyond the time of the clock to discover what tends to remain in the shadows and explicate some of the implicit temporalitites of educational practice. The amount of time spent on activities and interactions in the class-room is not solely dependent on bells, buzzers, calendars and clocks; they are merely the structural elements within which temporal plans, decisions and actions are executed. The when, how often, how long, in what order and at what speed, in other words, are also guided by times other than the abstract measure. That is to say, in addition to the physical parameters, direction is given to educational practice by norms, habits and conventions. These determine the timing and duration of preparations for the Christmas play, of when to teach *Romeo and Juliet*, of how often to have a parents' evening. Equally, clocks and calendars are not the only considerations behind the timing and sequencing of activities and the teaching of specific subjects. Thus, for example, career advice is not given to children in primary schools but during the last year of secondary education, and geometry is only taught after students have a basic grasp of addition, subtraction, multiplication and division. These norms for timing, sequencing and prioritizing in education are located in very specific, if implicit, theories of time. In addition to time as measure and as quantity they express an understanding of the unidirectionality of processes, of cause and effect, and of the cumulative nature of knowledge. They imply an understanding of time that acknowledges that 'you cannot step into the same river twice', that the past and future are inseparably tied to the present, and that there is a 'right' time for everything.

Furthermore, timing is not only a problem of timetables and a task for participants who need to be in the right place at the stipulated time and for the correct duration but also of the coordination and fusion of personal times. Thus, worried pupils who have overslept and forgotten some of their books and homework, students who are tired because they stayed up too long watching a late-night film, and others who are anxious about their biology examination and flustered because they have just been told off for running in the corridor have to join their time-worlds with that of a teacher who has had a confrontational encounter with a colleague and who is now seeking to capture everybody's attention with a lesson on the Pilgrim Fathers (and Mothers). The task for all participants is to suspend their extended, multiple, personal time-worlds and to enter collectively, under the guidance of the teacher, the time-world of the pilgrims. Such synchronization and switching of time-worlds is part of every lesson whether the subject is history, literature, mathematics or art.

In the class-room, the joining of personal times is extended to a collective temporality: we can speak of a creation of class-room times. Class-room times are constituted by a world of shared patterns of inter-action and communication, collective knowledge and common expec-tations. (See Collins and Green 1992; and Weade 1992: 94–5 for their innovative discussions on what constitutes a class-room.) That is to say, class-room times are not exhausted by how long members spend on certain activities, not even by the daily, weekly and yearly timetables that structure every aspect of educational activity. Rather, they are consti-tuted on the basis of individual and collective histories and futures which, in turn, have a central bearing on any one moment of time generated by the group. The class thus *creates* class-room times in a pregiven temporal setting based on clock and calendar time as well as schedules guided by norms, habits and tradition. It produces times that fundamentally extend beyond the visible present. These non-quantifiable aspects of time in education prove particularly troublesome, as I show below, for empirical studies of educational practice.

Beyond the complexity and simultaneity of class-room time, the join-ing of life-worlds and the normative dimension of educational time there is the time implicated in the key concepts of education: in teaching and learning, vocational training, assessment and records, student profiles, performance, achievement, curriculum and educational reform. Each one of these concepts is a temporal statement that irreducibly invokes not clock time but the past, present and future. To keep records, for example, is to fix present information for use in some future present. Assessing pupils' performances, educators not only judge actual ac-complishments with reference to the group but to the pupils' potential for achievement: 'could do better', 'has not worked hard enough in this subject' and 'has disappointed' are indicators that consideration is given to predicted capability based on the knowledge of past performance, not merely the actual but the temporally extended, projected achievement. The recipients of education are classified into bright students, underachievers and slow learners. Each of these categories contains a time extended by past and future penetration, and by a horizon of achievement and expectation while simultaneously entailing time as pace, as cumulative and unidirectional process, and as measured duration. The notion of reform implies that we can use our understanding of the past to create a new and better future, while ideas about the curriculum and learning in the educational context more generally are based on the belief in a causal relationship between teaching and learning (see Weade 1992 on myths about learning). They encompass implicit assumptions about a 'right age', a pre-existing 'appropriate base' upon which to build, and about 'proper sequencing'. They are premised on the supposition that a child who has not learnt to add up cannot be expected to grasp multiplication, that there has to be progression from the simple to the complex and from the concrete to the abstract. Piaget's theory of developmental stages has been incorporated into educational assumptions and practices as unquestioned and unquestionable 'fact'. These implicit time dimensions of education are rarely attended to. They are simply taken for granted by both educators and social scientists alike.

From this first glance at times in education there emerges a recognition first, that the dominant clock and calendar time are central but by no means the only kinds of time, and second, that even in its most quantitative form time displays a complexity of explicit practice, implicit norms and embedded temporalities that requires closer examination. Research in education, however, has barely begun to focus on the most explicit aspects of time in education (Ball et al. 1984; Ben-Baruch 1986–7; Delamont and Galton 1986; Morrison (ed.) 1992; Schuller 1990), let alone those aspects that form the untheorized, common-sensical substrata of educational practice. In this chapter, therefore, I want to bring together the implications of recognizing the complexity of social times for theory, methodology, empirical study and practice. As such the chapter forms a pivotal part of this book. We have to bear in mind, however, that the analysis offered here applies to all the topics investigated in this book; education is merely the exemplar through which I seek to make the specific theoretical and methodological points.

Research times beyond the clock-time measure

Timetables, schedules and programmes of work are, of course, not prerogatives of educational practice; they also permeate the research experience. It is in the form of measure, parameter and resource that time is used predominantly in educational research. Beyond these dominant expressions the complexity of times in research is constituted in forms less visible than those associated with calendars and clocks. It is implicated in observations of decision-making, teaching and learning. It enters methodological considerations, whether we engage in cross-sectional or longitudinal research, whether we conduct time-series analyses, trend or panel studies. It permeates observations and comparisons, the recording of data and their analyses, their evaluation and explanation. It is integral to the objects of observation as well as the observers, their methodologies and theories. Thus, the complexity of times in research must not be left implicit but needs to be given attention in its own right: the taken-for-granted needs to become an object of reflection. That is to say, reflexivity needs to be turned on the self, on social science praxis.

All research is structured, paced, timed, sequenced and prioritized within the overall framework of the research design, the task at hand and the funding. Specific activities are scheduled to preset durations, designed to follow certain sequences, and synchronized with the activities of the class and educational establishment to be investigated. This means that the when, how long, how often, in what order and at what speed of research is predesigned to fit the object of investigation, the research agenda and the stipulations of the funding body. Even the link between speed and efficiency is applicable to researchers and researched alike. Furthermore, the temporal location, duration, sequence, timing and periodicity of observation and interviews will have an effect on both the process and the outcome of the research. Class-room observation can serve as an example. *When* the research takes place as well as its *timing* – Monday, the second half of a double lesson in biology, at the beginning of the autumn term, taught by a new member of staff – have a significant bearing on the outcome. So have considerations about the *duration* of the research – the whole lesson or part of it, for one or more lessons, for the term or a whole year – since the length of the observation and of the research as a whole significantly influence the data. This applies equally to the question about *how often* the observations are to take place – once, ten or thirty times – and to whether their *repetition* is to be conducted regularly or intermittently. Each of these considerations, singly and collectively, will have a bearing on the observational data. Recognition of the significance of these time factors should therefore form an explicit part of any research design.

It matters further whether the research is based on observations of processes or comparisons between two states on a before-and-after basis, whether it seeks to establish causal connections or correlations, and whether it allows for the past and future to become an explicit part of the research design and the analysis. Moreover, these temporal dimensions may be implicated in decisions about the research design irrespective of whether or not the aim is to test hypotheses (future projection) or someone else's findings (past-based), whether or not the objective is to record (fixing the present) or predict (the future on the basis of our knowledge of the past), whether or not explicit attempts are being made to affect future practice and policy (the future acting as guide to actions in the present), and whether or not the research is to be contained within the scientific remit of description, analysis, explanation and the construction of models (reflective and selective, past-oriented hindsight, in part even ossifying processes). All these time aspects are constituents of empirical research and therefore need to be acknowledged as such in research practice.

As far as clock and calendar time are concerned, the research tool seems to suit the subject matter, in this case educational activities and events, with its strong emphasis on clock time-based timetables, schedules and the educational calendar. This fit disintegrates, however, when researchers encounter the complexity of times, temporalities, timings and tempos entailed within each moment of investigation. Such multiplicity is not easily contained within the single medium of empirical research where, at best, the various aspects can be identified separately and where the plurality has to be achieved on the basis of a recombination of single 'parts', where complexity can only ever be a simulation of complexity. To grasp the extent of the problem, it is necessary to appreciate the historically sedimented association between scientific research and clock time.

Since its earliest beginnings, science has been associated with the clock-time measure. That is to say, with its dependence on measurement, quantification and causal analyses, science is intimately tied to the uniform, abstracted, fragmentable, physically and spatially representable time of the clock. In classical science, as I show in detail elsewhere (Adam 1990: 50–5) and in other chapters of this book, time is conceived as a quantity: invariant, infinitely divisible into space-like units, measurable in length and expressible as number. It is time taken, the duration between events.

> When we speak, for example, of time intervals and durations or of time order and sequence, we have in mind an imaginary long straight axis of time with points on it locating events and distances along it measuring the elapsed time between events. The very words *interval, duration, sequence* evoke spatial images that help us to think about time and its measurement. In other words, for quantitative and related conceptual purposes, we picture time as a kind of one-dimensional continuous space. And one finds this spatial view of time throughout scientific literature. (Jones 1983: 79)

Social science research is not exempt from this scientific approach to time: it too relies on time as measured quantity, linear sequence and cyclical pattern. It too is concerned to measure rates of change, duration and periodicity, all of which are central expressions of the time of classical science. As quantity, resource and measure, dissociated from educational events and experiences, the time of scientific research is used to establish change on a before-and-after basis; it compares two static states of two points in time, one earlier and one later. It is the basis for educational tests and the ground upon which traditional research is conducted. Today, however, it is recognized that this time of the clock constitutes a very specific and partial aspect of the complexity of social times, that its validity as a research tool, therefore, is limited. The implications for research are clear: researchers have to begin to deal with the complexities of times. At the very least, they have to encompass temporality, timing, tempo, intensity and rhythmicity as well as the temporal extension of the present. Furthermore, and in addition to time as parameter, they need to recognize the constitutive character of time, that research is not merely conducted *in* time and *over* time but that it also *creates* time in interaction with its subject matter. This means that educational researchers need to begin to talk about the *construction* of classroom times, not merely time's use and abuse, and about the creation of research time, not merely its allocation and control.

We further need to appreciate that the past and future impact on every moment of the research process. We have to cope with the fact that as invisibles the past and future fall outside what clock time can express and measure. As such, they are particularly troublesome for a medium based on the senses as well as a materialist epistemology: we can neither see nor measure students' life-worlds, their personal biographies, their past experiences, their hopes, fears and ambitions. We can ask about it but the respondents' answers will always be retrospective rationalizations; the responses cannot be mirrors of reality even if the persons questioned consider themselves to be telling the truth. We have to grasp that when researchers observe class-room time they are joining a process time with a history, a temporal time created, re-created and maintained in interaction on the basis of collective and individual past knowledge and future-oriented projects. Researchers become participants, in other words, in a reality where invisible pasts and futures form the primary constituents of that reality. Both observers and observed are located in time and space and both are characterized by separate biographies, personal histories and future orientations which are in turn nested in uniquely relevant, wider socio-historical contexts. For the duration of the observation, however, their time-worlds meet. They may just run parallel as, for example, during the process of 'objective' outsider observation. Alternatively, participant observers may join their time-worlds with those of the observed, while interview situations will require a more substantial degree of joining of time-worlds by both interviewer and interviewee. Irrespective of the method, however, even a long-term study would still have to contend with the invisible life-worlds and biographies which staff, students and researchers bring to that collective time and which, in turn, influence what individual members see, understand and take to be relevant. This would be the case even in situations where the investigator had taken part in the development of that joint construction from the moment that teacher and students first met. This means, the observational moment is never just that: it is vastly extended in time and space and researchers have to draw on a 'wide variety of additional data sources', as Green et al. (1992: 147) point out, once they acknowledge the complexities and contextualities, the continuities and discontinuities, and the temporal extension within any one moment of class-room inter-action available for observation.

Such spatio-temporal extension becomes particularly pertinent in re-search on learning. Learning implies, as I argue above, an understanding of time as a unidirectional, cumulative process with a past and future extension. For research this means first, that it is meaningless to associate learning with points in time, second, that there can be no un-learning, only forgetting, just as there can be no un-living or growing younger, and third, that there is a problem, as Weade (1992) shows, with conceptualiz-ing learning in terms of cause and effect, input and output, with clearly identifiable points at either end and with teachers transmitting knowl-edge which students absorb. Weade recognizes learning as a tacit, elusive and largely invisible act and she accentuates the problem by asking the question 'When is learning?'. She emphasizes the cooperative and con-structive aspects of the learning process and she stresses the complexity of forces bearing on learning, influences that extend beyond the personal interaction and collective histories to the setting and even the materials involved. The message for research is unambiguously clear: learning is a process with a history and a future; it is thus not containable within observable moments. It entails a joining of life-worlds, a drawing on collective and individual past knowledges as well as projected visions, all of which are brought to bear on the interactive present. Learning further depends on intricate timing, considerations of speed and intensity, and finally on the comforting predictability of rhythm and routine. These multiple times, furthermore, cover the material, conceptual and emotional reality entailed in any learning situation. If, however, learning is invisible, and if it is not possible to identify moments or points of learning because learning is always temporally extended, then what is it that researchers are observing when they are investigating learning? What *is* observed and seen, it seems, depends on prior knowledge and theories. That is to say, what is observed extends beyond the boundaries of the observation. It is not only filtered through the observers' frames of reference but also temporally extended in a way that can *never* achieve a match between teachers', students' and observers' personal temporal extensions. This means, and I argue this more fully in Chapter 7, that we have to let go of the illusion of an objectively observable reality uncontaminated by observation and unaffected by times, most specifically, the invisibles of past and future.

Acceptance of the complexity of times, therefore, poses intransigent problems for the very foundations of empirical research: the practice of generalizing across time and space, objective observation and the measurement of change on a before-and-after basis. Acknowledgement of the multiplicity entails a growing sensitivity to the fundamental mismatch between the measure and that which it measures and to the irreducible implication of past and future in any (present) moment of investigation. Finally, it enforces recognition that invisibles and simultaneous complexities are beyond the capacity of empirical research and fundamentally depend on theory. Where empirical research is bound to the local and the specific, theory can reach out. It can transcend the empirical restrictions and explore the complex, the uncertain and the invisible. It can aspire to understanding and knowledge of the realm beyond sense data. It is here at the theoretical level, therefore, that we have to make sense of the multiple complexity of times in educational praxis and everyday life more generally.

Theoretical traditions and challenges

Some of the founders of social science have given more than just cursory attention to the nature of social time, a topic most contemporary social scientists consider too philosophical as a subject matter for study. Durkheim demonstrated the social synchronizing and integrative function of time. Marx stressed its commodification and Weber its rationalization. More recently, Mead focused on issues of ontology – the reality status and the constitution of the past, present and future – while Schutz concentrated on matters of epistemology, emphasizing the centrality of reflection, multiple time-worlds and the life-plan. These classical theories of time can provide us with necessary first steps towards developing theoretical frameworks for research that give explicit attention to time.

Collectively, they can help us to see in relation what has thus far been treated separately: the commodity, the resource, the lived experience, the rhythms of institutions and planetary motions, the beat of clocks and the patterns established by habits and norms. Classical time theories, furthermore, are continuous with existing approaches in the sociology of education. In other words, the time theories of Durkheim, Marx, Mead and Schutz, as well as their contemporary exponents, have their counterparts in the normative, critical, interpretative and constructivist approaches to education, detailed in Middleton (1987).

Thus, for example, functionalist emphases on temporal order, synchronization, integration, regulation, and on timetables, schedules, time-management and time-budgeting – the when, how long, in what order and at what speed – correspond to the liberal tradition in education and the normative approach in educational research. In the studies of social time by Durkheim (1915), Sorokin and Merton (1937), Moore (1963), Roth (1976), Lauer (1981), and Zerubavel (1979, 1981, 1985), for example, the concept of time tends to be used pretheoretically within the dominant, largely quantitative tradition of social science and to be premised on assumptions of an external, objectively observable reality, a social world uncontaminated by temporality and unaffected by the processes of observation. These theorists' time conceptualizations are predominantly those of time as parameter, as measure and as resource. Processes are translated into fixed states and compared on a before-and-after basis. From this perspective learning is established quantitatively by comparing two fixed points; the difference between them is taken as the measure of learning. Furthermore, there is a generalized concern to establish the social nature of time, to posit it in contradistinction to the times of the physical and living environment as well as to the psychologically-based times of memory, perception, cognition and intent. This nature–culture dualism, of course, is an approach I take issue with throughout this book, most specifically in Chapters 2 and 6 on health and the environment.

Time studies located in the theories of temporal order, synchronization and regulation not only exclude the body, the physical environment and all that is invisible to empirical study, they also tend to leave untouched questions of power *vis-à-vis* processes of knowledge formation. Analogous to approaches in the liberal tradition of education and the normative methodology in educational research, there is little attempt to address the historical development of power over time. Similarly, concern with questions about who controls whose time, who defines what as time for study, teaching or examination is absent from the research agenda. Equally lacking is an understanding of how learning is achieved, how it is constituted in interaction and how it is defined and redefined through communicative practices within and between historically located groups. In this dominant perspective, in other words, sustained attention is denied to that which transcends the immediate, the observable, the quantifiable and the material.

Some of these gaps in functionalist approaches to time are addressed in the critical tradition where emphasis is placed on the control of time and the historical development of time as an abstract exchange value. The Marxist stress on commodification, on the economic dimension of time, and on the role of the state can be compared to critical approaches in educational research and to theories of social and cultural reproduction as defined by MacDonald (1980). Contemporary theorists sympathetic to this social science tradition, as I show in other chapters but most specifically in Chapter 4 on work, focus on time as a medium that enables the translation of labour into a monetary value (see also Adam 1990: 104–26 and Schwartz 1979). In their development of Marx's (1857/ 1973: 140–3, 1867/1976: 39–40) analyses, writers such as Giddens (1981: 119–20, 130–4), Nowotny (1985) and Thompson (1967) argue that time as lived time, as the substance of being and social life, has become extended by time as abstract quantity and pure duration. In its modern, extended form, in other words, time is freely exchangeable with all other times and usable as an abstract medium for exchange. Moreover, they suggest that quantification is implicated in the contemporary, Western meaning of time: disconnected from the materiality of experience, time comes to be perceived as real, 'objective' time and associated with money. Finally, and in agreement with Mumford (1934/1955: 3–9, 1973: 272), the clock is accorded a central role for the coordination of labour power and machines as well as the standardized, metronomic rhythm of industrial work.

Despite the stress on power and the *processes* of commodification and control, however, time is still predominantly conceptualized as a parameter within which life is enacted and as a spatial quantity by which time is measured as distance. That is to say, the potential to theorize the connection between the transformative power of times and the external quantity is rarely utilized. Furthermore, even in critical analyses processes tend to get translated into comparisons of before-and-after states. Lastly, and most importantly, positivist beliefs in objectivity, causal connections and the attainability of truth are left unscathed (see particularly Chapter 7). With reference to our present focus on education it is important to recognize that time as resource, as money and as clock-based rhythm is not restricted to capitalist *industrial* production. As we have seen above, it equally pervades the institutional structures of education and the activities of its participants, thus functioning as a habituating environment, as preparation for an industrial way of life. The quantity-clock-power dimension, therefore, is essential for providing the link between the neutral quantity and its control. The control and power aspects of time, we can say, are inseparably implicated in temporal organization, order, synchronization and regulation, in the timetables, schedules and time-management of contemporary, Western-style education: functionalist and Marxist theories are mutually dependent on each other.

Neither the functionalist/normative nor the Marxist/critical approaches to time in education, however, encompass the past–future extension identified above. For that we have to turn to interpretative and constructivist positions which, in turn, draw extensively on Heidegger's (1927/1980, 1969/1972) philosophical theory of time and being. Heidegger emphasized the finitude of *Dasein*, our being unto death, as the source for our existence *in* time. Heidegger argued that out of our awareness of the finality of existence arise not only the meaning, the importance and the urgency of being but also time as the boundary to life. In other words, timetables and daily schedules, clocks and calendars, day and night, and the seasons are not the only sources of a time framework that locates us *in* time. This birth–death parameter, moreover, must not be thought of like a perimeter fence or a fixed structure. Rather, it has to be appreciated as permeating our being at every moment of projective existence and, most importantly, as fundamentally including becoming: we are extended by our past and future. This means that *Dasein* is both horizon and presencing, that birth and death enter creatively into every moment, and that the time-frame is continuously reconstituted in the present. From this theoretical perspective it makes little sense, for example, to establish learning quantitatively on a before-and-after basis since the temporal framework is conceived not as objective and fixed but as relative to the person in question. From this vantage-point, it clearly makes a difference whether students are ten, eighteen, forty or sixty years old when they learn about the stock-market crashes of the 1930s and 1980s, the destruction of the rain forests, or the rise and fall of the Berlin Wall, since their personal experience continuously impacts on and intersects with what they learn. That is to say, context, biography and the life-plan are *constitutive* of the temporality of education.

This phenomenological understanding of time has significant implications for researching time in education: it leaves us in no doubt that the past and future permeate the moment of observation, whether we are dealing with a life-plan, a curriculum review or the daily lesson. The past and future, as I have shown above, are active constituents in the creation of the present, a hidden dimension that is neither isolatable nor abstractable from observable actions or the effects of institutional structures. Teachers experience the constitutive power of the past and future permeation on a daily basis. It is implied, for example, in their efforts to merge their own time-worlds and that of their subject matter with the multiple time-worlds of their pupils. It is inextricable from their creation of a class-room, a common culture that builds on their collective past and projected future. It is fundamental to their record-keeping, assessment of pupils and planning of teaching. This means that parameters as fixed external temporal structures intersect with the creative moment of past and future penetration or, in Schutz and Luckmann's (1973: 47) words, 'knowledge of finitude stands out against the experience of the world's continuance. This knowledge is the fundamental moment of all projects within the framework of a life-plan, as it is itself determined by the time of the life-world.'

Schutz and Luckmann offer the concept of multiple life-worlds as the phenomenal moment where the private and collective, the fictional and the real interpenetrate. Beyond this, the concept encompasses an appreciation that the stream of consciousness intersects with the rhythms of the body, the seasons and society. For Schutz and Luckmann, therefore, time is never monolithic. The permeation by pasts and futures of the physiological rhythms of the body, planetary movements and the patterns of seasons, as well as routines, plans and reviews is inseparable from the social organization to bells, clocks and calendars. Mutually implicating, they constitute an important part of the complexity of educational times. Schutz and Luckmann's conceptualizations of the life-plan and the multiple times of the life-world thus provide an invaluable base from which to begin to theorize not only the complex interpenetration of the multiple levels of time but also the implicit time dimensions of, for example, planning strategies, assessment and reviews.

A second important dimension of time is covered in Schutz's (1971) phenomenological work on consciousness and reflection. Once more, the past, present and future play a central role. Schutz pointed out that whilst actions are processes in the direction of the future, that is, always oriented towards a project, an act can only be known reflectively, once it is in the past. This applies to past known acts as well as to those in the future present where they can be reflected on as possible acts: we can reflect in the past tense, the present-perfect tense and the future-perfect tense. This means, Schutz (1971: 172–3) suggested, that the present is 'inaccessible for the reflective attitude. We can only turn to the stream of our thought as if it had stopped with the last grasped experience. In other words, self-consciousness can only be experienced *modo praeterito*, in the past tense.' That is to say, first, that reflection and representation break the flowing unity of action, transforming it into partial elements, and second, that reflectively attributed meanings are by necessity selective. Third, it is to note that representations are ordered and sequenced according to priorities and a hierarchy of values and meanings.

All this points to the importance of the past and future at any one present moment. As I have shown above, any individually purposive action is simultaneously bounded by the socially constituted common stock of knowledge, by language and by the imposed relevances of the group, all of which are past-dependent. This means, first, that the past is fundamentally embodied in projects, and second, that the public and the private, the objective and the subjective, the past, present and future interpenetrate in actions and their representations: historically sedimented knowledge, goals and concerns permeate actions, interactions and communications. The constitution of a class-room and any inter/action therein is fundamentally temporally extended. On this basis we are able to refer not only to common pasts but also to collective futures. Moreover, it allows us to think in both the past and the future tense: we can conceive of past pasts, past presents and past futures, future pasts, future presents, present futures and future futures, or a number of other combinations. Once more, the implications for educational theory are striking: established dualisms become meaningless as choices, master narratives and the objective position untenable. Apart from this deconstructive effect on theory and understanding, Schutz's analysis is relevant for the theoretical elaboration of the reflexive moment in our subject matter and in our work as researchers. Moreover, it is indispensable for making explicit the invisible aspects of time in education.

While Schutz's work helps us to make visible what is taken for granted, Mead's (1932/1980) work facilitates an even more fundamental re-vision of established social science traditions. His *The Philosophy of the Present* presents the most radical of all social science conceptualizations of time. It is therefore worth our while to explore in more detail some of Mead's innovative thoughts. Where Schutz (1971) was concerned with epistemological problems, Mead (1932/1980: 1–32) focused predominantly on matters of ontology. In the essay 'The Present as Locus of Reality' he explored the status of the present, past and future. As the title suggests, for Mead reality exists in the present. Any reality that transcends the present, he argued, must exhibit itself as present in the present. Translated into an educational setting, Mead's thoughts on the past, present and future mean that the failures, achievements and potentials of educators and their charges can only be studied in and known from the standpoint of the present.

Mead allowed for the present to vary in its temporal spread, but insisted that it must include becoming, otherwise we would not be able to distinguish one event from another. For us to be able to conceive of events, change, continued existence, the present or even time, there has to be becoming and disappearing. An eternal present, Mead argued, cannot be a present at all. The present may be an incident in the classroom, a lesson, participation in assembly, the first year of teacher training, or the post-war period of education. For these presents to become the past something new has to happen: a break or another lesson, the intake of a new first year or a significant socio-political event by which we would define a 'new' educational era.

Emergence, Mead (1932/1980: 11) argued further, inevitably reflects into the past and changes its meaning. He showed how it is customary to think of the past as 'out there' and as not being subject to change, instead of recognizing that the past is continuously re-created and reformulated into a different past from the standpoint of the emergent present, that each moment is re-created afresh in the light of a new present. Old concerns about teaching methods, course contents and the curriculum do not get replaced but, instead, are reformulated in the light of each subsequent educational reform, be this welcomed, resisted or rejected. The past, we can therefore say, has no status apart from its relation to the present. The past 'in itself' is not a past at all; only its relation to the present is the ground for its pastness. What was novel in the old present has become part of the world of the new and different past. In its meaning and the way it is preserved, evoked and selected, therefore, the past is revocable and as hypothetical as the future. The 'real' past, just like the 'real' future, is unobtainable for us. Only through mind do we transcend the present and extend our environment. Only through mind is the past open to us in the present.

Taken on board, these thoughts have fundamental consequences at the level of empirical study and theory. Only a few examples can be mentioned here. The first problem we have already encountered above. It relates to the difficulty of 'objective' observation since neither the past nor the future is observable. Rather, they are accessible only through the 'subjective' accounts of the objects of observation or through records which, in turn, are either accounts or interpretations of accounts. Second, Mead's conceptualization of the past and future as relative means that this relative, subjective, created time needs to be distinguished from the external, imposed frame of clock-time units and calendar dates. It needs to be differentiated from and understood in relation to the time-frame by which we identify earlier and later states in time. Third, the time we *create* through our extended being, interacting and learning needs to be conceptualized in relation to the time by which we live *in* time.

Mead argued that we must locate the source of time in the interaction of organisms (human or otherwise) and their environments, in both the mutual forming and the content of that process. Even in something as insignificant as writing a sentence we act on our environment while it acts on us, and it is in the ensuing process of mutual adjustment and reorganization that all the past gets readjusted from the standpoint of the present. The world, Mead (1932/1980: 47) suggested, is irrevocably different because of it. This means that no routine action, tradition or regular recurrence is ever the same in any of its repeats. Between last year's lesson on the Norman Conquest and this year's, last week's first-year assembly and this week's, yesterday's registration and today's, the world has changed and so have the other participants, the environment and our collective past and futures. We have grown older. The context is different. This year's lesson on a specific multiplication problem is used unaltered or changed in the light of the previous years' experiences, changing approaches in the teaching of mathematics more generally, the knowledge of the present class, the situation at the time, and many more explicit and less conscious considerations. All one can state is that the more similar and unchanging the events, the more they allow for speculation on a similar future or, more accurately, on a continuously constituted and constitutive future that *appears* similar to past presents.

This locating of the source of time in the constitutive symmetry-breaking of interaction is intimately tied to Mead's conceptualization of sociality. For Mead, sociality must not be understood in purely human, cultural terms but rather as a quality that permeates all living existence, a quality central to the living world, to conscious being and to symbolic interaction. He conceptualizes sociality as the process of emergence and mutual adjustment at the levels of physical, living and conscious reality. 'The social character of the universe', he writes (1932/1980: 49), 'we find in the situation in which the novel event is in both the old order and the new which its advent heralds. Sociality is the capacity of being several things at once.' The sociality he has in mind has two essential aspects: passage and emergence (1932/1980: 77). Sociality, in other words, is fundamentally temporal and time is irreducibly social, since both are located in the interactive process of adjustment and not in its result, in the active moment of symmetry-breaking and not in its outcome.

The implications of Mead's conceptualization of the mutual implication of time and sociality are first, that sociality cannot be restricted to *human* intersubjectivity and second, that we have to take account of the unalterable direction in things, events, organisms and their interactions, and human knowledge. It means that we have to encompass in our theories the impossibility of un-being and un-becoming. We cannot un-know, only forget what we once knew. Third, acceptance of sociality as temporal entails a recognition that there can be no repetition of the same, no standing still, no fixing of moments. Such an understanding has implications beyond education for the issues I raise about theorizing 'other time', body time and the environment. Moreover, and as I have already indicated above, it poses methodological problems: it questions the validity of generalization across time and space and the idea of verifiability. Taken seriously, in other words, Mead's analysis threatens some of the key pillars of empirical research while, at the same time, explaining the difficulties researchers encounter in the monitoring and evaluation of educational practice. A fourth consequence relates to the quantification of time: no numbering or counting of units could possibly account for time since the chief reference is to the emergent event which is always more than the processes that have led up to it. Without emergence, Mead (1932/1980: 22) contends, there is no time, not even a quantity to be measured. He considers the quantification of time an 'unwarranted use of abstraction'. Mead, in other words, requires us to recognize this practice as a reification. It is unclear from his writing whether he would go so far as to argue that the clock-time measure is therefore an inappropriate tool for the elaboration of time in education. However, no such ambiguity exists with reference to temporality. Mead insists that we have to bring the creative, constitutive and transformative power of time to the centre of social science analysis. As such, his theory is particularly relevant for researchers working within a constructivist perspective of educational investigation.

In conclusion we can say that the exploration of classical social theory statements on time is a first, essential step towards taking seriously the complexity of times. It is an important step because some of the classical theorists, unlike their contemporary colleagues, focused on time *per se*. They did not consider it too metaphysical a topic for social science. They did not start from an *a priori* assumption of *social* time. Together, the classical theoretical approaches to social time present us with some of the conceptual tools with which to approach the complexity and multiplicity of times in everyday life which, in turn, are easily transferable to social science research generally and educational research in particular. Collectively, they take us out of the natural attitude. They make visible the breadth of temporal issues and allow us to see in relation what remains separate when social scientists place themselves automatically in one perspective. Once we have grasped the complexity we can *knowingly* choose a perspective that will provide us with the appropriate conceptual tool for a *specific* task. This enables us to discuss those *aspects* of the complexity *as* aspects without losing sight of the multiplicity. Focusing on the classical statements and applying them to the field of education, moreover, we can see the connection between approaches to time and the normative, critical, interpretative and constructivist traditions in the social sciences. To understand the assumptions that underpin these traditions means that we establish a base for critique: we recognize when the conceptualizations of time are at odds with the central premises that guide a particular tradition of thought. We appreciate when functionalist, Marxist and Weberian studies focus on and utilize exclusively the clock-time parameter and the quantitative measure, or when phenomenological, interactionist and constructivist investigations emphasize past and future extensions or the constitutive aspects of time at the expense of timetables and schedules, and/or the abstract exchange value and the commodified time of economic relations.

The second step takes us back to the sketch of time in education presented at the beginning of the chapter. This account suggested that order, control, structure and interaction are not available choices for researchers, that these aspects of educational life are present simultaneously. This recognition is, of course, not a new insight in educational research; it is central, for example, in constructivist approaches to education. The focus on time, however, pushes us more relentlessly than most other foci towards a search for theories and methodologies that can encompass creativity without losing sight of externally imposed structures, theories for which simultaneity and implication are fundamental. To seek such theories is different from suggesting that theory and reflection should or even could reproduce reality in its infinite complexity; representations are bound to separate, select and sequence what exists simultaneously. The way this is done, however, is in need of reconsideration. At the very least, analytic dissection can focus on the *relation* between the artificially created parts. It can create a web of reconnections rather than isolate and abstract meaning that is given through its multiple unity. For our purpose it is therefore crucial that we grasp the connections between the rationalization of school life to bells, clocks and calendars and the commodification of time which mediates contemporary relations of economic exchange; between the creation of the past, present and future and times as constituted in our consciousness and through our interactions. It is important that we recognize the link between all of these, the reflexive attitude and the relation to our own finitude. This entails that we extend the established concerns of social science research, that we focus explicitly on the multiple times inherent in our subject matter and on the complexity of times that pervade our praxis as social scientists. At the substantive level of everyday life we need to break through the habit of clock time if we are to find more appropriate and meaningful relations to health, work and the environment. As social scientists we have the opportunity to offer such a re-vision.

Key points

At the substantive level I have shown
- the breadth and depth of clock and other times in educational practice, research and theory: time lived, experienced, generated, reckoned, known, allocated, sold, controlled and used as an abstract medium for exchange; time in events and events in time
- the historical roots for time-discipline in the monastic rules of the Benedictine monks and the close links between the clock-time measure and science
- that approaches to social time mirror perspectives in education and educational research: normative, critical, interpretative and constructivist.

With reference to methodology I have argued
- that the methodological tool of clock time is out of sync with the multiple times of its subject matter and that researchers have to take account of the invisibles: the past and future extension, aspects of the multiple life-worlds
- that we need to treat with caution all generalizations across time and to let go of the belief in an objectively observable reality, uncontaminated by observation and unaffected by time
- that time is an ideal focus for facilitating cross-fertilization between theory, methodology, empirical study and practice, be it in education, health, work or environmental action.

4

The Time Economy of Work Relations

Time forms a largely unreflected aspect of our daily lives, of the chores, routines and decisions, the coordinations of actions, the deadlines and schedules, the commitments, plans and hopes for the future. As social scientists studying that world we need to reflect on the unreflected, make the implicit explicit. We need to understand the times embedded in those activities, conceptualizations and orientations and to theorize their inter-relationship. Work time constitutes such a substantial and important part of the times of everyday life that it forms an ideal focus for such an investigation: it is bargained for, sold and controlled, and in the ensuing disputes over working time the complexity of social times becomes visible. Sensitivity to this complexity is, in turn, an essential step towards establishing connections between work, time and social science assumptions.

In this chapter I would like to continue the task of establishing connections where none exist at present and to show how an explicit focus on time can help us to see relationships between incompatible research foci. The topic of time and work is, however, very different from the other time themes pursued in this book. While the others have attracted very little social science attention, research on work time has proliferated for several decades and spans the entire range of the social sciences: from anthropology (Evans Pritchard 1940/1969; Bourdieu 1979; Hall 1983), business studies and organization theory (Blyton 1989; Blyton et al. (eds.) 1989; Clark 1982; de Grazia 1974; Hassard 1989b; Hay and Usunier 1993; Starkey 1988), to economics (Hill 1989; Sharp 1981), geography (Carlstein et al. (eds.) 1978; Hägerstrand 1975; Harvey 1989), and history (Landes 1983; LeGoff 1980; Kern 1983; Thompson 1967), from social policy (Lee and Piachaud 1992; Rinderspacher 1989), to social psychology (Jahoda et al. 1933/1972; McGrath and Rotchford 1983; Yaker et al. (eds.) 1972), sociology (Cottrell 1939; Grossin 1969, 1974, 1992; Hassard 1989a; Moore 1963; Nguyen 1992; Rinderspacher 1985) and women's studies (Balbo and Nowotny (eds.) 1986; Davies 1990; Hantrais 1993; Leccardi and Rampazi 1993; Lefeuvre 1994; Nowotny 1986, 1989; Pasero 1994). This list, selected from an output of several hundred publications, stands opposed to fewer than twenty papers on time and education, a similarly small number on time and health, and virtually none on either global time or temporal issues relating to the environment.

It cannot be my aim to review this immense body of research on time and work or to give a comprehensive account of all the complexities of this field of study, since to do it justice would require writing not just one but several books. Instead, I select for attention a few themes that focus on time as lived, experienced, conceptualized and related to. Thus, a brief sketch of the rationalized aspects of work time and its sources is followed by an exploration of time inside and outside employment relations. Next, I discuss time with reference to the high regard for speed, and finally, I investigate time in relation to the development towards the ever-increasing flexibilization of work. All are constitutive aspects of work time and particularly suited to bringing to the surface what is normally disattended.

Working with rationalized time: clock-time rhythms and their sources

A significant proportion of studies on time and work tend to be preoccupied with the link between industrial/capitalist production and its organization to the time of the clock (Blyton 1985; Blyton et al. 1989; Clark 1982; Cottrell 1939; de Grazia 1974; Grossin 1969, 1974; Pollard 1963; Thompson 1967; Thrift 1981, 1988; Wright 1968) and many of these are further concerned to identify the historical sources for this development. The contemporary industrial way of work and its fundamental dependence on clock time is thus variously associated – singly or in clusters – with the development of cities and urbanization, with the rationalized way of monastic life and the Protestant work ethic, with writing and with the economic principle of competition (Harvey 1989; McLuhan 1964/ 1973; Nguyen 1992; van Rossum 1989; Thompson 1967; Thrift 1981, 1988; Weber 1904–5/1989; Zerubavel 1981). Irrespective of emphasis, however, in all these analyses the clock is accorded a central role.

Thompson, in a seminal essay entitled *Time, Work-Discipline and Industrial Capitalism*, argued that pre-industrial work was task- rather than clock-oriented, that the specific activity and not the standard of the clock governed the rhythms, routines and timings of pre-industrial work. He indicated that the change of approach to working time was a slow process that started in the Middle Ages and came to fruition in the late seventeenth century. 'The image of the clock-work extends', writes Thompson (1967: 57), 'until, with Newton, it has engrossed the universe.' The task-orientation, meanwhile, has not disappeared from industrial societies; it has merely been relegated to work in rural communities and to the more southern countries of Europe. This part of Thompson's analysis is substantiated by the work of Inhetveen who studies the time intersections of both tradition and progress (Inhetveen and Blasche 1983) and nature and culture (Inhetveen 1988, 1993, 1994) in the work of farming women in Southern Germany; and it is borne out by one of my interlocutors, a farmer's wife who said:

> 'Our time is primarily regulated by cows. Their need to be milked structures what we do and when we do it and it means we have to get up early seven days a week. Because they are our own cows we can get up a bit later to suit ourselves but not very much later – the leeway is about one hour. . . . We don't wear watches on the farm. I wear my watch for going out, as a piece of jewellery. Time is only important when we have to go somewhere and be there at a certain time. Despite the constant demand of the cows and the lack of weekends we have time to talk to people and appreciate things.'
>
> (*Abridged interview with Jane, forty-seven, farmer's wife,*
> *mother of two grown-up children*)

Thompson associated the clock-time attitude with time thrift, time-keeping and time discipline, with the clear demarcation between work and leisure and with the more general process of commodification, a development first explicitly theorized by Marx in *Capital* and *Grundrisse*. 'Puritanism in its marriage of convenience with industrial capitalism', Thompson (1967: 95) suggests, 'was the agent which converted men to new valuations of time; which taught children even in their infancy to improve each shining hour; and which saturated men's minds with the equation, time is money.' No longer the task but the value of time became dominant: time has been transformed into a currency, into something which is no longer passed but spent.

Where Thompson's important analysis becomes problematic is in its seeming dualism of capitalist clock time on the one hand and task-orientation on the other (for critiques see O'Malley 1990, 1992b; Thrift 1981, 1988). If we take the example of rural dairy farmers, there is no doubt that their lives are structured by the needs of the animals and the tasks at hand but they are also simultaneously under the spell and pressure of the time economy of the clock – not just when they go out but because they are embedded in a market economy organized to the principles of commodified time. Here as in all other instances of this kind we have to learn to conceive together what traditional analyses keep apart.

Thompson's analysis has precursors in socio-economic theories of Marx and Weber during the middle of the last and the beginning of this century. More than fifty years before Thompson's essay Weber (1904–5/ 1989) identified a link between capitalist principles and practices, the Protestant work ethic, and a utilitarian, economic approach to time. Weber cited at length the writings of Benjamin Franklin whom he considered an ideal exponent of that new spirit.

> Remember, that time is money. He that can earn ten shillings a day by his labour, and goes abroad, or sits idle, one half of that day, though he spends but sixpence during his diversion or idleness, ought not to reckon that the only expense; he has really spent, or rather thrown away, five shillings besides. Remember, that credit is money. If a man lets his money lie in my hands after it is due, he gives me the interest, or so much as I can make of it during that time. This amounts to a considerable sum where a man has good and large credit, and makes good use of it.
>
> Remember, that money is of the prolific, generating nature. Money can beget money, and its offspring can beget more, and so on. . . . (Franklin quoted in Weber 1904–5/1989: 48–9)

Time here is treated as a valuable resource, as a quantity irreducibly tied to work and economic exchange. Once time is quantified and used as an exchange value it becomes an economic variable like labour, capital and machinery, a resource that has to be handled economically: we can speak of a time economy. Thus Mumford (1934/1955: 5) writes, 'time-keeping passed into time-serving and time-accounting and time-rationing. As this took place, Eternity ceased gradually to serve as the measure and focus of human actions.' The contemporary approach to time clearly denotes a historical change away from working *in* time and towards a working *with* time. However, as I indicate above, this shift occurred slowly over a protracted period. It was a long-drawn-out process, the (Western) beginnings of which can be traced back to the very early Middle Ages (Hohn 1984; O'Malley 1992b; Thrift 1981, 1988). Moreover, as I demonstrate in other chapters, contemporary Western life continues to be conducted *in* time, that is, in the variable times of seasonal and diurnal cycles as well as in the objectified, rationalized time of calendars and clocks.

Though Weber did not focus explicitly on the time dimension of the rationalization of work in capitalist societies, his *The Protestant Ethic and the Spirit of Capitalism* is a central source for establishing an association between general processes of rationalization, the puritan attitude to work and the appreciation of time as a precious resource to be allocated and spent with diligence and frugality. It is also the first widely read social science text that connects a rational, economic approach to time with the rigidly organized life-style of monks (1904–5/1989: 118–19), namely, with the meticulous allocation of predefined sections of time for specific daily activities. (The closely associated connection between the time discipline of the monks and Western-style education is elaborated in Chapter 3.) Weber notes that the asceticism associated with the Protestant ethic is one not of contemplation and absence of activity but of *rationally calculable action*. Such action implies an expectation of predictable and controllable regularity within a universally applicable time, an empty time which measures the same abstract units anywhere and everywhere, a time that is applicable equally to work, leisure and caring activities.

Assumptions of predictability and calculability become visible in the requirement for punctuality, one of the highly praised virtues of the Protestant ethic. To expect punctuality is to take as given that people can calculate, and have control over, their future actions and that they can organize their lives in accordance with the requirement of keeping appointments at mutually agreed times. It is to relate to the future instrumentally and to hold an implicit belief that the future is not merely calculable but controllable. That is to say, people do not fundamentally see themselves in the hands of fate and at the mercy of external forces outside their control. They no longer primarily understand the future as either the realm of the unknown and unknowable or the return of the similar which characterizes living processes. Instead, valorization of punctuality presupposes a predictable future based on the return of the same and a time that allows for identification of generally applicable points in time. Universally rationalized and sectioned, empty time is thus a precondition for calculable actions geared towards the appropriation of a controllable and controlled future. As I show in Chapter 5, with the introduction of standardized world time and global time zones at the beginning of this century the rationalization of time was brought to its logical conclusion. Thus Weber's elaboration of the rationalization process clearly provides an important source for analyses of work time in industrialized capitalist societies.

It is not surprising, therefore, that much of contemporary research on work time is heavily indebted to his work: the relationship between the spirit and the organization of twentieth-century capitalist working life, the Protestant work ethic, the time discipline of monastic life and the economic approach to time is identified as central by numerous contemporary social scientists researching the sources of contemporary work's clock-time beat (Landes 1983; LeGoff 1980; Mumford 1934/1955; van Rossum 1989; Thompson 1967; Thrift 1981, 1988). The influence is most clearly evident in the work of Zerubavel (1981: 54–6) who writes of the 'activity cult' of the Protestant ethic, of its 'utilitarian' approach to time. Similarly to Weber, Zerubavel argues that the root of the daily schedule is to be sought in the medieval monasteries of St Benedict. The rigid regularities first introduced by the monks are alive and well, he suggests, not just in contemporary education but in work practices where they comprise four major forms, 'a) rigid sequential structuring, b) fixed duration, c) standard temporal location, and d) uniform rates of change' (Zerubavel 1981: xii). Like Weber, Zerubavel proposes that the Reformation transformed the monastic legacy into a worldly principle of work organization. But, unlike Weber, he focuses specifically on the role of time in that transformation. Referring to St Benedict's Rules he shows that time was treated by the monks as a resource, as something to be used efficiently and spent economically.

> The notion that one can allocate and budget one's time presupposes a certain philosophy of what time is. After all, these concepts definitely have some very clear economic overtones. And indeed, from the very start, the evolution of the schedule in the West has always been embedded within a pronouncedly economic philosophy of time. (Zerubavel 1981: 54)

That this assumption still persists in the contemporary attitude to time is evident, for example, in the way we speak about time: we spend it, waste it, invest it, budget it and save it. We equate it, in other words, with money.

Exchanging commodified time

The presupposition of a tight link between time and money permeates contemporary Western business. Labour is paid by the hour, the week and the month. Companies calculate their labour costs in 'man-hours'. Surplus value and profit cannot be established without reference to time. The life-span of a machine is reckoned in relation to the amount of work it produces within a specific period. Overtime, 'time out' through absenteeism, and strikes all form integral aspects of the calculation of a business's production costs, its efficiency and its performance in relation to competitors. All this, as I showed in Chapter 1, is possible only on the basis of 'empty time', a time separated from content and context. Only as an abstract, standardized unit can time become a medium for exchange and a neutral value in the calculation of efficiency and profit.

We tend to think that time as resource is linked to the passing of time, to the inevitability of death and to the diurnal cycle of night and day. These, however, are not the primary sources of this form of time. The transformation of lived time into a resource that we can use, allocate, control and exchange on the labour market has to be understood with respect to a very specific development: *the creation of a non-temporal time* and the orientation of social life to this very specific kind of time. The capacity to control people's time and the association with money, in other words, is only possible once time has become decontextualized and disembodied from events, once it has been established as a universally applicable, abstract, empty and neutral phenomenon that accords all hours the same value: where the hour between three and four o'clock is the same regardless of whether it refers to the afternoon or the night, in Alaska or Central Africa, during summer or winter. This is a time where content is irrelevant and where, as Luhmann (1982: 302) argues, the 'connection between what lies in the past and what lies in the future becomes in principle contingent'.

Luhmann identifies four characteristics associated with this mathematical, universalized world time: independence from context and content, chronological dating, translatability – the capacity to compare non-simultaneous stretches of time – and mental reversibility by which we are able to repeat what is fundamentally irreversible. Only in this abstract form can time mediate the translation between fundamentally different qualities of the environment and cultural life. Only in this decontextualized form, as Marx (1857/1973: 140–3) showed, can time become commodified, can it enable us to convert a variable quality into an invariable, abstract exchange value and mediate the value between different commodities. As abstract exchange value, time is no longer something that is merely used, passed or filled. It is a commodity. In Marx's analysis, therefore, clock time is the very expression of commodified time (see also Giddens 1981: 118–20 and 130–5; Harvey 1989; Hohn 1984: 145–61). Clock time and world time, rationalized and commodified time converge.

This decontextualized, commodified time of the clock is fundamentally implicated in contemporary, social science analyses of work time; it is implicated irrespective of whether the research emphasis is on synchronization, regulation, timetables, deadlines and priorities, on control and power, or on the role of time in the history of industrial capitalism. It means that commodified time is as much part of functionalist studies of the when, how long, in what order and at what speed of work time as it is of Weberian investigations of calculability and Marxian research on labour relations. It forms an integral part of labour history from the earliest revolts against the enforced new time discipline (Blyton et al. 1989; Thompson 1967), via disputes over the length of the working day and week (Blyton 1989; Elchardus 1991) and problems with rationalization (Hassard 1989b; O'Malley 1992a, 1992b; Rinderspacher 1985) to contemporary conflicts over flexibility (Elchardus 1991; Starkey 1988). The Marxian focus on commodification and power therefore needs to be taken on board in Weberian analyses of processes of rationalization and functionalist studies of the duration, sequencing, speed and rate of working time. All three traditions of social science thought are tied and committed to the dominant, clock time-based conceptualizations of time as money and power, as measure, as quantifiable resource and as a parameter within which working lives take place.

Clock time mediates complexity

This socially created, artefactual resource has become so all-embracing that it is now related to as if it were time *per se*, as if there were no other times. This has the effect that even the embedded, lived times of work and non-work are understood through the mediating filter of our own creation of non-temporal time. The metaphor, in other words, is transposed on to the subject of inquiry and we tend to forget that qualitative variation precedes the uniform, abstract quantity of human origin. We lose sight of the knowledge that much of the complexity of work time bears little relationship to the standardized measure, that it is fundamentally different from the artefactual time we use to compare, relate and quantify. Furthermore, this machine time is problematic not merely for studies of work time but more generally for analyses of all aspects of cultural life since social existence is transformed in repetition: social life, and by implication working time, is not invariable and abstract but fundamentally temporal and contextual. Habits and rhythms give a dynamic, temporal structure to our lives. The hours of darkness are passed differently from the hours of daylight and, as I show in Chapter 2 on health, our activities are affected by the seasons. Interactions are timed, sequenced and prioritized as change-continua. Time is simultaneously lived, created in interaction, treated as money, used as a resource, and budgeted, allocated, sold and controlled. Working to a deadline is different from stretching out a job during a spell of low orders. Periods of social upheaval or severe economic hardship are lived and experienced differently from the daily routines of 'normality' and relative economic prosperity. Writing a book with the aid of a computer, a typewriter or a pen means interacting with and generating different times. Most importantly, and as this book demonstrates, even during the most mundane activities, the multiple complexity of times bears on our lives *simultaneously*. Readers may find it beneficial at this point to revisit some of the interviews at the beginning of the book, particularly the reflections by Christoph and Mary.

The depth and breadth of implications of taking seriously the simultaneity of times in a context of multiplicity and difference have yet to be taken on as a problem by social scientists. Often, the complexity is reduced to perspective-based emphases, reformulated into dichotomies or simply transformed into an invariable measure. Where complexity is taken on as an issue (Clark 1982; Das 1986; Hassard 1989a; Hay and Usunier 1993; Starkey 1992; Whipp 1994), it tends to be retained within strictly disciplinary boundaries which rather delimits the scope of the analysis. I therefore suggest that there is a need to elevate everyday experience and tacit knowledge over the disciplines' traditions. There is an urgent requirement, that is, to alter the theories better to fit the findings and not vice versa. This may well entail turning to unconventional sources.

In addition to personal experience and the knowledgeable voices of ordinary people we might take note of the work of writers, poets, artists and colleagues in other academic disciplines and allow their insights to inform our social science understanding. Such an extension seems pertinent since present quests by contemporary researchers for qualitative, multiple times tend to be rendered inoperable by their traditional framework of analysis. Much that is central to working time is consequently rendered invisible.

And thus, driving through the city, he is both here and now, there and then. He carries yesterday with him, but pushed forward into today, and tomorrow, skipping as he will from one day to the other. He is in London, on a May morning of the late twentieth century, but is also in many other places, and at other times. He twitches the knob of the radio: New York speaks to him, five hours ago, is superseded by Australia tomorrow and presently by India this evening. He learns of events that have not yet taken place, of deaths, that have not yet occurred. He is Matthew Halland an English architect stuck in a traffic jam, a person of no great significance, and yet omniscient. For him, the world no longer turns; there is no day or night, everything and everywhere are instantaneous. He forges his way along Euston Road, in fits and starts, speeded up, then clogged again between panting taxis and a lorry with churning wasp-striped cement mixer. He is both trapped and ranging free. He fiddles again with the radio, runs through a lexicon of French song, Arab exhortation, invective in some language he cannot identify. Halted once more, he looks sideways and meets the thoughtful gaze of Jane Austen (1785–1817), ten feet high on a poster, improbably teamed with Isambard Kingdom Brunel, and George Frederick Handel, all of them dead, gone, but doing well – live and kicking in his head and up there guarding the building site that will become the British Library. And then another car cuts ahead of his, he hoots, accelerates, is channelled in another licensed burst of speed. Jane Austen is replaced by St Pancras.

Thus he coasts through the city, his body in one world and his head in many. He is told so much, and from so many sources, that he has learned to disregard, to let information filter through the mind and vanish, leaving impressions – a phase, a fact, an image. He knows much, and very little. He knows more than he can confront; his wisdoms have blunted his sensibility. He is an intelligent man, a man of compassion, but he can hear of a massacre on the other side of the globe and wonder as he listens if he remembered to switch on his answering machine. He is aware of this, and is disturbed. (Lively 1991: 2–3)

In conjunction with the interviews, this extract from *City of the Mind* gives an indication of what might be omitted in functionalist, Marxian and Weberian approaches to social time, and in contemporary analyses based on one or more of these theoretical traditions. It shows that the complexity of times in any one working moment extends beyond the reconnection of task to clock time, beyond images of circles combined with lines, beyond analytical fusion of quantitative and qualitative time. The unity of the permeation of the past, the global extension of individuals' presents, the simultaneity of impressions, feelings, memories and associations, and the focusing, selecting and discarding of information require more than the transformation of dualisms into multiple dualities. They necessitate, as I argue throughout, a way of seeing where focus on any one aspect does not exclude but *implicates* the rest, an approach that can fuse the insights of Marx, Weber and Durkheim with those of Schutz and Mead (see Chapter 3), and the traditions of the social sciences with those of the humanities and the arts. This is not to deny or devalue the importance of existing work that questions the linear–quantitative thesis (Clark 1982; Das 1991; Hay and Usunier 1993; Starkey 1988, 1989; Whipp 1994) but to argue that it does not go far enough. Thus when Hassard (1989a: 21) points out that industrial sociologists over-emphasize the rationalized aspects of working time at the expense of 'a wealth of work processes based on self-paced production', when he cites ethnographic evidence that demonstrates flexibility to remain widespread in a variety of professions, and when he shows how even the most externally controlled work processes allow room for workers to impose their own rhythms, he is taking a necessary first step away from single explanations and master narratives. The depth and the breadth of the problem, however, extend beyond the capacities of the traditional perspectives. One such difficulty is demonstrated by the failure of classical social theory to encompass within analyses of work time the complexity of times that fall *outside* the time economy of employment relations, another by the changing work-time patterns associated with flexibilization and the venerations of speed, which are the issues I turn to in the remaining sections of this chapter.

In the shadows of economic time

Not all time is money. Not all human relations are exclusively governed by the rationalized time of the clock. Not all times are equal. That is to say, all work relations touched by clock time are tied up with hegemony and power. This is clearly demonstrated in research on time in unemployment (Glass 1988; Jahoda et al. 1932/1972; Neumann 1988), in the lives of young people between school and work (Allatt 1992), in retirement (Young and Schuller 1991) and in farming (Inhetveen and Blasche 1988; Inhetveen 1993, 1994) to name just a few examples. This varied body of work identifies times that are constituted as the shadows of the time economy of employment relations, times not calculable in monetary terms yet evaluated through the mediating filter of both the rationalized time of the Protestant ethic and the commodified time of the market.

Feminist social scientists have provided the most coherent and wide-ranging accounts of these shadow times. It is for this reason that I am using the work on women's time as an exemplar for times lived, given and generated in the shadow of the hegemony of universal clock time. Thus, reading about studies on women's time, we have to bear in mind that much of what is identified in this research applies not just to women but to all those outside the time economy of employment relations, and we have to further appreciate that it does not apply to *all* women at *all* times of their lives. My purpose in this section is not to establish new dualisms and dualities – male and female time, productive and reproductive time, quantitative and qualitative time, instrumental and expressive time, employment time and its shadows – rather, it is to sensitize us to a complexity largely untheorized and left implicit in social science analyses that focus on some aspects of time to the exclusion of others.

In a perceptive study of women's experiences of time Davies (1990) shows that the working times of women as wives and mothers, both in and out of employment, cannot be placed in a meaningful way within perspectives that separate work from leisure, public from private time, subjective from objective time, and task from clock time. The cliché of 'women's work is never done' exemplifies the incompatibility with a work time that comes in finite units, a uniform and abstract time that can be measured, quantitatively evaluated, controlled and exchanged for money, accumulated for 'time out', and delimited against leisure time. Davies's (1990) research demonstrates that, as mothers, many women feel themselves on call twenty-four hours a day. Their times of caring, loving and educating, of household management and maintenance, and their female times of menstruation, pregnancy, childbirth and lactation are not so much time measured, spent, allocated and controlled as *time lived, time made and time generated* (see also Chapter 2). These are times that operate according to non-economic principles: they can be neither forced into timetables, schedules and deadlines nor allocated a monetary value. Rather, they need to be open-ended. Thus, for example, birthing, feeding and caring – all key features of maternal times – have to be given whatever amount of time they need. Such times, therefore, are consti-tuted outside the commodified, rationalized clock time of employment relations.

Moreover, when there is a need to coordinate multiple times – the times, for example, of paid work, leisure, school, meals, shopping, caring and voluntary work commitments – then we begin to see that not all times are equal, that some times are clearly privileged and deemed more important than others. This differential treatment of times becomes visible in the sequencing and prioritizing of certain times and in the compromises in time allocation that have to be achieved on a daily basis. The inequalities tend to be so taken for granted that they are no longer challenged. Thus it is rarely questioned that work, school and organized leisure times (in that order of importance) take priority over shopping and mealtimes, that the times which are governed by commodified time take precedence over those outside the time economy of employment relations.

Research on women's caring and emotional work demonstrates that times which are not convertible into currency have to remain outside the charmed circle: the basic assumptions and categories of classical social science render them invisible. That is to say, time-generating and time-giving activities have no place in the meaning cluster of quantity, measure, dates and deadlines, of calculability, abstract exchange value, efficiency and profit. They simply cannot feature in the analysis.

History tumbles outside of drawn lines and selective dialectic. For example, the dialectic of nature and history, of seasons and clock, of individual
and generation, of fecundity and decay. Knowledge of these is knowledge
of abstract time, time out of mind, not experienced time, not species time,
not common time. Men have used mind for the sorts of understanding of
reality embedded in the history of the conquest of time, men's history.
Women 'mind' the children. (O'Brien 1989a: 14)

Irrespective of social scientists' increasing sensitivity to work time as a
multiple rather than singular phenomenon, the full complexity will
continue to elude analyses of work time while they exclude times that
fall outside the time economy of employment relations, while they
emphasize self-paced production, flexibility and personal rhythms (see
Hassard 1989a: 21) but ignore the time-giving, time-constituting and
time-generating aspects of work relations. Studies of work time, in other
words, will remain locked in the clock-time framework of analysis as
long as they disregard research on times that fall outside the hegemony
of commodified time of which the work on women's time is a prime
exemplar.

Focus on the idea of 'free time' illuminates from a different angle of
vision the dominance of clock time and the general pervasiveness of its
meaning for all spheres of life – within the time economy of employment
relations *and* in the shadows of commodified time. From a historical
perspective, the steady shortening of working time – from seventy to
eighty hours per week and no holidays during the middle part of the
eighteenth century to thirty-nine hours and less plus weekends and holidays towards the end of the twentieth century – creates an appearance of
ever-increasing free time, even of 'time wealth'. The association of
commodified time with freedom and wealth, however, is misleading
since, as Rinderspacher (1989: 103) notes, it is a time produced through
increased efficiency and is not 'free' in the sense of belonging to people
in the first place. In other words, 'free time' and its correlate leisure time
are *derived* from commodified work time. They are *produced time*, time
that has been wrested from employer's time, a *not-work time* that exists
only in relation to the time of markets and employment (von Krockow
1989: 88). This means that outside the framework of economic time the
idea of 'free time' must remain relatively meaningless since its very
definition is tied to the history of labour and paid employment. Here too,
therefore, it clearly makes little sense to speak of women's free time,
when the women in question are not in paid employment. Yet, it is, of
course, not only women's times that fall outside the remit of 'free time'.
As Nowotny (1986/1989: 13) rightly argues, the discrepancy applies

equally to periods of childhood, education, unemployment and retirement, to all the times outside the direct control of the labour market.

Whilst the recognition that women's times are not the only times that
fall outside the rationalist framework should not detract from the
achievements of feminist social scientists, there are nevertheless conceptual problems that need to be addressed. That is to say, whilst feminist
social scientists need to be credited with pointing out the anomalies and
incompatibilities of women's working times in relation to the dominant
time economy of the clock, their analyses are not immune from the
theoretical problems dogging mainstream approaches to social time in
general and work time in particular. Based on their innovative research
on working time in the shadow of industrial employment relations, many
feminists conceptualize women's time as either predominantly cyclical
(Forman 1989; O'Brien 1989a and b) or as process- and task-oriented
(Davies 1990). Like Thompson's (1967) task- versus clock-time orientation, however, these inevitably dualistic definitions need to be treated
with caution. They are problematic first, because they re-create and
strengthen existing dichotomies, and second, because those antinomies
carry within them a conceptual baggage with a long history. The opposition of cyclical and linear time as well as those of process and structure,
or rational, instrumental and expressive, caring time belong to a tradition
of thought alien to the meaning being sought in those analyses. They
share a conceptual history and a common logic with male-stream social
science. To be effective, I suggest, critiques have to stay clear of offering
new dualisms, otherwise they are automatically reabsorbed in the very
framework of the analysis they seek to transcend. More recent feminist
work explicitly acknowledges this general problem (Ermarth 1989, 1992;
Leccardi and Rampazi 1993; Nicholson 1990: 1–2; Nicholson (ed.) 1990).

Again, I would stress the need to be sensitive to the complexity of
everyday life where the multiplicity of times forms an unproblematic,
cohesive unity and where the stresses and tensions between some of the
less compatible times are managed and expressed. The reflections on
time by my interlocutors show clearly the extent of the complexity of
times, the mutual permeation of its various aspects, and their simultaneous existence. They leave no room for doubt that the theoretical traditions which make us choose on an either-or basis are in need of revision.

'Time changes and it changes reality.' The role of time in my life
relates to my consciousness and emotional relationship to time as
well as to my concern about what I do with it, how I use it. Moreover, the concept changes and becomes a parameter of existence.
The structural value of the past, present and future influences me

more today than in earlier periods: a more conscious now, a more
focused tomorrow, and a more experienced, tempered yesterday.
Today I live more in the present than ten years ago. This helps me
to cope with the rapid passage of time. It avoids my getting fright-
ened by it and allows me to enjoy time more consciously. The view
of the past and the relationship to it provides a perspective – be
it public, personal or through the children. The future per se
can't give a perspective: only the past gives the future a depth
perspective.

'With reference to my work I feel that I do not have enough time
to live and to pass on the work I have begun. I am missing at least
ten years; I have started about ten years too late with both having
children and with my work as a therapist. The age at which one
starts key areas of education and vocational training are so important. Past a certain age many things are no longer viable, and linear
career structures need to be substituted with a creative puzzle of
bits and pieces of work and training.

'For me time is a parameter which I associate with both consciousness and structure. The structural dimension in turn is not
static but dynamic and it binds all pasts into a coherent whole. Time
relates to what I do and what I omit to do, to my values and my
moral judgements. I know that all my actions are irreversible: in my
actions I turn the total potential into an irreversible finality. The
wider I expand the time horizon – from the personal to the cosmic
– the more the real daily structures escape: horizons and potentials
become amorph.'

*(Inga, forty-nine years, therapist, mother of three
teenage daughters)*

Change, multiplicity and the past, present and future seem to be central
in this reflection on time. Time as a resource and a structural parameter
is acknowledged as integral to the complexity without being accorded
greater importance than any other aspect of this complex meaning of
time. The centrality of the 'right' and optimal time for certain actions and
life changes is recognized and brought into touch with experience and
time consciousness. The 'creative puzzle of bits and pieces' as a substitute for a linear career structure resonates with feminist writings that
challenge the assumption of work as a full-time, continuous occupation
with a linear career structure. This woman's reflection on time demonstrates a personal complexity of times that clearly exceeds even feminist
analyses of women's times.

For the moment, however, let us insist with contemporary feminists that work time is not gender-neutral while, at the same time, recognizing first, that neither caring nor healing, loving, educating and houseworking times are the sole prerogative of women and, second, that not all women at all times of their lives are involved in those activities. Let us further acknowledge with Forman (1989: 7) that, 'as a collective, women do not only live *in* time (from birth to death), they also *give* time and that act makes a radical difference to Being-in-the-World'. Let us consequently argue that women's time does not replace but shifts the emphasis from time as finite, rationalized, decontextualized exchange value to time as historically embedded and embodied, to a generative temporality that is nevertheless socially evaluated through the mediating filter of commodified time. Simultaneously, let us recognize that men, the prime architects of the decontextualized, rationalized, standardized time of employment relations, are not exempt from living and making time, not excluded from the capacity for creating life. They too generate open time in interaction. Finally, let us appreciate that the complexity of times applies not only to women and men – even to men in paid employment – but also to different categories of people, to people out of work or retired, to those working in professions and skills at the intersection of commodified and lived time, to preschool children and to young people between education and employment.

Moreover, while it may appear as if the multiple times identified thus far belonged to fundamentally different time systems – to clock time on the one hand and to the lived, constitutive, time-generating time on the other – this is not the case. The multitude of times interpenetrate and affect each other's quality and meaning. Furthermore, the lived, generative times do not merely intermesh with the commodity but are, as I demonstrate throughout, evaluated through the mediating filter of that economic time. Any time that cannot be accorded a money value is consequently suspect and held in low esteem. Such differential appreciation of work time inside and outside market and employment relations is in turn documented more generally in studies of women's work (Beechey 1986, 1987; Beechey and Whitelegg (eds.) 1986; Davies 1990), unemployment (Westergaard and Walker 1989), retirement (Young and Schuller 1991), and the 'third age' (Laslett 1989) which brings us back to the link between clock time and power, which is in turn central for establishing the connection between time and the economic goal of efficiency and profit. The interpenetration of multiple times and the mediating factor are further illuminated with reference to the valorization of speed and flexibility, the themes I turn to in the last section of this chapter.

Efficiency and profit: speed and flexibility

Speed

To be efficient is to produce something or to perform a task in the shortest possible time. To be profitable is to spend as little money as possible on labour time. To be competitive is to be faster than your rival. In 'Western societies' efficiency, profitability and competitiveness all carry a positive value. That is to say, in industrial and industrializing countries speed is valued over processes that take a long time and over procedures and actions whose duration cannot be accurately estimated and calculated. Such valorization of speed – from education to sport, work, services and politics – makes little sense until we grasp that time as quantitative resource, work as paid employment, and the money–efficiency–profit link are inseparably intertwined, that they are mutually defining. Let me explain.

Speed is not a value in itself. In some countries in the Middle East and Africa, for example, speed and haste carry a negative value. They denote a lack of decorum. Thus it is considered undignified to rush and carry out daily routines at great speed. In Western cultures, in contrast, faster means better: a faster aeroplane is 'better' than a slow one. A train that gets its passenger to a business meeting in two hours is 'superior' to one that takes two hours and nineteen minutes. A microwave cooker is an 'advance' on slower, traditional cookers. This year's world records in downhill skiing, in the 100-metre sprint, in speed-skating and swimming, for example, are 'vast improvements' on those of ten years ago. Fast learners are considered bright while the notion of the 'slow learner' stands for dull-wittedness, lack of intelligence and a negative deviance from the aspired norm. The valorization seems to be maintained irrespective of questions of quality; in other words, speed seems to hold its generalized high social value independent of the variable quality achieved by particular speedy actions and processes or the possibility of qualitative superiority by, for example, slower transport, cooking or learning. The veneration of speed is even more puzzling when we consider that the 'time saved' is usually achieved at a price, that it has to be paid for, as I show in Chapter 6 on the environment, with extra energy which puts an additional burden on environmental resources. Even the link between time and money does not necessarily explain the value of speed. If time were money, would it not make more sense to *invest* time/ energy in activities, to take longer to cook, travel and learn, thus enhancing their value? Equally puzzling and incomprehensible is the 'slow learner' stigma when we link it up with the traditional knowledge that 'a good thing takes time'.

In order to understand the underlying rationale of this contemporary speed fetishism, we need once more to enter the work–time–money–efficiency–profit circle. The concept of 'time economy' may help to shed light on the paradox. It alludes to the implication of time in the economic investment–return–profit cycle. In other words, between an investment and its return is a time-span, and the shorter that elapsed time, the greater is the profit. In addition to profit as a motivating force for the high value of speed, competition plays a central role. To produce something of equal quality in a shorter time allows for a reduction in the price of the product which increases its competitiveness. The more time you are left with after an activity the better, since this allows even more actions, transactions and productions to be fitted into the period of time thus freed up. What all these conceptions share is a purely quantitative approach to time. One of the rationales for the Western approach to speed is thus to be sought in the quantification, decontextualization, rationalization and commodification of time, in the calculation of time in relation to money, efficiency, competition and profit.

Recognition of the association of speed with economics and the quantitative time of the clock allows for a better appreciation of its conflict with the open-ended generative time of caring, the time of joining with phenomena and processes, the giving of time to people and activities and the time that is oriented towards birth and the production of life. Broadening out the issues, we can see further how the link between speed, economics and clock time operates against the principle of equal opportunity, whether this be in relation to different sexes, occupational groups, cultures or categories of people. In addition to the inequality between men and women, the valorization of speed with its tight link to economics militates against equality between professions and skills. This means, for example, that artists, carers and people providing services compete on unequal terms with occupational groups whose work is amenable to translation into the clock-time units.

Such inequality turns into a major problem where the principle of commodified time has been politically imposed across the board, irrespective of suitability: where it has been thrust upon business, education and health services, theatre companies and the visual arts community without regard for their unique temporal complexities, and where evaluation is conducted on the basis of commodified time. Equally, it obstructs equality between cultures, between societies which consider speed to be socially unacceptable and those which valorize it as a virtue at both a personal and collective level. This particular inequality is most clearly discernible in the relations between 'First' and 'Third' World countries: in the latter's difficulty to adapt and conform to the former's time discipline and speed fetishism as well as in the differential level of pay offered to workers of those respective countries. Finally, it prevents equality amongst categories of people with the very young, the elderly, the disabled and their respective carers being discriminated against.

Let us take disability as an example. For disabled persons to be given equal opportunity at work, it is not enough merely to supply them with the appropriate technological aids. As French (1993) insists, such aids are no substitute for bringing disabled persons 'up to speed' with their able-bodied colleagues. Bringing time to the centre of equal opportunity debates, she argues, is important if we are to take seriously the disadvantage of disabled persons in the work place.

> In my view the only way to give equal opportunities to visually impaired people engaged in employment normally requiring vision (which is most employment) is to pay them the same amount for less work, and the same applies for many other disabled people. Such is my past socialization as a disabled person, and my knowledge of other people's attitudes, that I would not, at the present time at least, feel able to accept this solution for myself. (French 1993: 3)

It is the socialization into a specific approach to time that is at issue here. To question and challenge the taken-for-granted view requires full understanding of the kind of times that underlie practices and traditions as well as their multiple alternatives. The task therefore is to understand the principles that underpin, maintain and perpetuate the dominant time and its impact as well as the characteristics of times that fall outside its remit. It is to demystify and make the taken-for-granted problematic which in turn creates the potential for alternative visions and, as I show in other chapters, for effective actions. To this purpose I want to explore one final issue related to the experience and conceptualization of work time in relation to efficiency and profit, namely, the rationalization and commodification of time associated with flexibility.

Flexibility

For more than two centuries of Western labour history we find a steady reduction in the time spent at work, a decline that has been regulated by both collective agreements and legislation. (In Britain, the Factory Acts of 1833 and 1844, the Ten-hour Act of 1847 and the Holiday Acts of 1871 and 1875 which introduced the four-day statutory holiday are examples for the beginning of a trend that continued throughout the Western world.) The detail may differ from country to country but the general direction remains the same: working time is being reduced (Bienefeld 1972; Blyton 1989; Elchardus 1991; ETUI 1979, 1984; Nguyen 1992; Solovyov 1962). During the last few decades, however, a new time trend has entered the sphere of employment and labour relations: the flexibilization of working time (Blandy 1984; Elchardus 1991; Müller-Wichmann 1991; Rinderspacher 1985; Starkey 1988). Part-time and shift-work as well as weekend and evening work are prime examples of working patterns associated with flexibilization.

Flexibilization of working time brings with it far-reaching changes to people's lives. The decoupling of work time from the time of the organization and from the collective rhythms of public and familial activities erodes communal activities in both the public and the private realm. For workers, flexi-time can have a number of different, even conflicting consequences: it can mean that workers are able to achieve greater control over the allocation of their own time on the one hand, while it may be used by their employers as a tool for improving efficiency on the other. It can take different forms and have different effects: it can mean decreased travel time, better child-care arrangements and/or improved choice on the one hand and an increase of weekend work and night shifts, unpredictability in the length of working time, and/or a shortening period of notice for temporary work schedules on the other. Uncertainty for the worker is at its worst, Elchardus (1991: 701) argues, 'when the working time is rendered directly sensitive to market fluctuations'. Elchardus (1991) designates the difference as one of flexibility *for* the worker on the one hand and flexibility *of* the worker on the other. While the former allows workers a greater degree of control over their time, the latter entails an increase in the unpredictability of working time. Rarely, however, are those two analytic categories neatly separated; instead, they interpenetrate and constitute simultaneous, multiple complexities.

The British Rail dispute over 'flexible rostering', detailed by Starkey (1988), shows the intricacy of these issues and highlights the problems that arise when the purely decontextualized, economic calculation of market time is imposed on the multiple, contextual and embodied times of people's everyday lives. British Rail's arguments about a neutral quantity time did not match up with the worker's bargaining over quality. It raised 'the spectre', proposes Starkey (1988: 108), 'of a return to a time commitment similar to that demanded by the feudal baronetcy of the Victorian era, a fear that impending changes presaged the railroader becoming, once again, the slave of railway time'. (I am writing at a time when the postal workers of south-east Wales are on strike over similarly inhumane, neutralized and decontextualized time-structure proposals by their employers.)

What is for employers an issue of rationalization and efficiency becomes for workers an unbearable, unfathomable burden for the very reason that workers – both male and female – do not operate exclusively in the commodified, rationalized and mechanized time of industrial employment but in a complexity of times which, in turn, need to be synchronized with the times of significant others and the society within which those employees live and work. When the multiple 'components' come adrift, the price to pay, as I show in other chapters, can range from illness and accidents, to divorce, strikes and socio-financial hardship. What had begun at the turn of this century (1885–1915) with Taylor's time-and-motion studies is taken to the extreme with 'flexible rostering' and other flexibilization strategies designed for greater profitability of the employing organization.

The cutting up of work processes and their 'creative' reassemblage for the purpose of achieving the greatest possible efficiency requires as a basic condition an empty, abstract time that is divisible into an infinite number of recombinable units. The processes of work, in other words, could be taken apart and rearranged in new ways only *after* an objective, standardized, decontextualized time had become the accepted norm. The general orientation towards clock time thus constitutes the foundation for the flexible organization of time. Since this process of recombining and assembling work time is similar to the task performed by editors of television and film, we could, with O'Malley (1992a) call it *time editing*. Just like the editing of television and film, such work-time editing is shrouded in an air of importance and inescapability. 'Dressed in the clothes of efficiency', writes O'Malley (1992a: 199), 'the editing of time could seem like a resort to a higher authority [rather] than mere convenience. In a contentious society of clashing interests, it could seem impartial and objective, free of local prejudice.' Such time-editing practices invariably meet with resistance for the simple reason that first, people are different from strips of celluloid: they *are* time, they *live* time, they *generate* time in interaction, they *fix* time in their artefacts. Second, people encounter ever greater difficulties in coordinating the flexible and inflexible elements of their lives of work, family, friends, leisure, cultural activities, public amenities' use and political engagement. The more flexible and/or unpredictable the work pattern, the more time has to be spent by those involved and their families on the task of synchronization.

Thus we can say in conclusion that the complexity of people's times becomes visible only at rare moments. We can recognize it when we probe the experiences and meanings of work time inside and outside employment relations. We can detect it when we investigate everyday conceptions of time as well as their literary representations. Finally, we become aware of it when the discord created by the extreme imposition of clock time – a time decontextualized and dissociated from people's actions and the temporal complexity of their lives – becomes too powerful to be reabsorbed into the taken-for-granted coherence. Once we make explicit what has thus far been 'treated merely as a category underlying our knowledge of social life' (Luhmann 1982: 290), and once we make problematic what has been assumed natural, the hegemony of the clock-time rhythm crumbles: we recognize its constructed character, appreciate its tie with economic production, and begin to understand why and how some people's times are constituted as the shadow of what is widely assumed to be time *per se*. Such understanding is essential for adequate analyses of work time inside and outside the time economy of employment relations and for bringing to the surface the power to define. It serves as a basis for challenging the validity and value of existing appropriations of clock time to the denial of all other times, and questions the existing discourse of disembodied, rationalized and commodified time. Reconceptualization is therefore an essential step towards changing practice and engendering a time politics that counteracts discrimination against large sections of Western industrial and, as I argue in Chapters 1, 5 and 6, against societies and beings whose lives are not organized to the metronomic beat of the clock.

Key points

At the substantive level I have shown
- that the market economy depends on a standardized, decontextualized, commodified time
- that a time that is generated and given cannot be encompassed within the time economy of employment relations, in other words, that women's times and the times of all those outside employment cannot be translated into a currency and that those times are constituted in the shadow of the market economy
- that a) free time has to be understood not as free *per se* but as *produced* time which makes the concept inapplicable for all those outside paid employment; and that b) the high value of speed as well as the quest for flexibility have to be appreciated in relation to the economic principles of profit, efficiency and competition.

With reference to methodology I have argued

- that Marxian, Weberian and functionalist analyses of work time are tied and committed to a conceptualization of time as resource and currency
- that the very important feminist deconstructions of social time are in danger of being reabsorbed into the very frameworks of analyses they make problematic as long as those alternatives are constructed along dualistic lines
- that in order to research the complexity of social times in general and working time in particular we need to draw on a multitude of unconventional social science sources ranging from people's personal accounts to poetry and that we have to alter the theories to better fit 'the evidence'.

5

Global Times and the Electronic Embrace

Television pictures of starving children move the sentiments of nations, and governments besieged by public sympathy and outrage give in to the pressure and send out a 'rescue mission' with aid. Such televised tragedies reaching the homes of viewers across the globe need to be set alongside the passage by Lively quoted in the previous chapter:

> He knows much and very little. He knows more than he can confront: his wisdoms have blunted his sensibility. He is an intelligent man, a man of compassion, but he can hear of a massacre on the other side of the globe and wonder as he listens if he has remembered to switch on his answering machine. He is aware of this, and is disturbed. (1991: 3)

Both situations show the influence of globalization on our daily lives; both are expressions of the fusion of local/personal with global times. Before I can explore the complexity and uniqueness of globalized times, however, I need to briefly outline social science approaches to the processes of globalization and discuss a range of meanings that have been attached to the concept.

Understanding globalization

The World Bank, OPEC (Organization of Petroleum Producing Countries), the United Nations, CND (Campaign for Nuclear Disarmament) and the World Commission on Environment are all indicative of contemporary transnational relations and interdependencies. They are social institutions and practices not bounded by the nation state but oriented towards global issues. This transcendence of nation states poses problems for disciplines that emerged in conjunction with the development of those bounded political structures. The challenge for sociology, Featherstone (1990: 2) therefore suggests, 'is to both theorize and work out modes of systematic investigation which can clarify these globalizing processes and distinctive forms of social life which render problematic what has long been regarded as the basic subject matter for sociology: society conceived almost exclusively as the bounded nation state'. Anything that exceeds those boundaries seems simultaneously to exceed the boundaries of social science in general and sociology in particular. Yet globalization is such an inescapable phenomenon that it cannot be ignored. Among social scientists who are concerned with understanding its development, there is much debate whether or not it is a new phenomenon and to what extent it is discontinuous with the world trade and colonialism of previous centuries. For some theorists like Hall (1991) globalization is integral to the rise (and decline) of contemporary Western nations like Britain.

> Certainly, from the perspective of any historical account of English culture, globalization is far from a new process. Indeed, it is almost impossible to think about the formation of English society, or of the United Kingdom and all the things that give it a kind of privileged place in the historical narratives of the world, outside of the processes that we identify with globalization. (Hall, 1991: 19)

This understanding of globalization with reference to world trade and imperialism has to be set against analyses that locate its contemporary distinctiveness in the development of electronic communication and globally networked money markets.

Furthermore, while there is widespread agreement that the contemporary world is shrinking, that it is interconnected through a network of trade, finance, social movements, travel, politics and information, there is little consensus about the specific form of that globalization, its motive force and its proper analysis. Thus theories of the 'world system' and ceaseless capital accumulation (Wallerstein 1974, 1990, 1991) compete with analyses of transnational processes and practices (Hannerz 1990, 1991; Keohane and Nye (eds.) 1971; Robertson 1990, 1991; Sklair 1991), and Beck's (1992a and b) analysis of the 'global risk society' with Giddens's (1990, 1991) theory of 'time-distantiation' and 'disembedding processes of high modernity'. Some writers identify new local–global connections (Giddens 1990; Hannerz 1990, 1991), others stress inequalities between centre and periphery (Hannerz 1990, 1991; Wallerstein

1990, 1991). The same terms, however, are not necessarily used from compatible perspectives and thus result in very different analyses. I am thinking here, for example, of the writings by Hannerz (1990, 1991) and Wallerstein (1990, 1991) on centre-periphery, or by Beck (1992a and b) and Giddens (1990) on risk. Within that entire body of thought, expressions of globalization are variably tied to capital accumulation, culture, technology or a combination of these and other forces.

It is not my objective in this chapter to discuss the work of the main protagonists of this debate. Nor is it my intention to take sides and locate myself in any one of the existing perspectives. Rather, I will take the substantive issues raised by that work and use them, where appropriate, as a basis for drawing out temporal features. Most particularly, however, I am interested in bringing into sharp relief the influence of technology on the development of global times. My main source of material, therefore, will be work which has focused on the impact of technology on contemporary globalized existence (Beck 1992a and b; Kern 1983; McLuhan 1964/1973; Nowotny 1989; O'Malley 1992a and b; Poster 1990; Rifkin 1987; Romanyshyn 1989; Wajcman 1991). In conjunction with an explicit exploration of the globalization of time, this focus on technological developments, which is generally regarded outside the concerns of social science, provides us with a novel access to existing debates. Once more, theorizing what is normally left implicit allows us to see the invisible, sidestep established traditions and suggest alternative explanations.

Two definitions: alternative visions

The different approaches to understanding the process of globalization can often be discerned from how globalization is defined. I want to pick out just two such definitions which allow for very divergent interpretations.

Globalization can ... be defined as the intensification of world-wide social relations which link distant localities in such a way that local happenings are shaped by events occurring many miles away and vice versa. This is a dialectical process because such local happenings may move in an obverse direction from the very distanciation relations that shape them. *Local transformation* is as much a part of globalization as the lateral expansion of social connections across time and space. Thus whoever studies cities today, in any part of the world, is aware that what happens in a local neighbourhood is likely to be influenced by factors – such as world money and commodity markets – operating at an infinite distance away from that neighbourhood itself. (Giddens 1990: 64)

On the basis of Giddens's definition globalization is clearly not confined to the twentieth century, not even just to the period since the industrial revolution. The missioneering activities of Christians, for example, already created those characteristics during the early Middle Ages. Christianity imposed a global rhythm of work, prayer and feast days. It thus was, and in a diminished capacity still is, a truly global influence on everyday practices and traditions in which, as Thrift (1988: 56) demonstrates, 'the basic routines of life revolved around the four great pivots of Christmas, Easter, Lammas and Michaelmas'. Protestantism, in contrast, as I already indicated in the last chapter, globalized not only a particular work ethic but also the relation to time as money (Weber 1904–5/1989). Moreover, those influences were felt in cities and rural areas the world over. Equally long-standing is the globalization of trade; that is to say, it too may be traced back to the early Middle Ages. Hohn's (1984) analysis shows how the expansion of Christianity and trade go hand in hand and how the former prepared the ground for the latter. A similar case for early globalization can be made about colonial processes which brought the world under the rule of a small number of European nations. This particular globalization in turn is closely tied to the expansion of world markets, a process dominated by a few nation states, with Britain as a key protagonist. 'It is that relationship between the formation and transformation of the world market and its domination by the economies of powerful nation states', Hall (1991: 20) argues, 'which constituted the era within which the formation of English culture took its existing shape.' On the basis of Giddens's definition, therefore, Western globalization is a process that began in the early Middle Ages, a process not unique to contemporary existence but merely intensifying during this century.

A second definition, this time not only about globalization as a social process but also about globalism as a value system, provides us with a different conclusion.

> I take it [globalism] to refer to those values which take the real world of 5 billion people as the object of concern, the whole earth as the physical environment, everyone living as world citizens, consumers and producers, with a common interest in collective action to solve global problems. (Albrow 1990: 8)

> 'Globalization' refers to all those processes by which the people of the world are incorporated into a single world society, global society. Globalism is one of the forces which assist in the development of globalisation. (Albrow 1990: 9)

Albrow's definition locates globalism and globalization firmly in the twentieth century and decouples it from any association with nation states. Analyses of globalization on those terms show that it entails new structures of social relations that circumvent the nation state. 'Global and local', Hall (1991: 27) suggests, 'are the two faces of the same movement from one epoch of globalization, the one which has been dominated by the nation state, the national economies, the national cultural identities, to something new.' Time, as I demonstrate below, plays a central role in this new development. The processes identified in Albrow's definition and the local–global connection crucially depend on changes that took place at the very end of the last and the beginning of this century. I am referring in particular to the development of the wireless telegraph and to the standardization of time. These two innovations are associated respectively with the global present and the rationalization of local times into standard time and world time.

Clock time standardized and globalized

At 12.15 a.m. local time on 14 April 1912 a distress signal was sent from a sinking ship in the North Atlantic. By early morning the news of the *Titanic's* tragic fate had covered the globe. A disaster that would have been destined to become a secret of the sea only a few decades earlier had become a collectively knowable, global event. In response to the tragedy people referred to 'a new sense of world unity', the possibility for 'the peoples of many lands to stand together in sympathetic union', 'to share a common grief', and to 'the need to wisely regulate this new servant of humanity' (quoted in Kern 1983: 67). The creation of a global present through the wireless telegraph, therefore, promoted a sense of global connectedness amongst people who formerly had been isolated by distance. In sharp contrast to the life-saving capacity of the telegraph and the associated sense of a shared present, the telegraph and telephone had a more dubious impact on other spheres of social life. The diplomatic activities preceding the outbreak of the First World War is one such example. Here, the established habits and traditions of diplomacy were not adequate to the new time-compressing tool at their disposal. As Kern (1983) brilliantly details in a chapter on 'The Temporality of the July Crisis',

> There is abundant evidence that one cause of World War I was a failure of diplomacy, and one of the causes of that failure was that diplomats could not cope with the volume and speed of electronic communication. Most of the aristocrats and gentlemen who made up the diplomatic corps in 1914 were of the old school [and were] in many respects, as wary of new

technology as some generals were wary of newfangled weapons and strategies. (Kern, 1983: 276)

Kern's data suggest that the speed of communication afforded by the
new technology left no room for the customary time for reflection, consultation and the diplomacy of conciliation. It played havoc with the
established art of carefully choreographed diplomatic timing. Time and
distance lost their established inseparability: distant events became immediate and decisions were required instantly. Never before had decisions about war and peace been made under such pressure of actuality
and immediacy. Never before had diplomacy been conducted 'under
circumstances of such extraordinary compression' (Kern 1983: 278). The
material basis for war and peace had changed almost beyond recognition. Spengler (1918: 176) compares that moment in history with earlier periods.

> In the classical world years played no role, in the Indian world decades
> scarcely mattered, but here the hour, the minute, even the second is of
> importance. Neither the Greek nor the Indian could have had any idea
> of the tragic tension of a historic crisis like that of August, 1914 when
> even moments seemed of overwhelming significance. (Quoted in Kern
> 1983: 257)

With the development of the wireless telegraph, the sending and
receiving of information became almost simultaneous. By the early part
of this century, this technological innovation had become an essential
part of a global network of communication that linked the cities of the
world as well as land stations and ships at sea. Equally important was the
development of the telephone. It too allowed for virtually instantaneous
communication across vast distances. Years, months and days of waiting
for a reply had been reduced to fractions of seconds, to a gap that was
almost imperceptible. Together, these innovations in communication
changed the relationship between time and movement across space:
succession and duration were replaced by seeming simultaneity and
instantaneity. The present was extended spatially to encircle the globe; it
became a *global present*. This opened up an unbridgeable gap between
the speeds at which information and physical bodies could travel across
space, a discrepancy ranging from the speed of light to the pace of
walking. Today, this gap is routinely incorporated into the anticipations,
plans and actions of members of industrial and industrializing societies,
whether these involve travel, satellite television, the movement of troops
and equipment to the scene of modern warfare or the interaction of
people with their computers.

Fraser (1987: 196) proposes that 'the width of the social present is determined by the time necessary to make people take concerted action. In its turn, that period depends on the distances involved and the speed with which messages may be carried.' Whilst letters between Europe and the United States took some forty days to arrive during the latter half of the eighteenth century, today telephone or facsimile communication is transmitted virtually instantaneously. The importance of technology for this development is therefore undeniable. 'The emergence of the global options', writes Henderson (1989: 3), 'would have been inconceivable without the development of information technologies, and particularly telecommunications. These technologies have been a major material condition for the emergence of the global option.' It is thus the capacity for global simultaneity which transformed the social present into a global one. The existence of such a global present meant not merely that business meetings could take place between people in Bangkok, Bonn and Boston without any of the participants having to leave their desks. It meant also that events in one part of the world could have almost instantaneous effects on the other side of the globe and send ripples through the entire network. Moreover, these processes are largely beyond the control of those involved since the combination of instantaneity of communication with simultaneity of networked relations no longer functions to the principles of clock time and mechanical interaction. Stock-markets are a case in point: excitement or problems in one financial centre have inescapable and often unpredictable effects on the rest. 'The new level of interconnectivity', as Poster (1990: 3) points out, 'heightens the fragility of social networks.' The enormous speed coupled with multiple, simultaneous, reflexive connections poses problems at the level of perception, understanding, expectation and action: it constitutes at all these levels an unconquered reality.

Not all moves towards global time, however, are of this complex nature. Some are based on the much more conventional nineteenth-century principle of rationalization. They include the very important developments of *standard time* and *world time*, the rationalization of clock and calendar time across the globe. Standard time brought to an end the myriad of local times and dates used by the peoples of the world. During the early part of the nineteenth century travellers moving from the East to the West coast of the United States, for example, encountered different local times in every town they went through until, in 1883, the US railroads inaugurated a uniform time. By 1884 Greenwich was installed as the zero meridian and the earth divided into twenty-four equal zones, each one hour apart. Although it took many years for this standard time to get adopted world-wide, its establishment constituted the beginning of the *global day*, a day made up of the same disembedded twelve hours irrespective of context and number of daylight hours. Closely associated with the globalization of the day is the development of a globally synchronized, unified time. At 10.00 a.m., 1 July 1913 the Eiffel Tower transmitted the first time-signal across the globe. Wireless signals travelling at the speed of light displaced local times and established one time for all people on this earth: 1913 is the beginning of *world time*. Standard time and world time are essential material conditions for the global network of communication in both information and transport. They underpin the planning and organization of transnational business and global organizations. They are fundamental to the concept of globalization and globalism as defined by Albrow above.

This network of information, transport and rationalized time changed the pre-existing global networks of religion, politics and economic relations: *global instantaneity and simultaneity became the norm and distance lost its barrier quality*. As distances were reduced by the speed of communication, so the personal, social, religious, political and economic horizons expanded. Giddens (1990) characterizes those processes through the concepts of time–space distantiation and disembedding. Time–space distantiation which he defines as 'the conditions under which time and space are organized so as to connect presence and absence' (1990: 14) is vastly expanded with electronic communication, while disembedding processes, defined as 'the lifting out of social relations from local contexts of interaction and their restructuring across indefinite spans of time–space' (1990: 21), are further advanced by the creation of standard and world time. World time, the universal day and the global present, therefore, provided the framework for the development of a *global perspective*. Such a global perspective became a potential reality once the whole world came into reach, in principle at least, at the everyday level. When people can hear on the radio or watch on their TV screen events and tragedies occurring on the other side of the globe, when it takes no more than two days to reach any destination, when, at the press of a button, a personal donation can affect the livelihood or survival of people in another part of the world, then a global perspective, Albrow's 'globalism', becomes part of everyday reality. The famines of the African subcontinent, the massacre at Tiananmen Square, the burning oil-fields in Kuwait, the plight of the civilians in the bitter civil war raging in the former Yugoslavia, Norway's decision to lift the ban on hunting certain species of whales, are inescapable, global events, subject for all to see, pass judgment on and exert pressure. We can no longer retain an attitude of non-involvement. Thus, McLuhan argued thirty years ago,

In the electric age, when our central nervous system is technologically extended to involve us in the whole of mankind and to incorporate the whole of mankind in us, we necessarily participate, in depth, in the consequences of our every action. It is no longer possible to adopt the aloof and dissociated role of the literate Westerner. (McLuhan 1964/1973: 12)

With a globalized present responsibility extends beyond representatives in local and national governments to the individual: it inescapably connects the global with the local and personal. This is why the architect in Lively's novel feels concerned: he *ought* to be moved by the massacre on the other side of the globe; he *ought* to be considering what action might be available to him to alleviate the suffering or to bring pressure to bear on the guilty. Worrying instead about his answering machine means he is failing in his responsibility as a citizen connected to global events. Knowing this, he is disturbed.

The globalization of information through technological developments had a particularly striking effect on the practices of surveillance and record-keeping. Technological innovations such as space travel and satellites extended the human reach into space. They created our earth as an external entity and freed the way for *global surveillance* in aid of war and peace purposes. Satellites, for example, can eavesdrop and detect movement of people and equipment on a global scale. Thus, during the Gulf War, US military personnel stationed in Australia advised Allied generals when and where to attack in Kuwait. Technologically based surveillance, however, does not only operate one way; it allows for some measure of surveillance in the other direction, that is, from the populace to those in charge of their surveillance. The example of live television illustrates the point since it cannot fully control what the public are to see: the faltering of Ceauşescu in the face of loyalty turning to hate, police and military atrocities against innocent citizens and civilians, the obvious lies of politicians, all are publicly available for everyone to see, react to and demand change to. Thus, live television, transmitted as it often is to global audiences, inextricably connects personal with collective, private with public, and local with global domains in a way that has irrevocably broken the traditional mould of power, surveillance and control.

A similar two-way, if equally unequal, capacity for surveillance is attached to record-keeping with the aid of networked computers. Initially, those developments of information networks and linked data banks promised expanded control on a scale unimaginable for previous generations. However, almost proportional to the expansion of the

sphere of control came a loss in security of the data since the information
is available to a far greater number of people than was/is the case with
records on paper. The electronic 'global embrace', in other words, entails
a surveillance where the access points can no longer be safeguarded for
only the select few. This loss of control over access thus creates the
potential for the two-way flow of information, for a wider base of surveillance which extends to individual and collective involvement at every
level of interaction. It implicates each one of us in the fate not just of our
own families and societies but of people and living beings in distant
places. The potential not just for vastly expanded control but for demo-
cratizing traditional power relationships is thus constituted through the
global embrace. Its democratic potential is poised to be realized. Central
to our contemporary globalized present, however, is not just a future
awaiting our actions but a *globalized future already realized.*

Global futures

We can speak of a global future when all or at least a significant number
of people across the globe share, in the short and long term, important
dimensions of their lives. I have in mind such examples as the future of
debt and destitution for countries on the receiving end of the Western
commitment to 'development' or the ecological effects of the industrial
way of life, the potential end in the present through the development of
nuclear power, and the lack of control for globally networked processes.
     When in 1949 President Truman defined a substantial part of the
world as 'underdeveloped', he set in progress the global agenda of
'development', the goal to bring the Third World up to the First or at
least the Second World's standards. He had thus begun a secular
missioneering project of proportions equal if not superior to that of the
Christian and Muslim religions: the world was to be westernized and
embrace industrialism, capitalism, technology and democracy. 'The guiding light of international development policy', Sachs (1992: 17) points
out, 'was to create societies of paid workers and consumers everywhere',
importing technology and experts from the West, producing industrial
goods with money borrowed from Western banks. From her Indian
experience and her position as a woman Shiva (1989: 84) argues that
'what is currently called development is essentially maldevelopment,
based on the introduction or accentuation of the domination of man over
nature and women'. Closely related to the Western understanding of
Third World underdevelopment is the discovery of its poverty: poverty
as lack of growth, lack of technology, lack of consumer goods and ma-

terial wealth, and poverty with reference to gross national product (GNP), a figure produced annually by the World Bank for every country. Since, however, the interest rates to be paid to Western banks over the years far outstrip the original loans, those countries pay for and finance the increasing material wealth of the West while they meanwhile descend on the well-documented spiral of debt and dependency. Far from narrowing the gap between rich and poor, 'development' has dramatically sharpened the inequalities of power and wealth. It is a global future that does not bode well for the majority of peoples on this earth.

Intimately connected to this global future of 'development' are the twin imperatives of growth and technological innovation with their respective effects on the global environment. As I show in the next chapter, it is a future of environmental crisis where GNP simultaneously constitutes a measure of gross national pollution. Dependence on continuing growth and consumption, in other words, cannot be separated from the inevitable need for obsolescence and the growth in waste. Moreover, since technology is regarded as the central tool for progress and as generator of successful development, it seems inevitable that the depletion of non-renewable resources, coupled with the attendant steep rise in pollution, should become an integral part of the global Westernized future. Those unintended consequences of the industrial way of life permeate the land, sea, earth, air and surrounding atmosphere of our planet. They affect perpetrator and innocent alike. Even societies not yet touched by industrialization and those resisting the Western path are nevertheless subject to the unplanned futures of technological development since its effects cannot be contained within their countries of origin.

Most pertinent to this creation of globalized present futures and future presents is, of course, the development of nuclear power and its associated threat of radiation. It is tested in the more remote regions of our world from where it permeates ecosystems and affects all of us to varying degrees of intensity. Nuclear material is located across the world on land, in the sea and in the air. It is stored deep in the earth and on the bottom of the oceans. It is harnessed for both benign and hostile power and it encircles our earth in satellites. It engulfs the globe, affecting all life on earth with its potential threat: the aftermath of radiation may be immediate or take decades, even millennia, to reveal. It is a *global future for all* irrespective of location, nationality and political persuasion. It forms an invisible reality that constitutes presents for hundreds, even thousands, of potential generations hence.

In conjunction with the nuclear threat, Beck (1992a and b) provides a powerful analysis of the limits to the contemporary principle of insurance. He argues for the difference between traditional dangers, industrially-induced problems and the contemporary threat of nuclear power, between, for example, the danger of being struck by lightning or having a car accident and the hazard of being affected by nuclear fall-out. While the former are considered calculable risks – by statistically establishing their probability of occurring – and are therefore covered by insurance, the latter falls outside the aegis of insurance, outside the possibility to prepare for and counteract an uncertain future. With the nuclear threat, he states, the industrial system is no longer capable of dealing with its own unforeseeable future.

> If a fire breaks out, the fire-brigade comes, if a traffic accident occurs, the insurance pays. This interplay between beforehand and afterwards, between the future and security in the here and now, because precautions have been taken even for the worst imaginable case, has been revoked in the age of nuclear, chemical and genetic technology. In all the brilliance of their perfection, nuclear power plants have suspended the principle of insurance not only in the economic, but also in the medical, psychological, cultural and religious sense. *The residual risk society has become an uninsured society*, with protection paradoxically diminishing as the danger grows. (Beck 1992a: 101)

This uninsurability for potential nuclear disasters is indicative of the fact that we have no institutions, now or in the foreseeable future, which could deal with the worst imaginable case of a nuclear war or even a major nuclear fall-out. As a global threat that permeates our present as well as our long-term future, the nuclear hazard creates the *potential end in the present*. This means, as I have argued elsewhere (Adam 1990: 141–2), that the belief in continuity, in the existence of a future as we know it, is a misplaced assumption: to the lack of certainty about *the future* has to be added the lack of certainty of *a future*.

Once the potential outcome of cultural activity is characterized by globalization and temporal uncertainty, and once the time-lags of cause and effect span from nanoseconds to millennia, both risk calculation and socio-political engineering become highly problematic social practices. Such globalized uncertainty poses barriers to effective action because our capacity to predict and control is dependent on processes governed by sequential, linear causality. In other words, the simultaneity and instantaneity of global information and environmental effects in conjunction with non-linear, networked processes render our efforts ineffective, elude our conventional modes of domination.

If our contemporary reality exhibits global features and is characterized by historically unprecedented characteristics, if it is marked by a multitude of times that coexist in an embedded, embodied and mutually

permeating way, and if we are personally implicated in and thus responsible for those globalized processes and their effects without being able
to rely on conventional modes of control, then these features must be
allowed to permeate not just our everyday, our economic and our political understanding but also our social science assumptions, our theories
and our methods. They need to become an integral part of social science
in the same way as the key features of the Enlightenment had penetrated
the work of the founding fathers and their successors. Such a shift in
conceptualization is crucial if we are to respond more appropriately to
the effects of globalization and the environmental crisis of the late twentieth century. This, however, is not yet the case. As Beck (1992a: 101)
points out, 'at the threshold of the twenty-first century, the challenges of
the age of atomic, genetic and chemical technology are being handled
with concepts and recipes that are derived from early industrial society of
the nineteenth and the early twentieth centuries'. The social sciences, in
other words, are still tied to the perspectives of their respective founding
fathers. Their key assumptions are still dominated by the technologies of
the early industrial period and the politics of nation states. And the
temporal complexity of this globalized reality has yet to penetrate their
theories and methodologies.

Enlightenment tradition and machine metaphors

Since their inception the social sciences have been tied to the project of
the Enlightenment thinkers; they have been associated with the development of objective science and with the control and rational organization
of every sphere of life. Sociology in particular was concerned to establish
itself as an objective science. Its aim, to some extent at least, was to offer
a social science equivalent to the natural sciences' control over nature.
Like the natural sciences, it focused on the rational elements of its
subject matter and emphasized the rational features of its theories and
methods. Its development and its fate therefore are linked to industrialization, to the rise of science as the dominant cosmology and to the
commodification and rationalization of every sphere of social life (see for
example, Giddens 1976, 1981, 1990, 1991; Harvey 1989; Marx 1857/1973,
1867/1976; Weber 1904–5/1989).

Analyses of social time tend to mirror those concerns by emphasizing
the organization of Western life to the metronomic beat of the clock
(Moore 1963; Young 1988; Zerubavel 1981). They stress the control over
time (Hohn 1984; Marx 1857/1973, 1867/ 1976; Nguyen 1992; O'Malley
1992a; Thompson 1967) and the rational standardization of time across

the globe (Kern 1983; O'Malley 1992b). The standardization of time at the turn of the century, the commodification of time in all areas of social exchange, and the separation of time and space through technological developments in communication and transport, all these form central components of analyses of social time (Bergmann 1992; Giddens 1979, 1981; Nowotny 1992). Time theories, in other words, reflect the social sciences' explicit concern with objectivity, rationality and the scientific study of Western, post-Enlightenment society (Adam 1988, 1990, 1992a). Simultaneity, instantaneity, networked information, time-spans from the imperceptibly short to the unimaginably long, and global presents implicating pasts as well as future presents and present futures in conjunction with embedded/embodied, local/personal times are characteristics of contemporary global times that cannot easily be encompassed by the rational, objective tradition of Enlightenment thought. The difficulty is compounded by the fact that time theories, like the social theories in which they are embedded, have been underpinned by the technological metaphors of the clock and the heat-engine.

When we explore these technological metaphors in more detail, we find that they entail different kinds of time, temporal features that are out of tune with the characteristics of global phenomena and processes identified above. Thus the time of the clock ticks away evenly and objectively. It is linked to abstract motion and to distance travelled in space. The clock marks time by dissociation, by abstracting it from human events and assigning it a number value. Emphasis on the clock-work highlights mechanical relationships: cogs and springs interacting to form an integrated whole. It accentuates parts. The smooth running of the whole depends on accurate timing, tempo, sequence, duration and periodicity. Breakdowns can usually be traced back to the source by logical pathways. And, if one fully understands the working of the clock, one can isolate the cause of the breakdown and – in principle at least – repair it by replacing the appropriate parts (for a more detailed discussion see Adam 1990: 48–55; Prigogine and Stengers 1984: 27–68).

If we turn to the image of the heat-engine we find that it not only retains all the functional characteristics of the clock but also contains some new features which are no longer reducible to those of the mechanical clock. The functional principles shared by the heat-engine and the clock are numerous: both use and dissipate energy. Both rely for their smooth functioning on accurate timing, tempo, sequence, duration, periodicity and the spatial measure of time. In contrast to the clock, however, heat-engines consume non-renewable resources and dissipate heat to the environment. Theirs is a system that is running down and as such it also changes the surrounding environment in the direction of a slow heat-death. These new features are intimately tied to the different tracking of time: the primary time of the heat-engine is that of unidirectional, irreversible change (for further detail see Adam 1990: 61–5; Prigogine and Stengers 1984: 257–90).

Clocks and heat-engines are metaphors for an inanimate reality, a world locked in predetermined pathways of change, of knowable futures where nothing new ever happens, where input connects to output and where cause and effect stand in a proportional relation to each other. They are expressions of a world of parts: simple, demystified, measurable and predictable. They represent a reality that can be taken apart and reassembled both physically and conceptually, a controllable reality that constitutes humans in the role of machine operator, even that of maker. Today, those conceptualizations are found wanting. They are inappropriate for understanding the processes of globalization on the one hand and ecological relations on the other. That is to say, clocks and heat-engines, the key metaphors for a world of bounded nation states and dominated by Newtonian and thermodynamic science, are no longer appropriate for a social world in which knowledge, information, politics, business, finance, transport and environmental problems are globally networked.

Electronic communication is one of the key technological factors in this contemporary globalization. It enmeshes our earth in a network of sounds and images. It is not subject to the constraints of time and space in the same way as were the earlier technologies: it is in principle available, storable and retrievable instantaneously all over the globe (McLuhan 1964/1973; Poster 1990; Rifkin 1987). Since the limit to the speed of that information transfer is the speed of light, those communications are virtually simultaneous and facilitate the transcendence of space. The age-old link between time and space is unsettled. Electronic information is dispersed across time and space. Decentred and infinitely multipliable, it no longer has a fixed location: it is 'everywhere and nowhere' (Poster 1990: 85). Similar to living processes I discuss in other chapters, it is both material and immaterial. Moreover, as Poster (1990: 17) notes, 'the new language structures refer back upon themselves, subverting referentiality and thereby acting upon the subject and constituting it in new and disorienting ways'. This brings with it a loss of certainty and predictability. It facilitates non-linear connections where the initial cause becomes disconnected from and irrelevant for the outcome and vastly increases the fragility of social networks: effects in one part of the world reverberate through the global network and insignificant local happenings may have dramatic impacts at the national and global level. The parallels with globalized processes are overwhelming. Moreover, in electronic communication cause and effect do not stand in a proportional relation; that is, small causes can have dramatic effects throughout the system. Unpredictability and uncertainty, the production of the unknown rather than the known, are therefore integral aspects of the networked connections of electronic information. Predictability, of course, has not disappeared, but unpredictability has taken prime position. A further irreducibly new feature of the technology associated with electronic communication relates to the loss of identity. Machines, be they mechanical or thermodynamic, are temporally organized *within* each machine without being rhythmically embedded in their environments. They may be coupled to other machines but this machine interdependence does not alter any of the machines' individual functional identities. Computers, in contrast, are so profoundly interconnected that their identities are no longer sacrosanct. Just like social interactive systems, they are able to pass on complex information, change each other in the process, even get 'infected'. In their mutuality they are subject even to epidemics (Poster 1990: 1–20).

With electronic communication, artefactual, living and globalized social systems have moved closer together. They all display features which cannot be grasped through the technological metaphors of the previous centuries. It means that a networked, globally connected social world that implicates each one of us in the ongoings of the whole is better served by the metaphor of electronic communication than that of the clock and/or the heat-engine. Like the metaphor of holography which I explored elsewhere (Adam 1990: 158–60), the metaphor of electronic communication allows for generative, non-linear, open, interactive, mutually implicating and productive processes where input and output do not stand in a 1:1 relation and where cause and effect are not proportional to each other. Closely allied to global processes, the electronic metaphor offers the potential for more appropriate intervention in the environmental, economic and political crises of the late twentieth century than did the metaphors of clocks and heat-engines. As such, it constitutes one small step on the path towards reconceptualization and new practices.

Other steps consist of understanding together what traditional analyses have kept apart, such as grasping the relationship between and the distinctiveness of the rationalization of time into standard world time and the electronically constituted global present. The task is not to replace the rationalized, decontextualized measure with the simultaneity, instantaneity and unpredictability of the global electronic embrace but to encompass their mutual implications and effects. It means conceptualizing the totalizing tendencies of globalization as inseparable from the local, the particular, the subjective, the embedded and embodied since the temporalities I outlined in this chapter are no longer meaningfully theorized in the either-or modes of Enlightenment thought.

> The twentieth century has been a unique period in world cultural history. Humankind has finally bid farewell to that world which could with some credibility be seen as a cultural mosaic of separate pieces with hard, well-defined edges. Because of the great increase in the traffic in culture, the large-scale transfer of meaning systems and symbolic forms, the world is increasingly becoming one not only in political and economic terms, as in the climatic period of colonialism, but in terms of its cultural construction as well, a global ecumene of persistent cultural interaction and exchange. (Hannerz 1991: 107)

This global ecumene demands that prediction, action and control be based on different temporal principles. As I argue in the next chapter, it necessitates response speeds outside the range of our physiological and mental capacity. It requires personal and collective responsibilities that span not just election cycles or, at best, a single generation, but hundreds of generations. It calls for a long-term perspective since our actions today determine the global presents and futures for a multitude of generations. It irrevocably links our personal/local times with global times and connects our individual concerns with collective responsibilities for the long-term future. These connections are not simulacra. 'We necessarily participate', as McLuhan (1964/1973: 12) insisted, 'in the consequences of our every action.' Knowing this, we are rightly disturbed when concern about the answering machine blots out a massacre at the other side of the globe or when debates about better interpretations of past theories substitute for theory as a basis for active engagement.

Key points

At the substantive level I have shown
- that at the turn of this century there emerged a number of globalized times – global time zones, standard time, world time – that formed the framework for a global perspective
- that the global present is premised on technological developments from the wireless telegraph to nuclear power
- that the global future in the present is realized when a significant number of people across the world share in the short and long term important dimensions of their lives such as 'development', market principles and environmental problems.

With reference to methodology I have argued

- that in the face of globalization the social sciences need to reconceptualize some of their basic premises: the dependence on the nation state as a primary unit of analysis, the exclusion of technological principles and the evasion of ontological questions
- that simultaneity, instantaneity, uncertainty and implication, the key features of global time, cannot be encompassed by classical theories based on a separation of past, present and future, linear causality and a positivist methodology
- that the technological metaphor of electronic communication can be utilized fruitfully for the conceptualization of globalized processes.

6

The Times of Global Environmental Change

Environmental change is one aspect of globalization that is difficult to ignore. It affects people's health and enforces changes in routine daily actions. Environmental issues are on the agenda for politicians, activists and journalists. From being local and national affairs, they have become global concerns during the 1980s. Widely accepted as causes for this concern are the pollution of land, air and water and prominent among these are the depletion of the ozone layer, global warming and the disposal and rendering harmless of waste. For social scientists to engage with the environment requires rethinking of some of the most basic premises of their disciplines. Focus on time can help us in this reconceptualization.

Approaches to the environment

While there is considerable agreement that phenomena such as ozone depletion, global warming and pollution constitute global problems, no such consensus has been reached over interpretations of the degree of the problems, their causes or their potential solutions.

> There are underlying disagreements over how problems are defined, their degree of seriousness, who is responsible for solving them, and how amenable they are to solution. These disagreements run deep; they are based on different moral principles, different values, different assumptions about how the world operates, and they are found not only at the international level, where cultural diversity is to be expected, but at all levels, within a single society or organisation, and within the actions and policies of a single corporate group. (Milton 1991: 4)

Often, some groups' answers are another's causes, and 'what is rational from one perspective is deeply irrational from another' (Porritt 1984: 15). The goals of industrially sustain*ed* growth and ecologically sustain*able* growth, for example, are difficult to reconcile. To propose a strategy of 'Best Available Technique Not Entailing Excessive Costs' (which goes under the acronym BATNEEC) is incompatible with proposals for new ecological ethics which insist on a shift from industrial product to ecological process, from planned obsolescence to durability, from short-term to long-term solutions and from understanding the measure of gross national product (GNP) as progress to viewing it as problem and pollution indicator.

Given this pervasive social debate, it is not surprising that sociologists are increasingly involved in the study and exploration not of environmental matters *per se* but of their attendant social relations, perspectives and actions. And yet there is unease about this social science approach to environmental research. How can sociologists make sense of the different definitions, approaches and proposals for solutions, asks Newby (1991), when their discipline has been established on the irreducible distinction between nature and culture, the natural and the symbolic environment, evolution and history, when the environment as a subject matter so clearly falls outside their traditional bounded domain? One strategy has been to stay clear of the substantive issues and to focus instead on environmentalism, the rise of green issues on the political agenda, on assumptions underpinning deep and shallow ecology, as well as the social construction of those scientific 'facts' (Cotgrove 1982; Dobson 1990). As Chapter 2 demonstrates, the exclusion of 'nature' from social science analyses of culture is not tenable once we give explicit attention to the time dimension of everyday life. With respect to environmental issues, however, such exclusion is even more problematic. That is to say, the social science approach of evading environmental issues *per se* seems highly misplaced when contemporary environmental hazards threaten our health and our survival – as members of an academic discipline, of families and societies, of a species and as living organisms on this planet – and when our present actions affect future generations thousands of years hence. Thus, beyond being a problematic subject matter for the social sciences, environmental issues confront us with questions about the 'objective', thus scientific, status of observers: Marx's comment that it is not enough merely to study society, but that it must be changed, never seemed more pertinent than when social scientists engage with environmental matters.

This means that concern with 'nature' and with engagement rather than detached explication demands some far-reaching changes at the very heart of the social sciences. Such a stance necessitates first that we open the disciplinary boundaries and extend our focus to the living, physical and artefactual environment. This, of course, is the approach pursued throughout this book. Second, it requires that we transcend the dualisms which constitute the very foundations of social science: nature–culture, fact–value, matter–mind, observer–observed, objectivity–subjectivity, to name just some of the most central of those antinomies. Again, this is an approach that arises as necessary from an explicit focus on the complexity of everyday times. Third, it means that we need to redefine the scientific component of our discipline and incorporate in that reassessment an engagement with the subject matter from the perspective of implicated participant. Engagement suggests a standpoint that unifies the investigator, the victim, the 'activist' and the bystander. This, finally, has implications for single-perspective understanding: we need to accept the multiplicity and irreconcilability of perspectives, find alternatives to the habituated expectancies of truth, proof, predictability and certainty and learn conceptually to embrace ourselves as creators of unknowable futures.

From this brief introductory outline of the issues it becomes apparent how much the conceptual implications of a focus on the environment overlap with the effects on social science by an engagement with everyday times. Together, these concerns provide us with an extremely powerful critique of existing social science praxis. I am therefore not concerned with the history of environmentalism or the social construction of scientific data. Instead I want to identify some of the implicit time dimensions of the environment–industrialism interpenetration and explore their implications for social theory. In the first part of this chapter I outline a number of distinguishing temporal features of artefacts, machines and living processes and suggest some connections to environmental problems. Although I talk about the 'natural' environment, this of course is a misnomer since there is virtually no aspect of the 'natural' environment that has not been affected by the industrial and agricultural way of life. Just as culture is infused with nature, so nature is socialized and acculturated (see also Chapter 2). Bearing in mind that permeation, I nevertheless want to make some distinctions that will help bring to the fore some of the factors that underpin the present global environmental change. In the main part of this chapter I thus make explicit the complexity of times that permeates specific aspects of contemporary environmental pollution. I conclude with a discussion of the conception of nature as 'other' and its inappropriateness for understanding global environmental change. My express purpose is to use the focus on time to span the gaps between personal, professional and environmental concerns in a way that suggests at each of these levels active participation in the creation of the future.

Of organic and artefactual time

In the chapter on time and health I show how the times of the body and the 'natural' environment are characterized by rhythmic variation, synchronization and an all-embracing, complex web of interconnections. Linear sequences take place but these are part of a wider network of cycles as well as finely tuned and synchronized temporal relations where ultimately everything connects to everything else: the structure of living systems is temporal and their 'parts' resonate with the whole and vice versa. Rhythmicity, therefore, forms nature's silent pulse. All organisms, from single cells to ecosystems, display interdependent rhythmic behaviour. Some of this rhythmicity constitutes the organism's unique identity, some relates to its life cycle, some binds the organism to the rhythms of the universe, and some functions as a physiological clock by which living beings 'tell' cosmic time. The 'natural' environment is thus a temporal realm of orchestrated rhythms of varying speeds and intensities as well as temporally constituted uniqueness. It is also a world of organisms endowed with the capacity for remembering and anticipating, of beings that time their actions, synchronize their interactions and reckon time. The very essence of life, furthermore, is growth and evolution. In organic processes, therefore, the entropic principle changes its direction from decay, uniformity and heat-death to growth, variation and life. This involves, as I show in previous chapters, the creation and regeneration of time: the use and depletion of time are counterbalanced by its generation and replenishment; decay is compensated by repair through healing and by 'superrepair' through the birth–death cycle. Moreover, 'natural' processes vary with context. This means that general principles find unique expression. The rhythmically changing constellations of the stars, for example, never repeat themselves in exactly the same way; springtime, the period when a large proportion of land-based nature comes to life, is incomparably different from winter-time when so much lies dormant. Finally, a vast range of time-spans 'coexist' simultaneously (this is, of course a problematic use of language since time-spans are not existents but an aspect of the framework of meaning). These time-spans extend from the imperceptibly fast to the unimaginably slow, covering processes that last from nanoseconds to millennia.

Artefacts as copies of nature

The artefactual world of human culture differs significantly from many of these temporal characteristics of living being. A brief outline of those differences may aid and enhance our understanding of environmental pollution. Though often conceived as copies of nature, artefacts do not remain embedded within the give-and-take, the transience of ecological interconnectedness and exchange. They are created apart, frozen for contemplation, fixed in their uniqueness. They take on a material existence with a difference: externalized, abstracted, bounded and isolated. They are created as islands of permanence in a sea of creative change. Their existence constitutes a finite time, encased in things and isolated from the processes of life and ecological interconnections. Consequently, their temporality is governed by entropy not by development and growth. The emphasis is no longer on process but on product. Except for their most recent expressions, cultural products encapsulate the aim of longevity. Paintings and books, cathedrals and nuclear power, all are moves towards immortality, all are efforts to overcome individual death (Becker 1973). Through their creations, moreover, human beings are able to gain knowledge, since to create in isolated and unchanging form what is interconnected, moving and changing facilitates reflection, contemplation and study. Such externalization of knowledge simultaneously advances the growth of understanding and provides the potential to have a relationship to that which is other than Self.

This cluster of time-related characteristics of artefacts – externalization, disembedding, detemporalization and emphasis on longevity and precision – is implicated in cultural activity from the construction of tools and the transformation of raw materials to the creation of cities. As such it is central to the human impact on nature and to the acculturation and socialization of the 'natural' world. Artefacts created with the aid of science are therefore not unique in this sense. They have merely intensified those discontinuities between human production and the temporal ongoings of living processes and with it they have vastly extended the effect of human activity on the environment. Like other products of culture, steam engines, cars and nuclear power 'plants' are not designed to be temporally embedded within the ecological give-and-take of their environments. Unlike many other artefacts, however, these products of science are conceived to be rhythmically organized and finely tuned *within* each isolated system. This makes machines and other science-based systems both similar to and different from living systems which are not only temporally organized but also by 'natural design' temporally embedded in a rhythmically organized energy exchange where the discarded energy of one system constitutes the source of energy for another.

This machine–organism distinction further contains a different meaning of efficiency. Life tends to depend on high-energy exchange within systems as well as between systems and their environments, whilst the efficiency of a machine relates to entropy and low-energy exchange: minimum entropy means maximum efficiency. In other words, there has to be just enough energy difference to make the machine work. The aim is to achieve a differential that is as close as possible to non-dissipation. An efficient car, therefore, uses the minimum of petrol for the maximum of distance travelled. An 'efficient' forest, in contrast, uses a maximum of carbon dioxide (waste energy of others) and transforms it into a maximum of oxygen (central life source for others). Entropy is implicated in yet another important organism–machine distinction. Machines start to deteriorate as soon as they are constructed and the sources to counteract this process – invariably energy-using and waste-producing – are always located outside the system rather than being generated from within: machines are not designed for death and regeneration. The success of living systems, in contrast, depends on their mortality and on the transience of their internal subsystems. 'The constant deterioration of the molecular and cellular components', Morin (1974: 563) suggests, 'is the weakness which gives living beings the advantage over machines.' Living being, he argues, is constituted on the basis of disorder whilst the design of machines is premised on 'the high reliability of their component parts'.

These distinctions, however, should not be conceived as simple dichotomies: temporal organization within systems or within and between systems, minimum or maximum entropy production, entropy or growth, order from order or order from disorder. The differences are far more multifaceted and mutually influencing: disorder tends to result from the creation of order. There is no growth without entropy production. Long-term stability is invariably based on short-term impermanence and uncertainty. Complexity and implication rather than opposites are thus necessary guides for understanding the role of human culture and contemporary science in the present environmental crisis.

A second feature, exacerbated by the scientific way of life, is the relation to the environment as external and 'other', and the treatment of nature as an inanimate source of exploitable resources. This Western relationship to nature as 'other' has a number of very deep-rooted sources in prescientific praxis (in the Marxian sense of unification of thought and practice). Central among these are the linear-perspective vision and the creation of a clock time. Both are powerful externalizers. Both separate subject from object. Both are devices that distance us from experience. Both facilitate mathematical description, quantification and standardization.

Linear-perspective vision

The linear-perspective vision of reality, a fifteenth-century technique to represent three-dimensional space on a two-dimensional plane, is a conceptual as well as an artistic method that enables us to employ a window ethic. It allows us to abstract observer from observed, and the part from the whole. Before its inception, the world and our place within it looked and felt differently: the person was always integral to the system of observation, which meant that knowledge was fundamentally relative. With the linear perspective the body was moved from the centre to the outside, from the midst of to outside the scheme of things. This entailed a transformation of participants into spectators, of active agents into passive observers (Romanyshyn 1989).

An analogous process occurred with the relationship to time when clock time became abstracted from the complexity of times that pervade our existence, when time became disembedded from the temporality, tempo, timing, rhythmicity, chronology and historicity of being and separated from the past, present and the future. With the creation of an independent machine time, the multiplicity of times was transformed into an objectified, measurable quantity that could be used as a social tool for orientation, coordination, synchronization and regulation. Temporalities thus mediated could then be translated into an object, a material commodity to be used, allocated, sold and controlled.

Whilst the linear perspective translated depth levels into spatial distance, clock time represented the passage of time as distance travelled in space, or as measurement of length. Emphasis on visual space, distance and detachment corresponded to the visual representation, externalization and decontextualization of time. The linear-perspective and clock-time vision found their coherent and full expression in the scientific world view. As conceptual tools, in other words, they encompass a number of principles that can be observed in scientific theories and designs: emphasis on abstraction, separation and otherness, elimination of surrounding context, and the allied pursuit of permanence and timeless truth. 'But the divorce of inner from outer, above from below', as Roszak (1992: 6) points out, 'could never be more than a temporary expedient, a way of getting on with fact gathering.'

Today, this particular cluster of characteristics is being questioned: it is considered inappropriate for the description and analysis of our globally networked reality. The subject–subject relation, for example, is no longer the prerogative of the human sciences: biologists and philosophers extend that relation to other living species, contemporary physicists like Brian Swimme to the physical environment both on earth and in the cosmos, talking of 'brother quark' and 'sister meson' (BBC TV *Soul* 1991). It is now the turn of sociologists (beyond the lone voice of Benton 1993) to extend their subject–subject relations to animals, plants and inorganic matter, to conceive of the environment as a community of subjects and to concern themselves with the re-embedding of cultural activities in the temporal ongoings of 'nature'. It is time for *engagement* with the environment. The focus on time can assist us in this endeavour.

Running out of time

'We are running out – not of resources but time.'
'All study, planning, negotiation and implementation of agreed
    action takes time.'
'We could not foresee the speed of depletion.'
'The rapid time scale of deterioration means that we have to cut
    our planned time scale of action by half.'
'We have to bring the cut-off date forward by five years to 1995.'
    (BBC Radio 1992)

Although these statements, made in a recent BBC radio programme on environmental issues, relate to the thinning of the ozone layer, they resonate equally with a number of other environmental threats such as global warming, deforestation, acid rain and the depletion of topsoil. Moreover, they are no less relevant to matters of waste: the export of Northern societies' waste to the poor countries of the South, the dumping of toxic waste in the oceans, and the hazardous accumulation of radioactive waste. Global problems need globally coordinated action which is difficult to achieve and extremely slow; it takes time. Such global action involves people from different nations getting together to discuss, explore and plan, feed back to their countries – nationally and locally – allow for discussion, consultation and more research, construct scenarios, explore feasibility and costs, suggest new solutions and compromises. After that, a next round of talks begins at the global level. *Invariably, the time-frame of the perceived danger is out of sync with the time-frame for action* and all too often the exigency of the crisis is traded against political and economic interests, established habits, national pride and legitimation (on this last point see also Hay 1994). This has the effect of widening the gaps between the time-scale of the problem, the time-span of concern and the horizon for action. Not surprisingly, a sense of urgency and a fear of being too late, of time running out for effective action, pervade some of the debates.

Ozone depletion

While all types of pollution share the difficulty of out-of-sync time-frames, none is as apparently easy to identify and solve as the depletion of ozone. None can be shown to have a single, direct and provable relation between input and output, cause and effect, between a human product, an environmental crisis and human health. None requires the phasing out of merely one product or action. This seems to make the thinning of the ozone layer unique among environmental effects and so attractive for political action: the proven cause presents a challenging but *manageable* problem and, most importantly, it can be tackled without a change of values, economic practices or political structures (see also Hay 1994 for a similar analysis). It needs, it is argued, no more than the 'speedy' phasing out of chlorofluorocarbons (CFCs) and the invention of an alternative substance to replace the many functions performed by CFCs. Not surprisingly, therefore, this particular environmental danger has sufficient global support to be carried through to what is at present envisaged to be a successful conclusion. By June 1990 a proposal to halt the production of CFCs by the year 2000 was agreed by ninety-three nations (Brown 1991: 19). By April 1992 this cut-off date had been brought forward to 1995 (BBC Radio 1992). It is important here to note the uniqueness of this problem. Its exceptional status means that it cannot be used as a model for responses to other environmental crises.

Despite the uniqueness of ozone depletion as an environmental threat, the history of CFCs shares many characteristics with other orig-inally benign human inventions whose unforeseen and unpredictable consequences have turned into environmental hazards: all were con-sidered technological triumphs, contributors to progress. Indeed, im-mense care and consideration had gone into their design. Only with hindsight could their dangers be recognized. The emergence of such unexpected problems is to be found equally in the history of steam, petrol and jet engines, the harnessing of electricity, gas and oil, and of many other scientific innovations. CFCs are synthetic gases which have a wide range of applications in aerosols, fridges, air-conditioning, insula-tion and fire extinguishers. They have, as Yearley (1991: 13–14) points out, an extraordinary range of benign qualities. Developed early this century, they were hailed to be non-inflammable, non-poisonous and non-reactive with other substances. Certain CFCs can be liquefied under pressure and when the pressure is released they evaporate rapidly. Most importantly, they do not break down easily. They are designed for longevity which makes them very cost-effective.

Their creators could not have envisaged the havoc this invention would wreak in the upper stratosphere of our earth. It was outside the predictive capacity of the designers, producers and promoters of this product to foresee that its most positive qualities – unreactiveness and longevity – would cause the dangerous thinning of the ozone layer with its attendant malignant effects on earth. It took highly sophisticated scientific analyses, unavailable at the time of invention, to identify the indirect, non-visible links between this particular cause-and-effect relation, between CFCs and their depleting action on the protective layer in the upper stratosphere which selectively screens out high-energy ultraviolet radiation from the sun, a process that enabled the evolution of our present form of life on this earth. At the beginning of the twentieth century this ozone-depleting future was unknowable in the same way as the effects of other human developments were unpredictable at the time of their proud inception. An unknown and unpredictable future thus constitutes an integral part of the history of novel scientific inventions.

The story of CFCs is notable for yet a further time characteristic: it is replete with time-lags. It is marked by time-lags not merely between cause and effect, or between invention and recognition of the problem, but also between the identification of the problem, its multinational acceptance and the global agreement to take action. It entails time-lags between the will to action and its collective execution, between actions and effects, between human corrective change and environmental recuperation. Despite corrective action, for example, there may be long periods of worsening effects before any sign of improvement can be registered. Such multiple time-lags constitute an integral part of most environmental problems. Time-lags, gaps and latency periods often mean that the links between causes and effects have become invisible, that their relationship is no longer amenable to scientific certainty and verification. In the specific case of CFCs the problem has been known since the early 1970s and extensive warnings have been voiced since that period, but it was not until 1985 when a major reduction in ozone was reported and the increase in skin cancers could no longer be ignored, that large numbers of countries agreed to phase out CFCs by the year 2000. Even then, however, there was still great reluctance and a general clamour for 'proof' (Churchill 1991: 157–60; Yearley 1991: 17–21).

This insistence on certainty and proof for situations characterized by out-of-sync time-frames, multiple time-lags, unpredictability and uncertainty is central to much of the political complacency about environmental problems: nothing is done until the connection is 'proven'. More research rather than action tends to be the response from business and politicians. Proof, in the conventional sense of empirical science, however, is impossible to achieve when there is no directly observable link between input and output, when the relation is not 1:1 but 1:many, when we are dealing not with static phenomena but with continuously changing situations and parameters, when the reactions are latent and invisible for long periods of time and when the effects are manifested not in the location of perpetration of the act but in neighbouring countries or even on the other side of the globe. The idea of proof takes on a new meaning when it is based not on the verification of observable 'facts' but on confirmation of speculative theories.

Global warming

Global warming is another case in point where those temporal features re-emerge. Here too, there is little consensus about the severity of the problem, its time-scale and the most cost-effective solutions. While governments seek proof as a precondition to instigating 'controlling' action, the scientific discourse is filled with expressions of uncertainty: 'Sooner or later it will affect vegetation and agriculture ...', 'cereal-growing areas of the USA may become too hot ...', 'it will probably affect weather systems ...', 'the climate may become more extreme ...', 'it would begin to melt the ice caps and sea levels would rise in step ...', 'it is difficult to establish how rapidly the effect is working ...' (Yearley 1991: 17–18). Moreover, there is a multitude of competing estimates and calculations based on different combinations of variables, most of which are characterized in turn by time-lags, latency periods and poorly understood relationships. The past in these cases is not a reliable predictor of the future and even where there is measured trust in past-based knowledge, scientists realize that the time-scales of their investigations outstrip the time available for action, that time will run out before they could provide reliable answers. As Pugh (1989: 29, in Yearley 1991: 18) explains about the spectre of rising sea levels, 'analyses of sea level trends need at least 20 years of measurements. There are no short cuts, no ways of speeding up the steady accretion of data.'

Here too, traditional approaches to knowledge seem to constitute a poor basis for analyses of out-of-sync time-frames and fundamental uncertainty: materialist assumptions, past-based knowledge and the sequential accumulation of data suit technological solutions and traditional politico-economic action but are ill-matched for the task of dealing with complex, multiple interaction networks characterized by unpredictable latency periods, invisibility and seeming non-causal connections. The stark compression of available time for action is accompanied by a massive expansion of the time-scale of concern needed to deal with the created, unintended consequences of scientific inventions. In other words, whilst the socio-economic, scientific and political development is towards ever-faster change and 'short-termism', actions required by environmental change need ever-longer time-spans of reference and consideration. This discrepancy is ever-widening and the responding actions are not bridging that dramatically increasing time horizon. We are clearly not, as many suggest we must be, 'mindful of the consequences our decisions will have on the generations of the future and their ability to respond to the conditions that our decisions [and actions] will create' (Maser 1991: 56). More than ever before, there will be a pressing need to shift from practices that foster short-term profit to those that aid the long-term ability of total systems to adapt to the industrially-induced changes to the environment. There is hope but not much trust that the economically inspired options based on BATNEEC, the 'Best Available Techniques Not Entailing Excessive Costs', and BPEO, the 'Best Practicable Environmental Option' (Churchill 1991; Holiday 1992; Warren 1991), will be ousted by REV, a more 'Radical Environmental Vision'. A central obstacle to such a vision is the economic, commodified relationship to time.

As I have shown in previous chapters, in societies with commodified time speed becomes an economic value: the faster goods move through the economy the better; speed increases profit and shows up positively in a country's GNP. A very different picture emerges, however, when speed is linked not to profit but to energy use. When time is associated with energy we become aware that the faster something moves or functions, the higher tends to be its use of resources: it transforms speed from something to be aspired to into a liability. Tied to energy, speed does not mean profit. Rather, it constitutes a deficit on the balance sheet: not gross national product but gross national pollution. (This time–energy link applies most specifically to traditional technologies but much less so to micro-chip information technology.)

Space too is implicated in that energy–time fusion. For the military, for example, increased speed means an increased land area for manoeuvre. As Renner (1991: 133) demonstrates, 'A World War II fighter plane required a manoeuvring radius of about 9 kilometres, compared with 75 kilometres today and a projected 150–185 kilometres for the next generation of jets.' The need for manoeuvring space on land has increased equally: from 1 square kilometre per 100,000 soldiers in ancient times to 55,500 square kilometres for the same number at a 1978 NATO manoeuvre in West Germany (Renner 1991: 134). A third relation exists between the speed of action and the scale of effect. Conventional and nuclear wars in their preparation and execution are cases in point where the speed of action stands in a direct relation to the spatial and temporal scales of their effects: the faster the action, the larger the effect. An equally devastating but inverse relationship seems to pertain between the human capacity to have an impact on the environment on the one hand and the loss of control over the effects on the other: the larger the impact, the less control we seem to have over the consequences. This relationship is nowhere more evident than in the history of nuclear power.

Nuclear power

With the invention of nuclear power, humans have created an invisible, alternative reality that reveals its secrets (but by no means all of them) exclusively to those capable of creating and maintaining it: the nuclear physicists. Other scientists may measure visible effects such as levels of pollution, contamination and mutations in living organisms. For the rest of humanity the hazardous world of radioactivity remains invisible until it materializes into symptoms of contamination. Even then, the linkages can be denied on the basis of insufficient proof by which could be demonstrated the direct link between input and output, between nuclear 'plants', nuclear accidents and, for example, the dramatic rise in child-hood leukaemias. While causal relationships cannot be ruled out, as the Black Report (1984) argued in the case of Sellafield, the connections could not be 'proven'. Similarly, in a recent landmark case brought against Nuclear Fuel at Sellafield by a family where the father had worked at the plant and whose three daughters developed leukaemia, the high court ruled in favour of Nuclear Fuel on the basis of insufficient proof (*Independent* 1993: 5). We are surrounded by the effects of nuclear power even though we cannot see, hear, touch, taste or smell them. This invisibility, the latency periods and the relativity of place give an illusion of safety and security (Macgill 1987). From a materialist scientific per-spective, therefore, the inherent, persistent, all-pervasive dangers of nu-clear power are difficult both to conceive and to quantify.

Risk assessment and evaluation of liability are public expressions of this difficulty. In the previous chapter I have already indicated the prob-lem about insurance. A similar situation has arisen with respect to liab-ility and compensation. The potential extent of a nuclear disaster and the enormity of the time-scale place it outside conventional legalized responsibility. Compensation for radiation damage inflicted by the military, for example, is no more than a distant dream for Eastern European citizens and an unlikely occurrence in the USA. A mere 200 million dollars of government trust funds were set up by the US government for specific groups of victims, and the military are shielded from additional liability to claims which could amount to billions of dollars (Renner 1991: 146). The situation is no better in the public sector. Due to the lack of operational experience and the extent of potential claims, argues May (1989: 13), the US government was 'forced to legislate for a limited liability' of 560 million dollars set up in a federal fund. 'The nuclear industry was to have no residual liability; the public would have no common-law right to bring any claim against the builders or operators of any accidentally damaged plant.' In Britain, the potential cost of accidents, the disposal of radioactive waste and the decommissioning of the 'plants' made nuclear power unviable for privatization. This exemption from conventional insurance and liability gives us an indication of the temporal discontinuity of nuclear technology with earlier scientific inventions central to industrial societies.

The longevity of nuclear materials as sources of energy and as waste has created environmental dangers for which there are no historical precedents. With nuclear power more than any other environmental threat, therefore, the past holds no clues for our actions in the present and affords no predictive power over the future. Present knowledge about the potential effects of nuclear waste disposal policies is based on guess-work and statistical probabilities. Moreover, we have no materials equal, let alone superior, to the life-span of the waste material we need to make safe. To encase high-level radioactive matter in glass (or medium-level waste in concrete) and to bury this deep under ground or at sea means our actions today create substantial health hazards and general environmental disasters for successive generations in the not too distant future. Nobody can know with certainty today how many generations may be secure on the basis of the durability of glass (and concrete). Nobody can be sure about the exact manifestations and the precise effects of the disintegration of those 'protective' materials on future generations at the receiving end of 'safety' measures implemented during the second half of the twentieth century. With nuclear power, science loses not only its 'sharp edges of clarity' (Macgill 1987: 13) but its privileged status of provider of truths and certainties. Notions of safety, control, predictability and proof are clearly incompatible with a threat that extends from nanoseconds to millennia, where the link between cause and effect is disconnected in time and space and where the potential of the impact stands in an inverse relation to the capacity for control.

Waste

More immediate and direct is the link between the industrial way of life and the problem of waste. Yet here too there are some interesting temporal connections with the environmental issues discussed above. Primary among them is the design of artefacts outside the give-and-take of the environment's dynamic structure which turns the longevity of products – be they nuclear, chemical, metal or plastic – into a problem of waste. Further sources of difficulty are to be sought in the brevity of their use and, of course, in the sheer quantity of consumer products. Up until a decade ago the fear was that the world would run out of non-renewable resources. Today there is a recognition that the environmental damage will become intolerable long before those natural resources are exhausted: we will be running out not of resources but time.

When products are conceived solely with reference to their function and utility, essential time dimensions are excluded from the design and costing; the product is detemporalized and decontextualized. To take the problem of waste, pollution seriously requires a temporal extension of planning, design and audit that includes the materials' entire history, that charts their paths from extraction to the rubbish dump, from the 'cradle to the grave'. There is a need, that is, to adopt a life-cycle rather than a point-in-time perspective. This is necessary because it is at those extreme ends – extraction and obsolescence – that most of the irreparable damage is inflicted on the environment. At present, those earliest stages in the conversion from embedded raw material to product and the final change from product to waste rarely feature in the economic calculations about the costs of materials and products despite the fact that environmentalists have presented strong cases in favour of the life-cycle approach. Adoption of such a wider time-frame demonstrates further that waste occurs not only at the end of the path, but that instead, a large proportion of waste is generated early in the production process. Mining, for example, generally requires the removal of more than double the quantity of unwanted material in relation to the resource being sought. In the USA mining amounts to approximately six to seven times the amount of municipal solid waste produced (Young 1991: 41–2).

Solutions to the problem of waste, therefore, must not be singular but multiple: to calculate costs from 'cradle to grave', to shift emphasis from product and profit to process and cost, to make things last longer by re-using and repairing them, to re-introduce the value of durability and, most importantly, to begin to design not for single, abstracted functions but rather for a product's temporal exchange with the environment. Such an approach, however, fits uneasily with the present economic ethic of maximum sales and the tight association between speed and profit. The dictum of maximum sales means the briefest possible use and the cheapest possible construction. It means advertising to create a need for consumption. It means replacement not repair, planned obsolescence not re-use. It means emphasis on export and long haulage of goods across the globe. While sustain*ed* development is an economic concept based on an expectancy of economic growth, the ecological concept of sustain*able* development is concerned with viable continuity into the long-term future. (For detailed discussions on the complexities and paradoxes of sustainability see, for example, Palmer 1992; Redclift 1987/1991; Shiva 1992.)

These differences, therefore, reach far deeper than UK environmental economists (Helm (ed.) 1991; Helm and Pearce 1991; Pearce et al. 1989) allow for. They demonstrate that an environmental ethic is difficult to reconcile with economics of both the capitalist and communist kind. Insistence that economics and the environment are fundamentally linked and recognition that GNP is an unsuitable indicator of a country's economic growth, wealth and quality of life (Pearce et al. 1989) constitute significant first steps by (conventional) economists towards an acceptance of those incompatibilities. Much bolder steps, however, are needed for REV, a more 'Radical Environmental Vision': environmental features of uncertainty, implication, invisibility, transience, temporal embeddedness and rhythmicity necessitate assumptions that allow us to relate to the globalized present, to historical and spatial extension, to the separation and reassemblage of time and space, to multiple time-spans, to speed, and to the gap between the time of information, machines and body movement across space. They require theories and metaphors that help us to extend simultaneously to the realm of the infinitely small and the unimaginably large: from nanoseconds to millennia and from the atomic and microscopic realm to the cosmos. This, however, is difficult to achieve without significant changes to the discipline. Everyday life rather than theoretical tradition may be one potent source for inspiration.

Everyday life as source for environmental theory

In our everyday understanding we have no difficulty in coping simultaneously with those complexities and inconsistencies. We move with ease between long-term and daily concerns, the memory of friends we have not seen for many years and their altered appearance, the sense of urgency associated with a particular problem and its attendant future dangers. We interact with computers whose operating speeds are outside the capacity of human reaction and computation. We deal with historical matters that predate us by a multitude of generations and we function in a material reality of our own making which outlasts us by millennia. We relate as subjects not just to our fellow human beings but to our pet cat, special plants and even our car: we know their life-span of existence, their ailments and signs of decline. We receive in our homes events that take place on the other side of the globe and we are able to distinguish between an actual news report, a record of an earlier event, a future projection, a fictional dramatization and a computer animation. There is no difficulty about communicating through several media: by telephone, letter or on audio-cassette. Nor is there a problem about distinguishing between the time of ageing, the 'right' time for action, and the commodified time of market exchanges.

All these times are equally available to us. We allow for the complexities to exist side by side, to interpenetrate and to inform each other. We cope with time-lags and latency periods without necessarily requiring proof of the link between manifestation and cause, between friends from long ago and their present appearances, between the measles epidemic and our offspring's fever and rash. While our disciplinary tradition forces us to chose between both dualities and different temporalities, our experience combines the incompatible, relates different levels of reality and connects what is separated by time and space. We manage this because we do not rely exclusively on analyses based on sequential, linear causality, on 1:1 relations, and on traditional materialism. While we continue in our professional capacity to isolate, separate, dichotomize, fragment and abstract, in our personal lives we are able to relate, combine, bridge gaps and extend our concerns beyond personal and national boundaries. Moreover, we do not expect to control all the outcomes of our plans and actions.

The complexity of everyday experience rather than perspective-driven tradition, therefore, is likely to provide the more appropriate guide to sociological engagement with present environmental crises. Once we take account in our analyses of the complexity of everyday experience, unify the personal and professional realms and move from the illusionary position of objective observer to implicated participant, we will find it less difficult to extend our concern to the millennia by which the scientific impact on nature will outlast us. As social scientists we need to overcome the clock-maker's reductionist view of nature and society and recognize our implication in the subject matter. We need to move ourselves from the outside to the midst of things, become re-embedded. We need to be not just observers but participants who recognize that every action has effects, if not necessarily in the same time and

place. We need to embrace the factuality of the global We that is nevertheless constituted on the basis of local, contextualized and embodied
difference.

The loss of 'other'

'With nuclear and chemical contamination we experience the "end of the
other", the end of all our carefully cultivated opportunities for distancing
ourselves and retreating behind this category' (Beck 1992b: 109). In the
late twentieth century the loss of boundaries and with it the loss of the
other is increasingly difficult to ignore. First, as I have already noted,
there is the inescapable impact of industrial culture on nature which
facilitates an 'acculturation' and 'socialization of nature' (Giddens 1991:
165). The 'invasion of the natural world by abstract systems', Giddens
(1991: 224) argues, 'brings nature to an end as a domain external to
human knowledge and involvement'. Recognition of these developments enforces acceptance of the inappropriateness of an 'antithesis of
nature and society' (Beck 1992a: 80) as well as the conceptualization of
'a world of objects existing outside the individual' (Elias 1992: 28). Technology is centrally implicated in these totalizing tendencies. Collectively,
those developments have serious consequences for a discipline focused
on classes, groups and nation states. They pose conceptual and methodological difficulties for a science established on the irreducible distinction
between nature and culture and a science used to excluding as irrelevant
to its concerns the physical and artefactual environment.

The problem goes deeper still: today it is not only the traditional
dualistic assumptions but even our language which turn out to be inappropriate since, to talk of nature *and* culture or of people's *relation to*
their environment still implies that both 'nature' and the artefactual
world are *separate and separable* from contemporary cultural activity.
Beck and Giddens both demonstrate the difficulty of such conceptualizations by pointing out the interpenetration of nature and culture
through the 'internally reflexive systems of modernity' (Giddens 1991:
165) and they consequently redefine nature as a historical product. 'At
the end of the twentieth century,' writes Beck (1992a: 80), 'nature is
neither given *nor* ascribed, but has instead become a historical product,
the interior furnishings of the civilizational world destroyed or en-
dangered in the natural conditions of its reproduction.'

Closely linked is Beck's suggestion that through the threat to people,
animals, plants and the elements that sustain life, Western societies are
re-experiencing their interdependence and oneness with nature. They

are encountering a knowledge that has been progressively eroded with their Judeo-Christian religious past and their classical Greek intellectual heritage. Today, fear and helplessness impress on us the realization of interconnectedness.

> In the threat people have the experience that they breathe like plants, and live *from* water as the fish live *in* water. The toxic threat makes them sense that they participate with their bodies in things – 'a metabolic process with consciousness and morality' – and consequently, that they can be eroded like the stones and the trees in the acid rain. A community among Earth, plant, animal and human beings becomes visible, a *solidarity of living things*, that affects everyone and everything equally in the threat. (Beck 1992a: 74, referring to the work of Schutz 1984)

This particular loss of other is the historical product of Western industrial activity which imposes on an earth community of living and inanimate beings the unintended consequences of its actions. The resultant collective We forces the social sciences to reconceptualize their strict separation of nature and culture, 'West and the rest', observer and observed, individual and society, local and global realms (see also Chapter 1, 'Social construction of other time' and Chapter 7).

An allied argument is presented by feminist scholars who identify the separation of nature and culture with patriarchal social structures and man's ambiguous relationship to nature. De Beauvoir's classic statement is illuminating here.

> Man seeks in woman the Other as Nature and as his fellow being. But we know what ambivalent feelings Nature inspires in man. He exploits her, but she crushes him, he is born of her and dies in her; she is the source of his being and the realm that he subjugates to his will; Nature is a vein of gross material in which the soul is imprisoned, and she is the supreme reality; she is contingence and Idea, the finite and the whole; she is what opposes the Spirit, and the Spirit itself. Now ally, now enemy, she appears as the dark chaos from whence life wells up, as this life itself, and as the over-yonder toward which life tends. Woman sums up Nature as Mother, Wife, and Idea; these forms now mingle and now conflict, and each of them wears a double visage. (de Beauvoir 1968: 144)

From the twin perspective of eco-feminism our relationship to non-human nature and human liberation are being rethought from women's points of view. This opens the way to develop a new ethics for the usage of and decision-making about technology.

In these analyses, the 'loss of other' covers not just other species and the universe around us but men and women of different races, different ages and different classes, living not just in the present but also in the future. In their reconceptualization of the human relationship to nature eco-feminists make visible the role of religion and science for our present alienation from living nature as well as for the contemporary efforts to reconstitute nature in artefactual and inanimate form. Moreover, eco-feminist analyses show the conflictual impulses that underpin the scientific quest for all-embracing knowledge and total control.

> The pursuit of scientific knowledge in our civilization is beset by an emotional dilemma. In order to control Nature, we must know Nature. But just as we are seeking to know, there is a knowledge we fear. We are afraid to remember what we, in our bodies and in our feelings, still know, but what, in our fragmented, civilized consciousness we have been persuaded to forget. That, like the forests we destroy, or the rivers we try to tame, *we* are Nature. (Griffin 1989: 10)

Eco-feminists thus present the interpenetration of nature and culture from a different angle of vision. In addition to the impact of culture on nature they impress on us the powerful interpenetration from the direction of nature. They stress cultural dependence on and continuity with nature: their analyses thus complement the social sciences' historical bias with an emphasis on the bio-physical dimension of human being. Like the focus on time and health (Chapter 2) eco-feminist analyses sensitize us to the earthly status of our being.

Naturalized social time and acculturated natural time

An explicit focus on social time supports and deepens those eco-feminist analyses on one hand and work that emphasizes the acculturation of nature on the other. Since I have written in detail on this subject elsewhere (Adam 1988; 1990, 1992a and b), however, I intend to provide here merely a brief summary of those arguments. Traditional approaches to social time define time in purely cultural terms and conceptualize it in distinction to natural time. As social construction, exclusive to the realm of culture, this approach to time mirrors the classical social science conceptualization of culture as irreducibly separate from nature. Recent work on social time, however, demonstrates that the temporalities of culture and nature interpenetrate and implicate each other, that they cannot be separated into social and natural time (Elias 1992; Kern 1983; Luce 1973; Nowotny 1989; Young 1988). From this research, social time emerges as a seemingly infinite complexity of times, a myriad of aspects, dimensions and meanings, all imbricated in the conditions of existence, in experience, action, transaction, language, social organization and control, with each containing a multitude of times within. This research shows that social time, in the words of Elias (1992: 8), 'cannot be understood on the basis of a conception of the world split into "subject" and "object". Its precondition are both physical processes, whether untouched or shaped by human beings, and people capable of mental synthesis, of seeing together what does not happen together.' The separation into natural and cultural time, Elias (1992: 8) continues, is an illusion, the 'artificial product of an erroneous development within science'.

This complexity and mutual implication of times from the most physical to the extremely cultural is made visible when we do not predefine time as an exclusively social construction but, as I have done in this book, seek its multiple expressions as they emerge from the breadth of academic disciplines and personal accounts. Such research highlights the intricate interpenetration and interdependence of multiple times which makes it meaningless to speak and write of 'natural' or 'social' time. As living beings we *are* time, we *live* time, we *feel* and *perceive* time; as human beings we *know* and *reckon* time; as members of contemporary Western societies we have *externalized* time, *created it in machine form* and now *relate to this time as a resource* to be sold, allocated and controlled.

This present research on social time shows human beings as activity-matter, as biological clocks that beat in off-beat to the rhythms of this earth, and as beings that get born, grow and die dynamically in interdependence with other systems of change-order. It suggests that we are locked into nature's silent pulse, that our activity and rest alterations, cyclical exchanges and transformations, seasonal and circadian sensitivities are tied to the rhythms of this earth and its solar system. 'We are connected', writes Griffin (1989: 17), 'not only by the fact of our dependency on this biosphere and our participation in one field of matter and energy, in which no boundary exists between my skin and the air and you, but also by what we know and what we feel.' The rhythmic cycles of matter and energy constitute living nature which *includes* human beings and our capacity to experience rhythms and to order impressions, actions and thoughts in a rhythmic fashion. As human beings we thus express what is separated in academic disciplines: the different realms of being. As rhythmicity and synchronization, growth and decay, 'natural time' is implicated in human being-becoming, experience and knowledge. As memory and anticipation it constitutes our temporal horizon. As physical measure and source for synchronization it is integral to social organization and the regulation of cultural activity. As externalized machine time it is linked to industrial production, to the role as abstract exchange value and to the social control of time. To recognize ourselves as having evolved and thus being *and* creating the times of nature allows for the humanly constructed and symbolized aspects of time to become one expression among others.

Focus on the temporality of being-becoming thus highlights the in-separability of physical, living and cultural existence, whilst focus on technologically constituted times emphasizes a global present, the stan-dardized day and world time affecting the peoples of this earth. Both document a loss of 'the other': the created time of industrial life demon-strates the global We among people; the time-generating temporality of life emphasize the global One and the interconnectedness of all living and non-living things. Both challenge the nature–culture dualism and the window ethic of the linear-perspective vision. Together, they enforce a re-vision from a time-sensitive ecological perspective where an under-standing of implication becomes of central importance.

Death and the quest for mastery

Feminist analyses of Western approaches to human temporality bring to the fore aspects of the nature–culture relation not attended elsewhere, aspects that shed new light on industrial societies' quest for mastery. They emphasize men's preoccupation with death – the denial of death and the explicit effort to control it – as central to the contemporary condition and the absolute separation of culture from nature (see Brodribb 1992). 'Patriarchal civilization', suggests King (1989: 21), 'is about the denial of men's mortality – of which women and nature are incessant reminders.' Recognition of this link between death and culture is, of course, not new. It has been previously identified by social scien-tists, notably by Becker (1973). Feminist theorists, however, are high-lighting features neglected in those earlier analyses, features which are particularly pertinent to understanding and conceptualizing problems associated with global environmental change.

For writers such as Irigaray (1983) and O'Brien (1989b) Heidegger's 'Being unto death' signifies the masculine approach to time which is rejected by feminist writers as an inappropriate perspective on human temporality and the human relationship to nature since it excludes birth and the *time-generating capacity* of procreation. To reintegrate birth as central to human temporality, they argue, is to find a new relationship to continuity. With reference to life and continuity, birthing takes priority over dying and unlike the creation of artefacts it is a process of external-ization without alienation. O'Brien (1981: 32–3) thus contrasts this fe-male principle of continuity with the masculine one of overcoming finitude by technological and abstract means such as art, artefacts, architecture and machines. Fixed in form and content, these ('male') cultural means of continuity are discontinuous with the principles of life and ecological interconnectedness. Separated from genetic continuity which creates the bond between past and future generations, continuity through artefacts sits uneasily within the transient give-and-take, the birth and death of living processes. Moreover, with its emphasis on isolated parts this approach to time ignores interdependencies and promotes a feeling of control. This sense of control, however, is illusionary since emphasis on death without birth signifies the ultimate loss of control. Finally, 'death without birth is not only abstract and unrealistic', as O'Brien (1989a: 84) points out, 'but it signals an odd unwillingness to give meaning to species persistence as the material substructure of temporality'. Thus the *generation* of time and not just its use, *organic continuity* and a tie with past and future generations, not just abstract continuity through artefacts, *cooperation* with nature and not just its control are integral to these feminist perspectives on human temporality.

From this investigation into the complexity of times associated with environmental change we can see how an explicit focus on time gives us a new social science access to contemporary environmental issues. A time perspective illuminates the shadow side of environmental phenomena, aspects of processes which are normally ignored. It enforces a revision of the mutual impact of nature and culture and demonstrates the inappropriateness of traditional, perspective-based analyses. It suggests points of departure, particularly the need to let go of our exclusive reliance on the past as guide to knowledge for the future and the necessity to change location and temporalities from external, static observer to involved, active agent. Once we shift position from exterior explicator to implicated participant, the environment no longer constitutes the 'other': it becomes an extension of physical, living, cultural selves, networked in never-ending relations. Importantly, this is achievable without losing sight of the workings of political interests and economic power. Finally, it involves social theorists in the transgression of disciplinary boundaries, the transcendence of dualisms, and a coming to terms with uncertainty: the very approach necessary for a theory adequate to environmental matters. Environmentally engaged and time-based social theory converge.

Key points

At the substantive level I have shown
- how focus on the temporality of cultural products can illuminate processes of pollution

- how the time characteristics of pollution – out-of-sync time-frames, time-lags, vastly expanded time horizons, uncertainty and longevity of materials – are handled with political 'short-termism', economic production for obsolescence, and positivist science
- how, in the face of global environmental hazards, the construction of nature as 'other' is losing its meaning and natural status.

With reference to methodology I have argued
- that we cannot use the past as source of knowledge for a science-based future
- that focus on time aids the necessary re-vision of social science assumptions about the relation between nature and culture and the role of nature for the social sciences
- the need to redefine the scientific component of social science in the light of global environmental change: multiple, irreconcilable perspectives, the fundamental interpenetration of nature and culture, and the uncertainty of a science-based future require social science engagement and concern with the im/material future.

7

The 'Temporal Turn': Mapping the Challenge for Social Science

The complexity of everyday times explored in these chapters presents a profound challenge to Enlightenment thought; it unsettles established conceptual traditions. Yet the object of the book is not a purely de(con)structive one. On the contrary, it is to find a basis for active engagement with contemporary issues and problems. It is to make the case for personal commitment to the subject of inquiry. That is to say, it seeks to ground sensitivity to the complexity of social times in theories more appropriate than the nineteenth-century frameworks of understanding, steeped as they are in the machine technology of Newtonian physics, the dualistic philosophy of Descartes and the political structures of nation states. Throughout the book I have therefore utilized the focus on time to delineate conceptual parameters for action based on embedded and embodied local/global relations, personal and collective life-worlds, im/material and ecological processes, and the technologies of today.

In this final chapter I want to explore the wider implications of that work, to set out the nature of the challenge within the context of other critiques of Enlightenment thought, and to identify key points of departure for a social science sensitive to the complexities of social time. Here, I construct my approach against a backdrop of the 'temporal turn' in postmodern theories (Belghazi 1993; Ermarth 1992; Wood 1989), the feminist struggle to situate contemporary feminist theory in relation to postmodernism (Butler and Scott (eds.) 1992; Ermarth 1992; Hayles 1990; Hekman 1990; Nicholson (ed.) 1990; Stanley and Wise 1993), chaos theories based on the mathematical theories outlined by Gleick (1987) and the Theory of Dissipative Structures presented by Prigogine and Stengers (1984). Since the purpose of this chapter is to work through some of the consequences for social theory of the arguments presented in this book, I do not discuss those allied critiques in their own right. Instead, I draw very generally on my readings of chaos theories and postmodernist thought in order to make visible the distinctiveness of the approach proffered here, and to show its utility and strengths for understanding and engaging with the contemporary.

The challenge is constituted by a number of key issues which will be discussed in more detail in the four sections of this final chapter. Pivotal among them are the subtle dissolution of dualisms, the loss of 'other' without erosion of difference, the dismantling of not only absolutes but also single perspectives and scientific objectivity, and, finally, acceptance of the simultaneity of material (sense data) *and* immaterial as well as visible *and* invisible constituting forces (from now on to be referred to as im/material and in/visible respectively). When dichotomies as central to social science as nature–culture, male–female, self–other, mind–matter, subject–object, continuity–change and local–global have been destabilized, then we can say without overstating the case that a major problem has developed for the Enlightenment episteme. Not only do we lose our traditional others, those generalized, simplified opposites against which we define ourselves, our gender, our culture and our species, but we also have to forfeit the convenience of working with certainties, with clear-cut, black and white categories, and with the hard tangibles of material sense data. Finally, we have to relinquish the comfort and alluring elegance of simplicity and begin to embrace the discomfiting untidiness, unwieldiness and awkwardness of complexity.

Emphasis on the complexity of social times brings together the personal and the global, the technological and the literary, the bodily and the scientific, totalizing tendencies and local particularities, coevalness and difference. It binds into a unified but conceptually unconventional whole what constitute antinomies, contradictions and incompatible categories in the traditions of Enlightenment thought. (See Figure 1.)

Recognition of the futility of thinking in opposites and locating oneself in a single perspective thus radically alters the background assumptions and the theoretical contexts within which social science is conducted, providing a pertinent critique of the social sciences' reliance on objectivity, linear causality, a-temporal truth and the absolute separation of observer from observed. This means that the conceptual tool-kit of the social sciences needs some creative renewal if it is to deal effectively with the contemporary temporalities discussed in this book.

The conceptual principle of implication has played a central part in this re-orientation. Throughout the book we can see how focus on the multiplicity of social times shifts the framework of understanding from

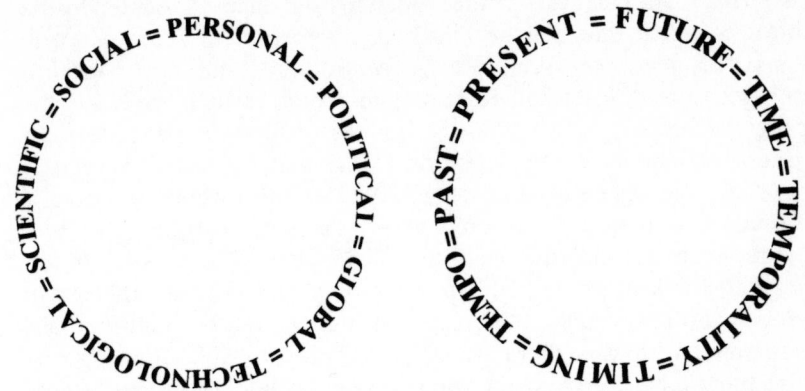

Figure 1 On the basis of everyday times we can construct a whole range of these cluster circles which can be entered anywhere and read in any direction.

dualisms and dualities to complex interrelations, permeations and resonating traces. Such a focus consequently brings to the fore the prevalence of implication – that the whole is implicated in any single phenomenon or event – and demonstrates how multiple meanings are inevitably lost when we approach social time from a single perspective. In these final pages I want to focus more explicitly on the principle of implication and show its relevance and utility for theorizing temporal complexity. This re-visionary concept, I suggest, is pivotal for a consistent and coherent dissent from the Enlightenment episteme. It transforms recognition of complexity from a rather non-committal and circumspect pluralism into a critical and radical social science criterion whose points of departure are both continuous with and distinct from allied postmodern and feminist critiques of that tradition of thought. I thus discuss the principle of implication in relation to the four problematic aspects of Enlightenment scientific thought outlined in this final chapter: the 'metaphysics of presence', the fear of relativism, the dependence on sense data, and the window ethic of uninvolved observers looking in. This de- and reconstruction brings me full circle back to the first chapter where I argued that the backdrop of implicit assumptions needs to be made explicit and given equal status in any analysis, and where I suggest that the reflective attitude has to be turned unto the Self, thus making self-less theory a thing of the past.

'Implication' displaces the 'metaphysics of presence'

Enlightenment thought – of both the philosophic and the scientific kind – starts from the premise of a *metaphysics of presence*, from the belief in an external reality that exists independent of and uncontaminated by the knower, a world that can be matched, mirrored and represented in theory. This presupposition forms a central focus for postmodernist deconstructions. Closely allied to the metaphysics of presence is the practice of employing a window ethic. As I showed in the previous chapter, this entails a representation of the material world seemingly independent of any point of observation, a viewpoint where anyone else observing that reality is expected to see the same corporeality. Both these premises are shown to be untenable in Chapters 1, 5 and 6. In this part of the book I want to highlight the way in which the metaphysics of presence and the window ethic are intimately connected and mutually reinforcing and to give them attention in their own right. Starting with the window ethic I ground the discussion in an understanding of temporal complexity and implication. That is to say, I locate it in an approach that stresses permeation, interpenetration, simultaneity and instantaneity, thus emphasizing the coexistence and unification of phenomena traditionally considered contradictory, incompatible and incommensurable.

The window ethic

The window ethic belongs to the instrumental world of measurement. Located in the linear-perspective vision, it presents a reality independent of the specific, contextual vantage-point of observation. Ermarth (1992) calls it a ' "Nobody's power": at once human and unspecific, powerfully present but not individualized' (p. 29), where 'the narrator remains disembodied and indistinguishable from the narrative process itself' (p. 27). 'This picture', suggests Ingold (1993: 155), 'is of a world as it could be directly apprehended only by a consciousness capable of being everywhere at once and nowhere in particular ... a consciousness at once immobile and omnipresent.' Yet to remove ourselves from the constitutive position in the midst of things to a neutral, no-where location can be a conceptual move only. As I show in these chapters, this conceptual strategy cannot 'truly' place us outside the scheme of things. That is to say, as contextual, embodied beings we cannot achieve uncontaminated, objective knowledge; our studies and observations affect the reality under investigation: the way we conceptualize time has an effect on how we relate to our bodies, to health, education, work and the environment. At one level, therefore, the framing of the subject matter is a device only and the elimination of our shadow therefore based on self-deception (see specifically Chapters 1, 5 and 6). This means that under the guise of being 'scientific' we pursue an impossible goal, a dream that some post-Newtonian physicists have given up more than fifty years ago (see Adam 1990: 55–69; Briggs and Peat 1985; Capra 1976). Throughout this book I show this objectivist perspective to be wanting and seek to re-embed observers as embodied participants and as creators of their observations, their knowledge and their historical situation. In other words, I argue for theorists' and scientists' implication in their subject matters and for the need to reflect the constitutive self in the analyses.

Unlike approaches which force us to choose on an either-or basis, however, focus on the complexity of times does not warrant the total eradication of the nobody/no-where perspective of the shadowless observer and its replacement by a view from within. Acknowledgement of the complexity demands that we find conceptual strategies that do not force us to choose between conflicting epistemes and that do not insist on commensurability. For this reason I have consistently stressed the centrality of the context within which theory is constructed. For today's social theories this means globalized times and social relations; technologies based on both Newtonian and non-Newtonian principles; environmental hazards created by the scientific and industrial way of life yet outside the control of science, economics and politics; satellites transmitting virtual realities, pictures of wars being fought across the globe, while real bombs still kill and maim people and destroy their lives, to name just a few of these contradictory complexities. To assert the need for social theorists to take account of, and for their theories to be in tune with, the historical context is, however, not an argument in favour of a metaphysics of presence. It is not to suggest that theories can represent and accurately mirror that reality; rather, it is to insist that social theory needs to be relevant and appropriate to the contemporary condition, that the conceptualizations need to be adequate to the reality they seek to encompass, explicate and constitute. It is therefore not to expect a 1:1 match between theory and subject matter but to require that the conceptual tools be suited to the temporal complexity of contemporary social life. Let me use an example to illustrate the point.

The TV screen as 'a window on the world' is the ultimate realization of the linear-perspective vision and its associated window ethic. With the development of film and television science has achieved the shadowless observer. It has effectively, if not totally, managed the separation of observer and observed (see Chapter 5). The television viewer is the supreme observer of 'facts', an objective spectator of replicated, fictional 'real-time', and simulated 'facts', all uncontaminated by the act of observation. This is the scientists' supposedly impossible dream come true: the goal of objective observation operationalized in television viewing. As such it forms an integral part of contemporary Western existence and it would make little sense, therefore, to exclude this principle from our theories simply because we have begun to recognize the inadequacy of the window ethic as a social science tool and, true to the dichotic tradition, have consequently argued the need for a shift in perspective from external voyeur to a view from inside. The answer cannot simply be to choose between opposites since to opt for the relative position of constitutive participant at the expense of objective observer would mean we are blind to the prevalence of the window ethic in our daily lives.

The complexity of the technological context

I have shown in relation to everyday time that it is clearly inappropriate to replace one position with its opposite and that we need to appreciate instead the complexity of the situation. This in turn involves taking account of the technological context as a constitutive feature of social life and appreciating the simultaneity of a multitude of phenomena that are incompatible and contradictory in terms of traditional conceptual categories and principles. Thus, for example, the linear-perspective and clock-time visions with their spectator approach are pivotal conceptual tools of Enlightenment thought and classical science. Yet the technology that brings those visions to fruition simultaneously creates relations, connections and effects that fall outside the capacity of classical science. As I show in previous chapters, the conceptual principles of a science based on temporal relations of cause and effect, succession and duration, and measurements on a before-and-after basis are ill-equipped to cope with instantaneity and simultaneity, feedback and amplification, with actions that create effects in different times and places without visible connections and empirically observable sense data: the rationale that underpins the system has created its own negation, conditions that can no longer be grasped with the Enlightenment principles of its inception. Poster (1990) argues a very similar case when he suggests that information technology can no longer be grasped with the rational conceptual tools of its creation.

> The mode of information undermines the time/space coordinates that have been employed to fix language in various contexts. It thereby opens up an understanding of language and society that has no reference in the grid of Renaissance perspective or the mimetic realism of Enlightenment reason. Subject no longer stands opposed to object, man to nature, or essence to existence. Words cannot any longer be located in space and time, whether it be the 'real time' of spoken utterances in a spatial context of presence or the abstract time of documents in a bureaucrat's file cabinet

and library's archive. Speech is framed by space/time coordinates of dramatic action. Writing is framed by space/time coordinates of books and sheets of paper. Both are available to logics of representation. Electronic language, on the contrary, does not lend itself to being so framed. It is everywhere and nowhere, always and never. It is truly material/immaterial. (Poster 1990: 85)

Consequently, contemporary social theory has to encompass multilevel, mutually implicating and incompatible processes: 'everywhere and nowhere, always and never', the in/visible and the im/material, the disembedded spectator and the contextual, embodied participant. This can be achieved only once we let go of the metaphysics of presence and the expectancy of 1:1 causal relations and once we think equally and simultaneously of non-linear interactions of 1:many with indeterminate periods of in/visibility, the knowledge of which is mediated by language and metaphors.

Technologies are clearly central to this complexity of contemporary existence and so is the physical environment in both its inorganic and organic acculturated form. Together, they constitute an important part of the material/cultural world of the late twentieth century. It is therefore no longer viable to exclude from social science concerns aspects of the complexity that form such crucial constituents of the contemporary environment. Once included, those two dimensions which are traditionally designated non-social and non-cultural need to be conceptualized in the complexity of their relations and permeations. It is for this reason that I argue for a full-scale implication approach that does not force choices between a view from no-where and now-here, but includes instead the constitutive power of the contextual, embodied theorist/researcher *as well as* the objectivist position, operationalized by such technologies as the clock, television and satellite.

Postmodern times

Let me bring the discussion back to the issue of time since this may help to crystallize the points under discussion here. For postmodernist theorists time constitutes an elusive incommensurability and irresolvable problematic that resists being unified into public time or the chronology of history (see Belghazi 1993 and Ermarth 1992 for analyses of those positions). Postmodernist theorists reject the *totalizing tendencies* of abstract time, affirm the contingencies of the event and emphasize indeterminacy, incompleteness and fragmentation. In agreement with the time theories of Bergson (1910), Heidegger (1927/1980, 1969/1972) and Mead

(1932/1980), they consider time to be not merely a theme but a condition for thought, not merely an external, neutral, homogeneous medium but, in Ermarth's (1992: 11) words, 'a function of position . . . a dimension of particular events' .

Postmodern theories thus resonate with and differ from the approach presented here since my focus on the complexity of social times supports the stress on incommensurability, contingency and indeterminacy without in any way minimizing the importance of the unified measure and the totalizing tendency of quantified, spatialized time. I emphasize the uniqueness and relativity of time creation while simultaneously pointing towards the central importance and hegemony of the abstract, decontextualized, neutral medium of clock time. To valorize the fractured difference of embedded and embodied times *at the expense* of the constitutive power of that totalizing and standardizing time, I want to argue, is not only to fall back into dualistic modes of analyses but, more importantly, to falsify the contemporary experience. Such surreptitious binary thinking produces a theory no longer adequate to its subject matter. Irrespective of its political attraction, therefore, we have to resist such conceptual oscillation since it by-passes everyday experience and no amount of talk about '*displacement*' rather than *re*placement, can make this approach more than a healthy antidote to the abstracting and rationalizing tendencies of Enlightenment thought.

If social theory is to remain pertinent and relevant to changing contemporary conditions then it must include the features and characteristics that play such a central, constitutive part in our everyday lives: embodied and embedded in local difference, fragmentation and contingency, we are simultaneously facing globalization on an unprecedented scale. That is to say, social life today is conducted in a context of globalized phenomena – finance, markets and the market principle, communication, transport, surveillance, pollution, and the nuclear threat, consumerism and fundamentalism in a multitude of guises – all demanding conceptual principles appropriate to the task of explicating that social existence. Moreover, life itself is generated and sustained not just by differentiation but by globalized and generalized elements, namely, water, air and earth. Thus it is important for social theorists to find a way of grasping the contextualized difference *in conjunction with and permeated by* those central totalizing tendencies, the complexity of embedded times *together* with the rationalized and standardized time that enmeshes our earth, the unique Me *implicated in and implicating* the global We.

This means that as social theorists located in a historical context of globalized, networked processes and social relations, we need not only to comprehend the constitutive power and the dangers of the shadowless spectator vision but also actively to promote what has been denied existence in the classical tradition: we need to highlight the creativity of the implicated participant, of the embedded, embodied maker of uncertain and unknowable global futures. Such re-vision is important since neither public time nor logocentrism – the valorization of reason and rationality – has so far been theorized out of existence. Despite sustained conceptual critiques and negations, they are still very much part of our daily existence, as is demonstrated by the examples of clock time and standardized world time, both material expressions of the contemporary trend towards rationalization. That is to say, irrespective of being denied reality status in contemporary philosophy and postmodernist theory, public time and logocentrism underpin much of Western science, politics and industrial action. This rationalist and commodifying tendency, as I show in several of the chapters, is in many ways counter-productive and even harmful at the personal and global level as well as being a force against equal opportunity between sexes, cultures and species. Its hegemony therefore needs to be exposed, its complexity explicated, its vulnerable access points explored, so that its pervasive hold may be broken. This requires a critical approach to theory, the explicit goal of not merely explaining but changing reality.

To this end it is useful, for example, first to show the unintended consequences of the rationalist tendencies, to establish that the application of rationalist science cannot be handled and controlled on the basis of rationalist principles – nuclear power being a case in point. Second, it is important to be able to demonstrate that such complexity demands conceptual tools that transcend the tradition of seeking certainties, simplicity and control, that it needs to allow instead for the coexistence of certainty and control with contingency, indeterminacy and a multitude of other incompatibles. Third, it is helpful to recognize the constitutive power of the framework of analysis *as* a framework, the defining force of metaphors *as* metaphors and the limit of all conceptual tools *as* tools. Together those conceptual strategies provide not only a superior explanatory tool for the contemporary condition but, more importantly, supply us with the means for effective action. The conceptual principle of implication is central to this approach and can take us further in the quest for understanding the complexity of contemporary life and being able to affect the direction of change than the postmodern critiques of the metaphysics of presence, logocentrism and historical time.

Concerns of postmodernist feminist theorists in many respects echo the more general postmodernist critique of the Enlightenment episteme. Most importantly, however, the feminist corrective is explicitly political; it is critical theory oriented towards achieving desired goals. As such it resonates with the approach presented in this book. The joining of feminist critical theory with the postmodern critique of the metaphysics of presence, however, brings to the surface some major conceptual problems which have yet to be resolved. Thus Flax (1992: 446) notes how the 'dreams of innocence' of uncontaminated knowledge leading to truth claims are still retained. This means that the thinking in binary opposites is not displaced: the dualisms of emancipation versus domination, difference versus generalization, constructivism versus essentialism, relativism versus absolutism, cultural versus biological determinism, and a view from now-here versus a view from no-where are still firmly in place. Postmodernist feminist discourse has merely reformulated those clearly identifiable Enlightenment antinomies into a postmodernist critique of the 'imperialist tendencies of generalizations' and 'essentialism', and into worries about the 'biological fallacy', the 'spectre of relativism' and the decontextualized 'view from everywhere' (see for example Hekman 1990, and essays in Nicholson (ed.) 1990). To illustrate the problem, I would like to respond to just one of these goals, namely, the purge of generalizations with their attendant imperialist tendencies.

In defence of universals and generalizations

There can be no question that it is important to recognize and condemn the established (naturalized) practice of generalizing from the Western, white, male, middle-class, heterosexual experience as unacceptable imperialism. The wrongness of this and other such practices, however, does not invalidate the principle of generalization. Even the most rigorous position in defence of a complexity of times, as I show throughout this book, could not justify a temporally based difference without universals: globally standardized, decontextualized clock time permeates even the most personal, contextual time of birthing; the universalized artefactual time invades the uniquely variable time of the mindful body. To argue against the principle of generalization is to be based in a metaphysics of presence; it is to take an absolutist view of theory, seeking a match between social phenomena and their representation. Moreover, it is to fail to recognize that the framework of observation determines the generality of the statement or, to put it in postmodernist terms, that truth is an effect of discourse.

The principle of implication is crucial here since thinking in terms of implication is not dependent on dualisms or single perspectives. It is a theoretical approach (rather than a theory) that stresses the mutual permeation and thus inseparability of such dichotomies: it unites the local with the global, difference with universals and stability, the One with the whole. It is a view from somewhere specific *and* everywhere. Moreover, it acknowledges multiplicities, including contradictions, and it insists on the relative position of the centre. It allows us to theorize together what traditional analyses have kept apart, to emphasize constitutive difference without having to abandon statements of a universal kind. As a method, it constitutes the difference between focus and abstraction. When we are focusing, the rest of our sensory field is not disappearing in the way it does when we are isolating and abstracting one part or event in order to study it. It is the difference between an embedded and reflected understanding where both the thinker/researcher and the subject matter remain integral to the totality, and one that severs those infinite connections (see also Mackie 1985). Focus means that everything remains dynamically tied and implicated in that which is being explicated.

There is, of course, a difficulty here with the very language we use to establish the specificity of this approach. By the simple act of comparison we fall back into the very thought structure we seek to render problematic: not like this *but* like that, focus *versus* abstraction, somewhere *and* everywhere. And yet, post-complexity dualisms are no longer constituted naively; they are recognized as problematic and limited conceptual strategies. There is 'no stepping into the same river twice'. Once denaturalized, dualities have been changed: there can be no return to the unproblematized natural attitude of Cartesian dualisms. The conceptual ground has shifted, the terms upon which those comparisons are made has irrevocably altered.

To work with a base assumption of implication is, moreover, an intensely political approach. As I demonstrate throughout this book, it acknowledges the theorists/researchers' part in the construction of their subject matter and the role each one of us plays in the constitution of local/global processes and the contemporary condition more generally. As such, it dissolves the clear-cut boundary between science and policy (see also Wynne and Mayer 1993: 33) and shows how concern with the question 'How shall we live?' is an inescapable duty for everyone (on that question see also Beck 1992a: 28; Giddens 1991: 215, 223; Weber 1919/1985: 143 and 152–3). The recognition that social science (and science generally) is an inescapably moral enterprise is a position that has been articulated not only by Weber (1919/1985, 1904/1969) at the turn of the century but also by feminist social scientists for some considerable time. To conceptualize social life in terms of implication gives theoretical coherence to this approach *without* being reabsorbed into the very tradition which is the object of the critique. Thus, when Stanley and

Wise (1993: 226) argue that 'the relationship between ontology, epistemology, and ethics is no relationship in our view for these are merely
different terms for the same thing and are entirely sustainable for each
other ... mutually subsumed within the other: a perfect union', they do
not really mean that ontology, epistemology and ethics are 'the same
thing'. Rather, when they explain about being 'mutually subsumed
within the other', Stanley and Wise are identifying mutual implication.

To recognize the mutual implication of the One and the whole and to
appreciate that everything is connected is a contemporary holistic approach that unites the thought traditions of the world from Buddhism to
Amerindian cosmology and does so without being totalizing or pre-
senting a new metanarrative (see especially Bohm 1983 and Spretnak
1991). It is an ancient tradition of thought still adhered to in a large
number of contemporary cultures and 'rediscovered' in the West
through, for example, the conceptual implications arising from the
globalization of environmental hazards, alternative medicine, the mathematical modelling of fractal geometry (Hayles 1990: Chapters 6 and 8),
and the technology of holography (Adam 1990: 158–60; Bohm 1983: 140–
57). We need to be aware, however, that this holism is very different from
the holism of traditional social science where parts are understood to be
causally connected to the whole, and where both the function of the
system and its past are thought to determine its future. The holism
theorized through the concept of implication is dynamic and times-
based. It is historical, non-determinist, and can accommodate contradiction as well as non-linear, networked relations. In this holism, reality is
created in the present, affecting all pasts and futures (see especially
Chapter 3, section on Mead). Here, dichotomous thinking and the language of abstraction, logocentrism and the metaphysics of presence do
not even need to be refuted; in its classical decontextualized form that
discourse has no longer any bases for existence. Finally, focus on the
complexity of social times grounds that holism in everyday experience.

Relativity beyond discourse

Acceptance of temporal complexity and the premise of ecological
interconnectedness leads us to a specific understanding of truth and a
particular approach to relativity. From such an ecological social science
perspective Truth (with a capital T) is tied to the capacity to grasp the
whole in its complexity; truth (with a lower case t) is delimited by
conceptual systems; and relativity is associated with the boundedness,
temporality and finitude of human embodied existence. In the contem-

porary context of science and technology, such relativity necessarily includes the 'objective' view from nowhere, promoted by artificially decontextualized, disembodied scientific observers. Moreover, the approach promulgated in this book acknowledges life to be characterized by temporality, by an ongoing and irreversible, creative process which means that no matter how hard we try, our explications are necessarily fragmentary and contingent. Finally, it accepts that the whole is not accessible in its entirety to (social) scientific study and linguistic representation. This has the effect that explication – even explication that implicates the whole – is always contextually situated, always partial, always selective, therefore always contestable: it clearly makes a difference to understanding the temporality of everyday life, whether this knowledge is constructed from within a Shanghai or a Venetian trading culture of the eighteenth century, a Hopi Indian tribe of the nineteenth century, a CBS television news-room, or from contemporary Japanese factories in different parts of the world producing micro-chips for computers.

To appreciate the contextual, temporal and partial nature of knowledge has consequences for the meaning of truth and for the role of relativism in (social) scientific theory. It means first, that explications can always be contradicted with other explications, and that what is rational from one perspective is irrational from another. Second, it indicates that theories and studies which abstract phenomena from their networked relations are negating a central characteristic of their subject matter, thus by default giving an 'untrue' account. Third, it recognizes that rationalist linguistic representation (particularly in the Western tradition) with its dependence on sequential linearity and the a-temporality of concepts predisposes understanding towards an extremely restricted temporal code. Fourth, it means that truth is tied to scale and, as I have demonstrated in several chapters, to time-horizons and speed.

Let me elaborate this last point. Ingold (1993), referring to the work of Ho (1989: 19–20), writes about the relativity of time-scale and tempo in the following way:

What appear to us the fixed forms of landscape, passive and unchanging unless acted upon from outside, are themselves in motion, albeit on a scale immeasurably slower and more majestic than that on which our own activities are conducted. Imagine a film of the landscape, shot over years, centuries, even millennia. Slightly speeded up, plants appear to engage in very animal-like movements, trees flex their limbs without any prompting from the winds. Speeded up more, glaciers flow like rivers and even the earth begins to move. At greater speeds the solid rock bends,

buckles and flows like molten metal. The world itself begins to breathe.
(Ingold 1993: 164)

Thus, whether we see movement and change or stable continuity is relative to the temporal framework of observation.

An equally telling example of relativity based on scale is provided by Hayles (1990: 210) who details the difference between Euclidian and Fractal geometry. In chaos theories, she explains, 'different levels tend to act in different ways, so that locality intrudes itself as a necessary descriptive feature defeating totalization'. Drawing on the work of Mandelbrot (1983: 25–33) she shows that the length of Britain's coast-line, like all other complex systems, is scale-dependent.

> If we use a mile-long ruler to measure the coast-line, we get a shorter answer than we do if we use a yardstick, for the mile ruler cuts across irregularities that the yardstick measures around. If we use an inch ruler the answer is still longer, because small pebbles are measured around; and if a micrometer is used, even irregularities within a single pebble count. In fact, Britain's coast-line *continues to grow without limit* as the ruler scale decreases, at least down to molecular scales. Unless the length of the ruler is specified, the question cannot be accurately answered. (Hayles 1990: 210)

Focus on the complexity of times and spaces, therefore, entails a fundamental recognition of embedded, interactive knowledge which is principally relative. Since, at the level of complex systems, it could not be otherwise, relativity is appreciated as a 'fact' of the complexity of life, not as a predicament.

This is a position on relativity that deviates from the feminist perspectives expressed by Harding (1987) who suggests that relativism is a problem only for those who have a vested interest in maintaining the status quo.

> Historically, relativism appears as an intellectual possibility, as a 'problem', only for dominating groups at the point where the hegemony (the universality) of their views is being challenged. As a modern intellectual position, it emerged in the belated recognition by nineteenth-century Europeans that the apparently bizarre beliefs and behaviours of non-Europeans had a rationality or logic of their own. (Harding 1987: 10)

From an ecological, time-sensitive social science, 'the spectre of relativity' poses a problem beyond hegemonic groups since it is more generally tied to perspectives that associate Truth with the possibility of a 1:1

relation between phenomena and their representations, that is to say, perspectives tied to logocentrism and the metaphysics of presence. When social life is understood as connected to the universe – to 'brother quark' and 'sister meson' – then relativity becomes part of what it means to be human and Truth the preserve of God(s), prophets, mystics and shamans since they are the only beings capable of enlightenment, of being able to grasp the whole in its complex totality.

This does not mean, however, that we cannot agree on things, rather, that such consensus is tied to cultural, linguistic and moral communities. If I say, 'I am getting old', and if my German self says, 'Ich werde alt', then which one of us would be 'right', which one would be telling the 'Truth'? In an intellectual context of one Truth it would make sense, be important even, to face that question. To focus on the issue of translation, and therefore to argue that both of us are right, misses the point. Since all knowledge is located in communities of shared meaning, translation inevitably privileges one over the other. This is most clearly visible in 'translations' of research on people from other cultures, classes, ages, sexual orientation and political persuasion into the meaning-frames of the researchers' own meaning-community, but it is generally fudged as an issue in the thought traditions of absolute Truth. Yet what can 'Truth' possibly mean, we need to ask, in the context of such (inevitable) translation? Anthropology is the discipline where a significant number of members have been acutely aware of the problem of Truth in relation to translation and the contextuality of meaning (Clifford and Marcus (eds.) 1986; Fabian 1983; Marcus and Fischer 1986, among others).

Deconstructionist and postmodernist theorists have taken yet another route to arrive at the realization that knowledge is relative. They have emphasized the contextual textuality of all knowledge and the discursively bounded nature of truth. This postmodernist 'linguistic turn' has been an important development in social theory. Yet, in agreement with Stanley and Wise (1993: 198) and others who have come to the conclusion that social life is constituted by more than language alone, my work foregrounds important non-discursive sources of knowledge: the physicality of everyday times which has so far been neglected in the social sciences' quest for the symbolic and textual dimension of cultural life. The above chapters on the temporality of the mindful body and the contextual, embodied person, of technology and environmental processes give an account of what, beyond language, might contribute to social life, to its creation and maintenance as well as the knowledge we acquire about it.

I have further touched on the metaphoric character of knowledge. Since 'the metaphors we live by' (Lakoff and Johnson 1980) are central not just to the discussion on relativity but also to the debate about the textuality of knowledge, they deserve some further attention here. My work shows that all meaning is mediated but not all mediation is based exclusively on the rationalist mode of discourse. Metaphors, as Lakoff and Johnson (1980: 117) argue, 'allow us to understand one domain of experience in terms of another'. The domains of experience they have in mind relate to our bodies, our interactions with the environment and our interactions with other people. As such they overlap with the domains I have discussed in relation to the complexity of everyday times. Metaphors as key sources to understanding are therefore often expressly *not* bound by the limits of language and our capacity for explanation. This is clearly so, for example, in the case of clocks, computers or water; they are so powerful as metaphors precisely because they work on the basis of non-verbal imagery. They function as dynamic images that induce in us a non-linear understanding of systems and their principles, help us to grasp processually and holistically how things work (see Chapter 5; Adam 1990: 157–60; Jones 1983). And it is this capacity for holistic, instan-taneous systems imaging which makes metaphors such effective concep-tual tools because it facilitates understanding of complex systems in their interactions.

Metaphors as conceptual tools cease to serve their purpose and proper function, however, when they become naturalized, when they become absorbed into the phenomenon, and when we consequently no longer recognize them as metaphors, as aids to a specific conceptual task. This is the case, for example, when the machine metaphor of clock time is related to as time *per se* and when, as I show most specifically in Chapter 4 on work, the embedded and lived times are evaluated through the filter of that quantitative time of economic relations and then deemed insignificant and inconsequential from that naturalized clock-time frame of meaning.

It is therefore crucial that we appreciate the mediated and deeply metaphorical nature of our knowledge and that we acknowledge theory not as faithful replicator of reality but as a kit full of specialized concep-tual tools for the task of grasping specific realities and for establishing a base from which to engage with and participate in the creation and maintenance of that world. Metaphors are particularly important for the task of conceptualizing contemporary existence in a way that is *adequate* to the created temporality of the industrial way of life. This is because the (Western) languages at our disposal are singularly unsuited to the job of conceptualizing networked temporal complexity, associated as they are with the rationalist, linear, causal and a-temporal tradition of Enlighten-ment thought and Newtonian science. (Western) rationalist and purely discursive knowledge, in other words, is not the means by which we will be able to transcend that particular tradition. Rather, we will need to draw extensively on a range of additional sources of knowledge, the sort of sources I have begun to utilize in these pages: the mindful body, everyday experience, a multitude of metaphors, and non-materialist knowledge grounded in moral consciousness, ethical awareness and spiritual wisdom. What those other sources and metaphors have in common is a capacity to facilitate dynamic holistic understanding. As such they are ideal aids to active *engagement* with a complexity where everything ultimately connects to everything else.

Recognition of metaphors as metaphors is thus an important step towards transcending not only the metaphysics of presence and logocentrism but also the fear of constructivism and the relativity of knowledge. It acknowledges that 'truth is always relative to a conceptual system' (Lakoff and Johnson 1980: 193), counteracts the myths of both objectivism and subjectivism and insists instead that we know the world through our interactions with it. We know it, insist Lakoff and Johnson (1980: 230), through a 'constant interaction with the physical environment and with other people'. Such interaction with the environment inevitably involves mutual change. 'You cannot function within the environment', Lakoff and Johnson (1980: 230) continue, 'without changing it or being changed by it.' Acknowledging the temporal, constitutive, contextual, selective and metaphorical nature of knowledge, we are moving one step closer to a non-imperialist epistemology without having to forgo the use of generalizations and universal categories.

In/visibility outside the materialist episteme

So far I have mapped the challenge of understanding contemporary social life in relation to the principle of implication and the inescapable relativity of knowledge. That challenge is intensified by the ever-increasing in/visible, im/material, future-creating phenomena and processes that escape the staunch materialism of the Enlightenment episteme. In the social sciences, moreover, this dependence on sense data is not only too exclusive but simultaneously not rigorous enough since the constitutive power of both the mindful body and the physical environment – organic, inorganic and artefactual – is excluded from analyses. Let me deal with those issues in reverse order and start with the argument that the social sciences' materialism is not extensive enough.

To eliminate from social science thought the temporal, material character of human social being, to reject it in the name of antifoundationalism and anti-essentialism and in a move against the 'natural fallacy' is analogous to privileging the roof or windows of a house to the exclusion of the rest and pretending to be dealing with a house. This treatise on the complexity of social time suggests that knowledge is embodied, embedded and contextually specific. This makes the mindful body and the technologies which structure so much of our lives central subject matters for the social sciences. Referring to anthropology in particular, Ingold (1993: 158) argues that it was a great mistake 'to insist upon the separation between the domains of technical and social activity, a separation that has blinded us to the fact that one of the outstanding features of human technical practices lies in their embeddedness in the current sociality'. Rejection of those material aspects of social life constitutes an inability to come to terms with the temporal complexity of everyday existence. Yet it is clearly possible (with some effort, determination and imagination) to achieve such an extension to social science concerns without need for major adjustments to the materialism that underpins those disciplines. Incorporation of phenomena that extend beyond our senses and beyond what is generally considered to be empirical reality, in contrast, cannot be so encompassed within the materialist episteme.

In the chapters on globalization and the environment I argue that our senses are no longer sufficient for dealing with information technologies operating at near the speed of light on the one hand and time-lags between polluting action and visible symptoms lasting for indefinite periods on the other, time-spans that might range from nanoseconds to millennia. I suggest further that instantaneity and simultaneity fall outside the designs, plans and actions based on materialist/empiricist, causal analyses and linear, quantitative time. Despite (or possibly because?) of this contemporary prevalence of phenomena and processes that are beyond the capacity of an exclusively materialist/empiricist conception of life, there is a general clamour for proof: insistence on certainty for situations characterized by in/determinacy and un/predictability, by latency and potentiality. This demand for 'proof' of that which we cannot see, touch, taste, smell or hear, as I argue in the previous chapter with reference to radioactive pollution, is bound to an exclusively materialist conception of life in which the in/visible and virtual are denied reality status. Steeped in the narrow, materialist conception of reality, we remain impervious to the im/materiality of the contemporary condition.

Yet hazards such as radioactive pollution from nuclear power plants which operate outside the time of human perception are ignored at our peril. As in/visible hazards those products of the industrial way of life pose a threat not merely to some distant future, they already permeate our present. In addition to the loss of an absolute distinction between nature and culture, parts and wholes, local and global phenomena, they negate the neat separation between past, present and future: inclusive of the past, actions now create presents for future generations; they constitute posterity as well as the potential end in the present. The future therefore becomes an integral feature of contemporary existence, a central area of concern. As such, it forms an inescapable subject matter for the social sciences.

However, to take account of the future is to encompass the unknown. This poses intense problems for materialist/empiricist systems of knowledge which are exclusively based on the recorded past, on past-based models of change, and on before-and-after measurements. At the turn of the century, for example, Europeans could not have envisaged the Russian Revolution, let alone Hiroshima or the depletion of the ozone. It was beyond the imagination of ordinary people even to think that a system of air transport would connect the cities of the world, that people could watch in their living-rooms events that are taking place on the other side of the globe, and that astronauts would take photographs of the earth from outer space. Taking account of the future is thus problematic on a number of counts: first, it is troublesome because technological innovations are not predictable on the basis of past knowledge. A second difficulty relates to the scale of the changes and their speed, to the fact that the transformations have taken place not over several generations but during the lifetime of a single one. Additional problems arise from the assumptions underpinning technological design. Let me expand on this last point.

Classical science, as I argue in previous chapters, conceived of machines as isolatable, bounded units and devised them according to their desired functions *without* cognizance of their multiple interrelations and effects. Despite their conception as isolated, bounded inventions, however, these technologies are not abstractable from their environment. Their development and use have consequences that become integrated into the complex web of ecological interconnections which in turn impact on social life.

> Max Weber's concept of 'rationalization' no longer grasps this late modern reality, produced by successful rationalization. *Along with the growing capacity of technological options [Zweckrationality] grows the incalculability of their consequences.* Compared to these global consequences, the hazards of primary industrialization indeed belonged to a different age. The dangers of highly developed nuclear and chemical productive forces abolish the foundations and categories according to which we have thought and acted to this point, such as time and space, work and leisure time,

factory and nation state, indeed even the borders between continents. To put it differently, in the risk society the unknown and unintended consequences come to be the dominant force in history and society. (Beck 1992a: 22)

The difficulties in extending our active concern to an unknown future are thus substantial. The formidability of the task, however, must not detract from the fact that our creations today make us inescapably responsible for their known and unknown effects. This means that taking account of the futures of successors is not just a positive thing to do; rather, it is an ineluctable obligation. To take this responsibility seriously requires a change in the taken-for-granted scientific assumptions I discuss throughout this book. In order fully to comprehend the nature of that necessary change it is useful to briefly refocus on the past and future in the materialist episteme.

Five features of the materialist/empiricist conception of the past and future seem of particular relevance to this discussion: the tendency to privilege the past, the tradition to conceptualize change on a before-and-after basis, the inherent dualisms of that approach, the construction of 'others', and the view of the future as a realm for prediction and control. Let us look at each of these points in turn. First, if one is located in such a materialist epistemology, then the past as that which can be known through its material records is considered more suitable for conceptual appropriation than is the virtual, potential and indeterminate future. Accordingly, knowledge of the past is utilized for the prediction and control of the future. Since, however, true innovations create unknowable futures, they are not predictable on the basis of past knowledge. This means that past experience is incapable of serving as an indicator for effects of scientific developments. Instead, the past can only demonstrate the uncertainty of the future for societies wed to the industrial way of life and for all other societies implicated in the effects of that particular social organization.

Second, a similar difficulty is encountered with the materialist/empiricist approach to change and its attendant measurement. Change is conceptualized as being caused by the past in a sequential and cumulative way and as such it is measured on a before-and-after basis: decide on two cut-off points, compare the difference between those two static states and you have the measurement of change. The conceptualization of change is thus achieved by stabilizing and generalizing into detemporalized and decontextualized form what are ongoing, dynamic, past- and future-inclusive, specific, embodied and embedded relationships and processes. The future is irrelevant to such past-based analyses because the model of change and the measurement are based on a purely quantitative theory of time: neither can encompass the process of creating the unknown, the very essence of innovation.

Third, retrospectively to fix processes and developments into historical categories positions members of those categories simultaneously along dualistic and hierarchical lines: postmodern against and as a development from modern, industrial against and as a development from agrarian, capitalist against and as a development from feudal societies. This is a practice generally discredited by contemporary social theorists – most specifically feminist scholars – and shown to be meaningless when we take account of the complexity of social times. Terms that fix historical periods are not only inherently non-temporal in their approach, they also attract a lot of academic disputes about definitions of the boundaries. Compare discussions about postmodernity with a focus on 'the contemporary', 'the now', or 'the present'. While the concept of postmodernity is inextricably tied to chronological, historical time, terms like 'contemporary', 'now' and 'the present' are mobile, relative and flexible: they wander and develop with us, so to speak, accompanied by their fluid boundaries and horizons. They are not fixed by the conceptual tool into specific historical locations. Rather, their boundaries are job-specific. They move with the present and are defined variably by the task at hand. Such temporally open conceptual tools do not only avoid the danger of losing sight of the subject matter through getting caught up in arguments about definitions, they are also more appropriate for analyses that deal with the interpretation of the past, present and future. They are amenable to analyses that want to convey the multi-layered, complex, ever-shifting phenomena of globalized social processes and their environmental effects.

The fourth aspect of materialist/empiricist approaches to the past and future relates to the tradition of understanding the 'then and there' as other to the 'here and now': the past and future and its inhabitants as 'other', as distinct from us in *our* present in an absolute way. This means that the dualistic approach is continued in relation to the past and future. It is a dichotomy that is not only premised on assumptions about them (then and there) and us (here and now) but also, and equally importantly, it precludes any acknowledgement of past-present-future implications and interpenetrations. It thus inhibits an understanding of selves and societies *being* their pasts and futures, of mutual implication, of coevalness, of unity and relatedness with difference. Finally, the future is conceived as a realm to be conquered and colonized. It is considered to be a calculable realm of potential, a world amenable to prediction and control on the basis of past experiences.

Collectively, these characteristics of the materialist/empiricist approach do not bode well for dealing with contemporary features that are not knowable on the basis of the past, or for grasping a globalized reality where everything is linked to everything else. They mitigate against our ability to get a purchase on situations where actions in one place – the here and now – have effects not just in different places but different historical times. They are unsuitable for encompassing conditions where there is an interpenetration and coexistence of tradition and self-conscious construction, of present in the future and future in the present, and where that which is visible and empirically available for study constitutes only a tiny proportion of the phenomena and processes under investigation.

Nuclear power is the most pertinent example to illustrate the points. With nuclear power the past is no longer a reliable, meaningful guide to the times ahead. Measurements on a before-and-after basis become not just complicated but insufficient, irrelevant even, when the effects may outlast their causes by millennia. Predictability, certainty and proof become misplaced goals when present knowledge about potential aftermaths of contamination through nuclear waste disposal policies, for example, is based on nothing more than guess-work and statistical probability, when the 'safety' of this technology cannot be tested but has to be 'established' on the basis of theory and mathematical calculation. The idea of proof takes on a new meaning when it is dependent not on the verification of observable 'facts' but on confirmation of speculative theories. Furthermore, the life of a product has always been considered in positive terms and did not enter the business calculation as cost. The longevity of nuclear materials has reversed this tradition by upsetting established sequences and time-scales, producing mismatches between the time-scales of invention, productivity and the periods of waste and pollution, between benefits and hazards, between threats and ameliorative action, between contamination and visible effects, between effects and control, between obsolescence and invention. Finally, dichotomization into them and us – then and there, here and now – becomes meaningless when the effects of nuclear power permeate the then and there as well as the here and now, when 'others' dissolve under the invisible, imperceptible force of radiation.

It is not surprising therefore that the social sciences are silent on issues regarding the future. With their assumptions firmly grounded in the natural sciences, and their knowledge fundamentally tied to the past, they cannot take account of a future for which the only certainty is its indeterminacy. As the temporal dimension least amenable to materialist/empiricist analyses, the future clearly falls outside their boundaries of inquiry. Yet when local actions have global effects on contemporaries and their descendants for many generations hence and when policies of 'making the earth inhabitable' (Beck 1992a: 38) have become standard for industrial and industrializing countries alike, then objective descriptions of the present, of a decontextualized Now, are as misplaced as they are impossible. When the future is constituted in and constitutive of the social present it is *de facto* the subject matter of the social sciences.

Thus we can see that tradition fails us when the old bounded categories interpenetrate, when past, present and future, time and space, nature and culture, individual and society, local and global, observer and observed, process and structure, material and immaterial, visible and invisible, abstraction and embeddedness, epistemology and ontology implicate each other, when the One implies the whole and when thinking in terms of cause and effect is no longer sufficient. The reflexive turn which I write about at the beginning of this book thus needs to be extended to those implicit assumptions guiding social science analyses and understanding. For the social sciences to become adequate to their subject matter they need to bring those implicit assumptions to the fore and begin to see relations and connections; they need to grasp their spiralling temporal unfolding, see multiple processes simultaneously, embrace contradictions and paradoxes, the unknowable and unknown. They need to encompass the latent and the invisible, loosening the dependence on an exclusively materialist epistemology. With the loss of clear boundaries, control and certainty, however, social scientists face not just analytical but moral problems; they have to re-address for their discipline questions about the role of values and political engagement. Time, as I show in these chapters, is fundamentally implicated in such a re-vision.

Responsibility in the context of objective science

Focus on the complexity of times provides us with a cluster of reasons for the return of moral issues to the heart of the social sciences: the situated, constitutive self which can no longer hide behind the imperialism of 'objective' knowledge, the dissolution of the category of 'other' in globalized temporalities, collective *Dasein* in the face of electronic and nuclear technologies, the loss of rationalist control and certainty based on knowledge of the past, and, finally, the displacement of a dualistic and materialist epistemology. Such a focus offers a substantive base from which to reconnect with the value debate, brought to prominence in the social sciences by Weber (1904/1969, 1917/1969, 1919/1985) at the beginning of this century. The issues raised in this book form a coherent starting-point from which to advance beyond the terms on which Weber has set out the issues and to enter what Giddens (1991) calls life politics. These politics have been most prominently pioneered by feminists, environmentalists and anti-nuclear campaigners but have so far lacked comprehensive integration into social science theory and practice.

I have agreed with feminist analyses that suggest the quest for the Real to be a desire for mastery in the same way as the reductionist, rationalist imposition of order is an exercise in control and domination. I have demonstrated how the presuppositions of Enlightenment thought and Newtonian science are being undermined by the unintended consequences of the material expressions of those systems of thought. Focus on the complexity of everyday time thus gives us an indication of the pervasiveness, cohesion and power of that tradition as well as its fragility and futility and it offers a substantive base from which to theorize the displacement of the episteme with its premise of a dualistic, external reality and its language of objectivity and control. Moreover, Schutz's work which 'socializes' phenomenology for social science research takes on board not only Husserl's (1928/1964) challenge to the subject–object dualism but also demonstrates the crucial role of the past and future for everyday consciousness (see Chapter 3). Mead's (1932/1980) conjoining of temporality with sociality, meanwhile, correlates with Heidegger's (1927/1980) insistence that beings do not merely exist in time, that they *are* time and that temporality is the ground of their being-in-the-world. Those theorists assault the linear and quantitative time of physics. Their subject is always contextual, always situated. *Dasein* is being-in-the-world, to use Heidegger's terminology, and there is no other kind of existence, no transcendence from which objectivity could be verified.

> If the 'subject' gets conceived ontologically as an existing *Dasein* whose Being is grounded in temporality, then one must say that the world is 'subjective'. But in that case, this 'subjective' world, as one that is temporally transcendent, is 'more Objective' than any possible 'Object'. (Heidegger 1927/1980: 418)

The temporal subject is thus reconceptualized into a fundamentally situated self in which any subjective reality cannot be separated from its social activities and moral/political engagements. Its creative being, in turn, is temporal and time-constituting.

> Twentieth-century phenomenology has [thus] massively revised the modern formulations of time and consciousness inherited largely from the seventeenth century, which formulated time as a categorical imperative

'natural' to human thought and inseparable from the conception of the individual subject, the founding *cogito*, that has developed its powers since then. By focusing on the phenomenal 'event' in which subjectivity and objectivity cannot be distinguished, phenomenology anticipates the always-embedded and in-process postmodern subjectivity. (Ermarth 1992: 8)

With these changes in conceptualization knowledge ceased to be neutral: anthropology and literature emphasize the constitutive and inventive mode. Atkinson (1990) writes about *The Ethnographic Imagination*; Fabian (1983) on *How Anthropology Makes its Object*; Clifford and Marcus (eds.) (1986) on *The Poetics and Politics of Ethnography*. With these changes in the social sciences we see the beginning of not just the constitutive subject but a subject that faces the inevitability of responsibility. As Ermarth (1992: 23) notes, 'once we begin to see our mental manoeuvers as inventions, they become not "neutral" and "natural" ways of behaving but, instead, modes of exercising responsibility and freedom'. Science is still incapable of providing answers to the question 'How shall we live?', to concerns with values, morals and ethical dilemmas; but, in addition, today's science no longer holds the position of provider of Truth. Like all other forms of knowledge it is contextually situated and it faces the uncertainty, indeterminacy and contingency of its own making. It has lost its defining power by which all other knowledge was constructed as inferior and the control through which its hegemony was established, that is to say, the material creations of absolute knowledge, rationality and control transcend the principles upon which they are built: the rational development towards simultaneity and instantaneity, for example, is no longer graspable by traditional rational means, by causal, quantitative, objective analyses. Similarly, the vast expansion of control over nature brought with it an unprecedented loss of control at every level of socio-political action. This is the context of inescapable responsibility.

> To take responsibility is to firmly situate ourselves within contingent and imperfect contexts, to acknowledge differential privileges of race, gender, geographic location and sexual identities and to resist the delusionary and dangerous recurrent hope of redemption to a world not of our own making. (Flax 1992: 460)

Where mastery used to substitute for morality (Giddens 1991: 202), loss of control raises the spectre of values. The question then becomes how we are to move from the traditional mode of social science analysis towards an approach that demands situated engagement, towards accountable knowledge that 'reveals the labour process of its own production' (Stanley and Wise 1993: 201) and, most difficult of all, how we are to take account of posterity. This would involve explicit cognizance of the future, not the prediction of the future based on knowledge of the past but a mindfulness of the future, a regard for the future which takes responsibility for potential outcomes of present actions and incorporates this into present plans and decisions.

This is clearly an impossible task as long as understanding is grounded in Newtonian science and Cartesian philosophy: unknowable futures, the scale and speed of changes, the connectivity and interrelatedness of processes, time-lags and periods of invisibility, all these characteristics of the contemporary global condition elude the Enlightenment vision. The formidability of the task, however, must not detract from the fact that our creations today make us irrevocably responsible for their known and unknown effects. This means that taking account of the futures of successors is not just a laudable aim, it is a moral imperative, not a choice but an inescapable duty. *Where mastery fails morals become an imperative.* If, however, science has no basis upon which to ground values and morals, then science and the materialist episteme have to be extended or displaced and transcended until such questions can be addressed head-on. They have to be surpassed by a system of knowledge and practice that can encompass the im/material and accept the personal as political, ecological and global.

This requires far-reaching changes to the taken-for-granted scientific assumptions I have been discussing throughout this book. First, it necessitates moving our exclusive trust in materiality to include as central the in/visible, im/material, virtual and spiritual. Second, it requires a shift in emphasis from the past to the future and from short- to long-term concerns that extend beyond personal interests and those of our immediate offspring to people and beings unknown. Third, it demands an extension beyond individualist, Eurocentric and humanist concerns to an interest in *all* of humanity, *all* of life and the cosmos, *all* time past and future, a move from exclusive to inclusive being. Fourth, it involves recognition that a present which extends into the long-term past and the even longer-term future is no longer bounded by our individual lifetime, that *Dasein* has ceased to be exclusively individual, that it has become social, public and global. Acknowledgement of the connectivity of Being beyond species boundaries, however, has further consequences: it turns the universe from a community of objects which we can observe and control into a community of subjects of which we are an integral part. It transforms our world into a reality that is fundamentally implicated in all present actions and concerns. It shifts our position from outside observers to participants and it acknowledges that the relation between knower and known is not only interactive but inseparable. It recognizes all entities in a process of multiple, simultaneous shaping, constructing and inventing so that it becomes clear that talk in terms of causes and effects is no longer sufficient but has to be extended by the language of creativity and a focus on the future. Finally, it demonstrates that the principal assumptions of Enlightenment thought are out of sync with some key characteristics of contemporary material existence for which they are employed as conceptual tools. Globalized presents and futures, the construction of impervious posterities, time-spans and time-scales outside the range of human consciousness and perception, the loss of other without the loss of difference, the negation of rationality through the processes of rationalization, the simultaneous increase and loss of mastery, the inescapability of morals, and the rise within the materialist culture of the invisible and immaterial, are all expressions of the inadequacy of nineteenth-century Enlightenment thought for grasping the dynamic complexity of everyday times.

Coda

'When you think a lot about time it goes by that much quicker which means I grow older that much faster.'

(David)

***

'What time is, that is more difficult to say. It is not a person, not a thing, not a vegetable. It's a period and units, the day chopped up into hours, minutes and seconds. But it also divides the past from the future. . . . I think it's an illusion since there isn't anything to be chopped up.'

(Miriam)

***

'Time is about those things that happen to you and around you, those things over which we have no control. People die. Accidents happen. . . . Time has to do with movement. If everything stood still there would be no time, only matter. It's a mystery which we don't think and talk about. . . . Today everything goes by the clock but, if this hadn't been started, we might organize our lives only by the sun or something else. Time then would be something quite different.'

(Tobias)

***

'Time is a scarce resource. I associate it with pressure and with the desire to use it in a meaningful way. . . . For me time is a dimension within which everything moves and happens. In conjunction with space it is a universal framework. . . . I think that the chronic shortage of time is linked to a steady increase of options and growth in the potential for choice and action. . . . The positive evaluation of tempo and speed – the faster the better – which permeates our contemporary life, derives from a purely economic approach to time: the bigger the quantity and the shorter the production time the better for business. This artificial, economic creation of speed as a positive value has been unquestioningly incorporated into our everyday lives.'

(Christoph)

***

'Time enters my life in two significant ways. One has to do with ageing and the life-span and the other with time passing and coping with things to be done in a day. . . . On reflection I relate time to the day and night and the sense of the year. Whatever you do, time passes – goes on outside our control. . . . Night-time seems to be a different sort of time from daytime, even in a physical sort of way.'

(Mary)

***

'A cancer patient can't generalize time any more. Time becomes specific: the idea of mortality, cognizance of existence. . . . Time assumes a different meaning. Time is the passage of phases and interludes until it all stops. . . . Daytime is positive in its distracting quality. Night-time, in contrast, is a reaffirmation of everything that is internalized. It is a period when you surface to encompass yourself and understand yourself. Night-time enforces a one-to-one relation: you and your conscience, your consciousness, your unconscious, your reality. . . . Time for me used to mean action and action is excitement. Today time is awareness, comfortableness, memory.'

(Brian)

***

'I feel squashed by time: time running out and time lasting too long. . . . There is so little time to accomplish things while simultaneously time is dragging on – waiting for death . . . School time is more hectic but it is alive and purposeful. . . . Time to me is about life-span and the ageing of individuals against the background of the history of our world, the universe, eternity.'

(Dominique)

***

'When there is more to do than I can achieve by a given deadline then time enters my life as panic. The older I get the faster time passes. . . . Time to me means seasons; everything is cyclical. My being and death is incidental to it. If the world gets blown up tomorrow there will still be time. Time is perpetual. Everything repeats itself.'

(Marie)

***

'Time changes and it changes reality. The role of time in my life relates to my consciousness and emotional relationship to time as well as to my concern about what to do with it, how to use it. . . . The future *per se* can't give a perspective: only the past gives the future a depth perspective. . . . For me time is a parameter which I associate with both consciousness and structure. The structural dimension in turn is not static but dynamic and it binds all pasts into a coherent whole. . . . Time relates to what I do and what I omit to do, to my values and my moral judgments. I know that all my actions are irreversible: in my actions I turn the total potential into an irreversible finality.'

(Inga)

*****

References

Adam, B. (1988) 'Social Versus Natural Time: A Traditional Distinction Re-examined', pp. 198–226 in M. Young and T. Schuller (eds.), *The Rhythms of Society*, London/New York: Routledge & Kegan Paul.

Adam, B. (1989) 'Feminist Social Theory Needs Time. Reflections on the Relation between Feminist Thought, Social Theory and Time as an Important Parameter in Social Analysis', *Sociological Review*, 37: 458–73.

Adam, B. (1990) *Time and Social Theory*, Cambridge: Polity; Philadelphia: Temple UP.

Adam, B. (1992a) 'Modern Times: The Technology Connection and its Implications for Social Theory', *Time and Society*, 1: 175–92.

Adam, B. (1992b) 'Time, Health Implicated: A Conceptual Critique', pp. 153–64 in R. Frankenberg (ed.), *Time and Health and Medicine*, London: Sage.

Adam, B. (1992c) 'There is More to Time in Education than Calendars and Clocks', pp. 18–34 in M. Morrison (ed.), *Managing Time for Education*, CEDAR Working Paper Series, Coventry: University of Warwick.

Adam, B. (1993a) 'Within and Beyond the Time Economy of Employment Relations', *Social Science Information*, 32: 163–84.

Adam, B. (1993b) 'Time and Environmental Crisis: An Exploration with Special Reference to Pollution', *Innovation in Social Science Research*, 6: 399–414.

Adam, B. (1994a) 'Perceptions of Time', pp. 503–26 in T. Ingold (ed.), *Companion Encyclopedia of Anthropology, Humanity, Culture and Social Life*, London: Routledge.

Adam, B. (1994b) 'Re-Vision: The Centrality of Time for an Ecological Social Science Perspective', in S. Lash, R. Grove-White, and B. Wynn (eds.), *Risk, Environment and Modernity: Towards a New Ecology*, London: Sage, in press.

Adam, B. (1994c) 'Running Out of Time: Environmental Crisis and the Need for Active Engagement', in T. Benton and M. Redclift (eds.), *Social Theory and the Environment*, London: Routledge, in press.

Aguessy, H. (1977) 'Sociological Interpretations of Time and Pathology of Time in Developing Countries', pp. 93–105 in *Time and the Philosophies. At the Crossroads of Cultures*, London: UNESCO.

Albrow, M. (1990) 'Globalization, Knowledge and Society. Introduction', pp. 3–13 in M. Albrow and E. King (eds.), *Globalization, Knowledge and Society*, London: Sage.

Allatt, P. (1992) 'The Dis-ease of Social Change: Time and Labour Markets in the Lives of Young Adults and their Families', pp. 139–53 in R. Frankenberg (ed.), *Time, Health and Medicine*, London: Sage.

Aries, P. (1976) *Western Attitudes toward Death. From the Middle Ages to the present*, transl. P. M. Ranum, London: Marion Boyars.

Aschoff, J. (1983) 'Die innere Uhr des Menschen', pp. 133–44 in A. Peisl and A. Mohler (eds.), *Die Zeit*, Munich: Oldenburg.

Aschoff, J. (ed.) (1965) *Circadian Clocks*, Amsterdam: North Holland Publishing Co.

Aschoff, J. (ed.) (1981) *Biological Rhythms, Handbook of Behavioural Neurobiology*, vol. IV, New York: Plenum Press.

Atkinson, P. (1990) *The Ethnographic Imagination. Textual Constructions of Reality*, London: Routledge.

Balbo, L. and H. Nowotny (eds.) (1986) *Time to Care in Tomorrow's Welfare System*, Vienna: Eurosocial.

Ball, S., R. Hull, M. Skelton and R. Tudor (1984) 'The Tyranny of the "Devil's Mill": Time and Task at School', pp. 41–57 in S. Delamont (ed.), *Readings in Interaction in the Classroom*, London: Methuen.

Barnes, J. A. (1971) 'Time Flies Like an Arrow', *MAN* (NF), 6: 537–52.

BBC Radio 4, (1992) 15 April: 19.00.

BBC TV, (1991) *Soul* Series on Science and God.

Beauvoir, S. de (1968) *The Second Sex*, New York: Random House.

Beck, U. (1992a) *Risk Society. Towards a New Modernity*, transl. M. Ritter, London: Sage.

Beck, U. (1992b) 'From Industrial Society to Risk Society: Questions of Survival, Social Structure and Ecological Enlightenment', *Theory, Culture and Society*, 9: 97–123.

Becker, E. (1973) *The Denial of Death*, New York: Free Press, Macmillan.

Beechey, V. (1986) 'Women's Employment in Contemporary Britain', pp. 77–131 in V. Beechey and E. Whitelegg (eds.), *Women in Britain Today*, Milton Keynes: Open University Press.

Beechey, V. (1987) *Unequal Work*, London: Verso.

Beechey, V. and E. Whitelegg (eds.) (1986) *Women in Britain Today*, Milton Keynes: Open University Press.

Belghazi, T. (1993) *Time and Postmodernism*. Ph.D. Thesis, University of Wales, Cardiff.

Bellaby, P. (1992) 'Broken Rhythms and unmet Deadlines: Workers' and Managers' Time Perspectives', pp. 108–22 in R. Frankenberg (ed.), *Time, Health and Medicine*, London: Sage.

Ben-Baruch, E. (1986–7) 'Conceptions of Time', *National Forum of Educational Administration and Supervision*, 4: 119–27.

Benton, T. (1993) *Natural Relations. Ecology, Animal Rights and Social Justice*, London: Verso.

Bergmann, W. (1992) 'The Problem of Time in Sociology: An Overview of Literature on the State of Theory and Research on the "Sociology of Time", 1900–82', *Time and Society*, 1: 81–135.

Bergson, H. (1910) *Time and Free Will*, London: Swan Sonnenschein.

Bienefeld, M. A. (1972) *Working Hours in British Industry. An Economic History*, London: Weidenfeld and Nicolson.

Black Report (1984) Investigation of the Possible Increased Incidence of Cancer in West Cumbria (Report of the Independent Advisory Group, chairman Sir Douglas Black, DHSS), London: HMSO.

Blandy, A. (1984) 'New Technology and Flexible Patterns of Working Time', *Employment Gazette*, 92: 439–44.

Blyton, P. (1985) *Changes in Working Time: An International Review*, London: Croom Helm.

Blyton, P. (1989) 'Time and Labour Relations', pp. 105–31 in P. Blyton, J. Hassard, S. Hill and K. Starkey (eds.), *Time, Work and Organization*, London: Routledge.

Blyton, P., J. Hassard, S. Hill and K. Starkey (eds.) (1989) *Time, Work and Organization*, London: Routledge.

Bohm, D. (1983) *Wholeness and the Implicate Order*, London: ARK Paperbacks.

Bourdieu, P. (1979) *Algeria 1960*, Cambridge: Cambridge University Press.

Briggs, J. P. and F. D. Peat (1985) *Looking Glass Universe. The Emerging Science of Wholeness*, London: Fontana.

Brodribb, S. (1992) 'The Birth of Time: Generation(s) and Genealogy in Mary O'Brien and Luce Irigaray', *Time and Society*, 1: 257–70.

Brown, F. A. Jr, J. W. Hastings and J. D. Palmer (1970) *The Biological Clock*, New York: Academic.

Brown, L. R. (1991) 'The New World Order', pp. 3–21, in *The State of the World 1991*, London: Earthscan.

Butler, J. and J. W. Scott (eds.) (1992) *Feminists Theorize the Political*, London: Routledge.

Capra, F. (1976) *The Tao of Physics*, London: Fontana.

Carlstein, T., D. Parkes and N. Thrift (eds.) (1978) 3 vols. I. *Making Sense of Time*, II. *Human Activity and Time Geography*, III. *Time and Regional Dynamics*, London: Edward Arnold.

Churchill, R. (1991) 'International Environmental Law and the United Kingdom', *Journal of Law and Society*, Special Issue: Law Polity and the Environment, 18: 155–73.

Clark, P. A. (1982) *A Review of the Theories of Time and Structure for Organizational Sociology*, Birmingham: The University of Aston Management Centre Working Paper.

Clifford, J. and G. E. Marcus (eds.) (1986) *Writing Culture: The Poetics and Politics of Ethnography*, Berkeley: University of California Press.

Cloudsley-Thompson, J. L. (1980) *Biological Clocks. Their Functions in Nature*, London: Weidenfeld and Nicolson.

Cohen, A. P. (1990a) The Future of The Self. Paper presented at the Association of Social Anthropologists, University of Edinburgh, 2–5 April.

Cohen, A. P. (1990b) 'Self-Conscious Anthropology', pp. 221–41 in J. Okley and H. Callaway (eds.), *Anthropology and Autobiography*, London: Routledge.

Collins, E. C. and J. L. Green (1992) 'Metaphors: The Construction of a Perspective', *Theory into Practice*, 29: 71–7.

Conroy, R. and J. M. Mills (1971) *Human Circadian Rhythms*, Baltimore: Williams and Wilkins.

Cotgrove, S. (1982) *Catastrophe or Cornucopia. The Environment, Politics and the Future*, Chichester: John Wiley & Sons.

Cottle, T. J. and S. L. Klineberg (1974) *The Present of Things Future. Explorations of Time in Human Experience*, New York: Free Press, Macmillan.

Cottrell, W. F. (1939) 'Of Time and the Railroader', *American Journal of Sociology*, 4: 190–8.

Das, T. K. (1986) *The Subjective Side of Strategy Marketing: Future Orientations and Perceptions of Executives*, New York: Praeger.

Das, T. K. (1991) 'Time: The Hidden Dimension in Strategic Planning', *Long Range Planning*, 24: 49–57.

Davies, K. (1990) *Women and Time. The Weaving of the Strands of Everyday Life*, Aldershot: Avebury.

Delamont, S. and M. Galton (1986) *Inside the Secondary Classroom*, London: Routledge & Kegan Paul.

Derrida, J. (1982) *Margins of Philosophy*, transl. A. Bass, Brighton: Harvester.

Dirken, J. M. (1966) 'Industrial Shift Work: Decrease in Well-being and Specific Effects', *Ergonomics*, 9/2: 115–24.

Dobson, A. (1990) *Green Political Thought*, London: Unwin Hyman.

Dossey, L. (1982) *Space, Time and Medicine*, London: Shambala.

Dunne, J. S. (1973) *Time and Myth. A Meditation on Storytelling as an Exploration of Life and Death*, London: SCM Press Ltd.

Durkheim, E. (1915) *The Elementary Forms of Religious Life. A Study in Religious Sociology*, transl. J. W. Swain, London: George Allen and Unwin.

Eigen, M. (1983) 'Evolution und Zeitlichkeit', pp. 35–57 in A. Peisl and A. Mohler (eds.), *Die Zeit*, Munich: Oldenburg.

Elchardus, M. (1991) 'Flexible Men and Women. The Changing Temporal Organization of Work and Culture: an Empirical Analysis', *Social Science Information*, 30: 701–26.

Eliade, M. (1954/1989) *Cosmos and History. The Myth of Eternal Return*, transl. W. R. Trask, London: Arkana.

Elias, N. (1992) *Time: An Essay*, transl. E. Jephcott, Oxford: Blackwell.

Ermarth, E. D. (1989) 'The Solitude of Women and Social Time', pp. 37–46 in F. J. Forman and C. Sowton (eds.), *Taking Our Time. Feminist Perspectives on Temporality*, Oxford/New York: Pergamon.

Ermarth, E. D. (1992) *Sequel to History. Postmodernism and the Crisis of Representational Time*, Princeton: Princeton UP.

ETUI (European Trade Union Institute) (1979) *The Reduction of Working Time in Western Europe: Part I*, Brussels: ETUI.

ETUI (European Trade Union Institute) (1984) *Practical Experiences with the Reduction of Working Time in Western Europe*, Brussels: ETUI.

Evans-Pritchard, E. E. (1940/1969) *The Nuer*, Oxford: Oxford UP.

Fabian, J. (1983) *Time and the Other. How Anthropology Makes its Object*, New York: Columbia UP.

Featherstone, M. (1990) 'Global Culture: An Introduction', pp. 1–14 in M. Featherstone (ed.), *Global Culture. Nationalism, Globalization and Modernity*, London: Sage.

Flax, J. (1992) 'The End of Innocence', pp. 445–63 in J. Butler and J. W. Scott (eds.), *Feminists Theorize the Political*, London: Routledge.

Folkard, S. and T. Monk (eds.) (1985) *Hours of Work. Temporal Factors in Work Scheduling*, Chichester: John Wiley & Sons.

Forman, F. J. (1989) 'Feminizing Time: An Introduction', pp. 1–10 in F. J. Forman with C. Sowton (eds.), *Taking Our Time. Feminist Perspectives on Temporality*, Oxford: Pergamon.

Forman, F. J. and C. Sowton (eds.) (1989) *Taking Our Time. Feminist Perspectives on Temporality*, Oxford: Pergamon.

Foucault, M. (1977) *Discipline and Punish. The Birth of the Prison*, London: Allen Lane.

Fox, M. (1989) 'Unreliable Allies: Subjective and Objective Time', pp. 123–35 in 'Childbirth' in F. J. Forman and C. Sowton (eds.), *Taking Our Time. Feminist Perspectives on Temporality*, Oxford: Pergamon.

Frankenberg, R. (1992) 'Your Time or Mine: Temporal Contradictions of Biomedical Practice', pp. 1–30 in R. Frankenberg (ed.), *Time, Health and Medicine*, London: Sage.

Frankenberg, R. (ed.) (1992) *Time, Health and Medicine*, London: Sage.

Fraser, J. T. (1982) *The Genesis and Evolution of Time*, Brighton: Harvester Press.

Fraser, J. T. (1987) *Time, the Familiar Stranger*, Amherst: University of Massachusetts Press.

French, S. (1993) 'The Problem of Time', *AUT Woman*, 29: 3.

Giddens, A. (1976) *New Rules of Sociological Method*, London: Hutchinson.

Giddens, A. (1979) *Central Problems in Social Theory. Action, Structure and Contradiction in Social Analysis*, London: Macmillan.

Giddens, A. (1981) *A Contemporary Critique of Historical Materialism*, vol 1: *Power, Property and the State*, London: Macmillan.

Giddens, A. (1990) *The Consequences of Modernity*, Cambridge: Polity Press.

Giddens, A. (1991) *Modernity and Self-Identity. Self and Society in the Late Modern Age*, Cambridge: Polity Press.

Gioscia, V. (1972) 'On Social Time', pp. 73–141 in H. Yaker, H. Osmond and F. Cheek (eds.), *The Future of Time*, New York: Anchor Books.

Glass, C. (1988) 'Zeit in der Unzeit: Arbeitslosigkeit', pp. 276–92 in R. Zoll (ed.), *Zerstörung und Wiederaneignung von Zeit*, Frankfurt a. M.: Suhrkamp.

Gleick, J. (1987) *Chaos: Making a New Science*, London: Penguin Books.

Graham, H. (1990) *Time, Energy and the Psychology of Healing*, London: Jessica Kingsley.

Grazia, S. de (1974) *Of Time, Work and Leisure*. New York: Anchor Books.

Green, J., C. Dixon, L. Lin, A. Floriani and M. Bradley with S. Paxton, D. Mattern and H. Bergamo (1992) 'Constructing Literacy in Classrooms: Literate Action as Social Accomplishment', pp. 119–49 in H. H. Marshall (ed.), *Redefining Student Learning: Roots of Educational Change*, Norwood, NJ: Ablex.

Griffin, S. (1989) 'Split Culture', pp. 7–17 in J. Plant (ed.), *Healing the Wounds. The Promise of Eco-Feminism*, Philadelphia: New Society Publishers.

Grossin, W. (1969) *Le Travail et le Temps: Horaires-Durées-Rhythmes*, Paris: Editions Anthropos.

Grossin, W. (1974) *Les Temps de la Vie Quotidienne*, Paris: Mouton.

Grossin, W. (1992) 'Technological Evolution, Working Time and Remuneration', *Time and Society*, 2: 159–78.

Habermas, J. (1973) 'A Postscript to Knowledge and Human Interests', *Philosophy of the Social Sciences*, 3: 157–89.

Hägerstrand, T. (1975) *Dynamic Allocation of Urban Space*, Farnborough: Saxon House.

Hägerstrand, T. (1985) 'Time and Culture', pp. 1–15 in G. Kirsch, P. Nijkamp, and K. Zimmermann (eds.), *Time Preferences: An Interdisciplinary Theoretical and Empirical Approach*, Berlin: Wissenschaftszentrum.

Hall, E. T. (1983) *The Dance of Life. The Other Dimension of Time*, London: Doubleday.

Hall, S. (1991) 'The Local and Global: Globalization and Ethnicity', pp. 19–40 in A. King (ed.), *Culture, Globalization and the World-System*, Basingstoke: Macmillan.

Hannerz, U. (1990) 'Cosmopolitans and Locals in the World Culture', pp. 237–52 in M. Featherstone (ed.), *Global Culture. Nationalism, Globalization and Modernity*, London: Sage.

Hannerz, U. (1991) 'Scenarios for Peripheral Cultures', pp. 107–28 in A. King (ed.), *Culture, Globalization and the World-System*, Basingstoke: Macmillan.

Hantrais, L. (1993) 'The Gender of Time in Professional Occupations', *Time and Society*, 2: 139–57.

Harris-Jones, P. (1985) 'From Cultural Translator to Advocate: Changing Circles of Interpretation, pp. 224–48 in R. Paine (ed.), *Advocacy and Anthropology*, St Johns: ISER, Memorial University.

Harris-Jones, P. (1992) 'Sustainable Anthropology: Ecology and Anthropology in the Future', pp. 157–71 in S. Wallmann (ed.), *Contemporary Futures: Perspectives from Social Anthropology*, London: Routledge, ASA Monographs No. 30.

Harvey, D. (1989) *The Condition of Postmodernity*, Oxford: Blackwell.

Hassard, J. (1989a) 'Time and Industrial Society', pp. 13–34 in P. Blyton, J. Hassard, S. Hill and K. Starkey (eds.), *Time, Work and Organization*, London: Routledge.

Hassard, J. (1989b) 'Time and Organization', pp. 79–104 in P. Blyton, J. Hassard, S. Hill and K. Starkey (eds.), *Time, Work and Organization*, London: Routledge.

Harding, S. (1987) 'Introduction: Is There a Feminist Method?', pp. 1–14 in S. Harding (ed.), *Feminism and Methodology*, Bloomington Ind.: Indiana UP.

Hawking, S. W. (1988) *A Brief History of Time. From the Big Bang to Black Holes*. London/New York: Bantam Press.

Hay, C. (1994) 'Environmental Security and State Legitimacy', in M. O'Connor (ed.), *Is Sustainable Capitalism Possible?*, New York: Guildford (in press).

Hay, M. and J. C. Usunier (1993) 'Time and Strategic Action: A Cross-cultural View', *Time and Society*, 2: 313–34.

Hayles, K. (1990) *Chaos Bound. Orderly Disorder in Contemporary Literature and Science*, Ithaca/London: Cornell UP.

Heidegger, M. (1927/1980) *Being and Time*, transl. J. Macquarrie and E. Robinson, Oxford: Blackwell.

Heidegger, M. (1969/1972) *On Time and Being*, transl. J. Stambaugh, New York: Harper and Row.

Hekman, S. J. (1990) *Gender and Knowledge. Elements of a Postmodern Feminism*, Cambridge: Polity.

Held, M. and K-H. Geissler (eds.) (1993) *Ökologie der Zeit. Vom Finden der rechten Zeitmasse*, Stuttgart: Universitas, Hirzel.

Helm, D. and D. Pearce (1991) 'Economic Policy Towards the Environment, An Overview', pp. 1–24 in D. Helm (ed.), *Economic Policy Towards the Environment*, Oxford: Blackwell.

Helm, D. (ed.) (1991) *Economic Policy Towards the Environment*, Oxford: Blackwell.

Helman, C. (1992) 'Heart Disease and the Cultural Construction of Time', pp. 31–55 in R. Frankenberg (ed.), *Time, Health and Medicine*, London: Sage.

Henderson, J. (1989) *The Globalization of High Technology Production*. London/New York: Routledge.

Hill, S. (1989) 'Time and Work: an Economic Analysis', pp. 57–78 in P. Blyton, J. Hassard, S. Hill and K. Starkey (eds.), *Time, Work and Organization*, London: Routledge.

Ho, M.-W. (1989) 'Reanimating Nature: the Integration of Science with Human Experience', *Beshara*, 8: 16–25.

Hohn, H.-W. (1984) *Die Zerstörung der Zeit. Wie aus einem göttlichen Gut eine Handelsware wurde*, Frankfurt a. M.: Fischer Alternativ.

Holiday, F. G. T. (1992) 'The Dumping of Radioactive Waste in the Deep Ocean: Scientific Advice and Ideological Persuasion', pp. 51–65 in D. E. Cooper and J. A. Palmer (eds.), *The Environment in Question. Ethics and Global Issues*, London: Routledge.

Husserl, E. (1928/1964) *The Phenomenology of Internal Time Consciousness*, M. Heidegger (ed.), transl. J. S. Churchill, The Hague: Martinus Nijhoff.

Independent (1993) 'Sellafield Families Lose Cancer Damages Fight', 9 October: 5.

Ingold, T. (1986) *Evolution and Social Life*, Cambridge: Cambridge UP.

Ingold, T. (1993) 'The Temporality of Landscape', *World Archeology*, 25: 152–74.

Inhetveen, H. and M. Blasche (1983) *Frauen in der kleinbürgerlichen Landwirtschaft*, Opladen: Westdeutscher Verlag.

Inhetveen, H. (1988) 'Schöne Zeiten, schlimme Zeiten – Zeiterfahrungen von Bäuerinnen', pp. 193–217 in R. Zoll (ed.), *Zerstörung und Wiederaneignung von Zeit*, Frankfurt a. M.: Suhrkamp.

Inhetveen, H. (1993) 'Die Zeit der Bäuerin und die "Reagrarisierung" des Bewusstseins'. Paper presented to the Evangelische Akademie Tutzing, conference on *Ökologie der Zeit*, May 1993.

Inhetveen, H. (1994) 'The Times of Farming Women', *Time and Society*, 3: 259–76.

Irigaray, L. (1983) 'L'Oubli de l'air, chez Martin Heidegger', Paris: Les Editions de Minuit.

Irigaray, L. (1989) *Le Temps de la Différence. Pour une Révolution Pacifique*, Paris: Librairie Générale Française.

Jahoda, M., P. F. Lasarsfeld and H. Zeisl (1933/1972) *Marienthal: the Sociology of an Unemployed Community*, London: Tavistock.

Jones, R. S. (1983) *Physics as Metaphor*, London: Abacus.

Kant, I. (1781/1966) *The Critique of Pure Reason*, transl. F. M. Müller, New York: Doubleday Anchor.

Keenoy, T. (1985) *Invitation to Industrial Relations*, Oxford: Blackwell.

Keohane, R. O. and J. S. Jr. Nye (eds.) (1971) *Transnational Relations and World Politics*, Cambridge, Mass.: Harvard UP.

Kern, S. (1983) *The Culture of Time and Space 1880–1919*, London: Weidenfeld and Nicolson.

King, Y. (1989) 'The Ecology of Feminism and the Feminism of Ecology', pp. 18–28 in J. Plant (ed.), *Healing the Wounds. The Promise of Eco-Feminism*, Philadelphia: New Society Publishers.

Kinget, G. M. (1975) *On Being Human. A Systematic View*, New York: Harcourt Brace Jovanovich.

Kitzinger, S. (1993) *Homebirth and Other Alternatives to Hospital*, London: Dorling Kindersley.

Kluckhohn, F. R. and F. L. Strodtbeck (1961) *Variations in Value Orientations*, New York: Harper and Row.

Kristeva, J. (1981) 'Women's Time', transl. A. Jardine and H. Blake, *Signs*, 7: 5–35.

Krockow, C. von (1989) 'Wie uns die Stunde schlägt', pp. 79–90 in R. Wendorff (ed.), *Im Netz der Zeit*, Stuttgart: Universitas, Hirzel.

Lakoff, G. and M. Johnson (1980) *Metaphors We Live By*, Chicago: Chicago UP.

Landes, D. S. (1983) *Revolution in Time. Clocks and the Making of the Modern World*, Cambridge, Mass.: Harvard UP.

Laslett, P. (1989) *A Fresh Map of Life: the Emergence of the Third Age*. Cambridge: Cambridge UP.

Lauer, R. H. (1981) *Temporal Man. The Meaning and Uses of Social Time*, New York: Praeger.

Leccardi C. and M. Rampazi (1993) 'Past and Future in Young Women's Experience of Time', *Time and Society*, 2: 353–80.

Lee, T. and Piachaud, D. (1992) 'The Time-Consequences of Social Services', *Time and Society*, 1: 65–80.

LeFeuvre, N. (1994) 'Leisure, Work and Gender: a Sociological Study of Women's Time in France', *Time and Society* 3: 151–78.

LeGoff, J. (1980) *Time, Work and Culture in the Middle Ages*, Chicago: Chicago UP.

Lévi-Strauss, C. (1963/1972) *Structural Anthropology*, Harmondsworth: Penguin.

Lively, P. (1991) *City of the Mind*, London: André Deutsch.

Luce, G. G. (1973) *Body Time. The Natural Rhythms of the Body*, St Albans: Paladin.

Luhmann, N. (1982) 'World-Time and System History', pp. 289–324 in *The Differentiation of Society*, New York: Columbia UP.

MacDonald, M. (1980) 'Sociocultural Reproduction and Women's Education, pp. 13–25 in R. Deem (ed.), *Schooling for Women's Work*, London: Routledge & Kegan Paul.

Macgill, S. M. (1987) *The Politics of Anxiety. Sellafield's Cancer-link Controversy*, London: Pion.

Mackie, F. (1985) *The Status of Everyday Life. A Sociological Excavation of the Prevailing Framework of Perception*, London: Routledge & Kegan Paul.

Mandelbrot, B. B. (1983) *The Fractal Geometry of Nature*, New York: W. H. Freeman.

Marcus, G. E. and M. M. J. Fischer (1986) *Anthropology as Cultural Critique: An Experimental Moment in the Human Sciences*, Chicago: Chicago UP.

Marshack, A. (1972) *The Roots of Civilization*, New York: McGraw Hill.

Marx, K. (1857/1973) *Grundrisse*, Harmondsworth: Penguin.

Marx, K. (1867/1976) *Capital*, vol. I. Harmondsworth: Penguin.

Maser, C. (1991) 'Adaptable Landscapes are the Key to Sustainable Forests', *Journal of Sustainable Forestry*, 1: 47–59.

May, J. (1989) *The Greenpeace Book of the Nuclear Age. The Hidden History. The Human Cost*, London: Victor Gollancz.

Mbiti, J. S. (1969/1985) *African Religions and Philosophy*, London: Heinemann.

McCann, J. (1970) *The Rule of Saint Benedict*, London: Steed and Ward.

McElwain, T. (1988) 'Seneca Iroquois Concepts of Time', *Cosmos* 4. *Amerindian Cosmology*, Edinburgh: Traditional Cosmology Society.

McGrath, J. E. and N. L. Rotchford (1983) 'Time and Behaviour in Organizations', *Research in Organizational Behaviour*, 5: 57–101.

McLuhan, M. (1964/1973) *Understanding Media*, London: Routledge & Kegan Paul.

Mead, G. H. (1932/1980) *The Philosophy of the Present*, A. E. Murphy (ed.), Preface John Dewey, Chicago: Chicago UP.

Melbin, M. (1987) *Night as Frontier. Colonizing the World after Dark*, New York: Free Press, Macmillan.

Middleton, S. (1987) 'The Sociology of Women's Education as a Field of Academic Study', pp. 74–91 in M. Arnot and G. Weiner (eds.), *Gender and the Politics of Schooling*, London: Hutchinson.

Midgley, M. (1979) *Beast and Man. The Roots of Human Nature*, London: Methuen.

Milton, K. (1991) 'Interpreting Environmental Policy: A Social Scientific

Approach', *Journal of Law and Society*, Special Issue: Law Polity and the Environment, 18: 4–18.

Mitford, J. (1963) *The American Way of Death*, New York: Fawcett.

Moore, W. E. (1963) *Man, Time and Society*, New York: John Wiley & Sons.

Morin, E. (1974) 'Complexity', *International Social Science Journal*, XXVI.4: 555–82.

Morrison, M. (ed.) (1992) *Managing Time for Education*, CEDAR Working Paper Series, Coventry: University of Warwick.

Müller-Wichmann, C. (1991) 'Der Streit um die Zeit: Konflikte um Arbeit und Leben', *Zeittheorie, Zeitdiagnose*, 2: 2–9.

Mumford, L. (1934/1955) 'The Monastery and the Clock', pp. 3–10 in *The Human Prospect*, Boston: Beacon Press.

Mumford, L. (1973) *Interpretations and Forecasts*, London: Secker and Warburg.

Neumann, E. (1988) 'Arbeitslos – Zeitlos', pp. 267–92 in R. Zoll (ed.), *Zerstörung und Wiederaneignung von Zeit*, Frankfurt a. M.: Suhrkamp.

Newby, H. (1991) 'One World Two Cultures: Sociology and the Environment', *Network*, 50: 1–8.

Nguyen, D. T. (1992) 'The Spatialization of Metric Time: The Conquest of Land and Labour in Europe and the United States', *Time and Society*, 1: 29–50.

Nicholson, L. J. (1990) 'Introduction', pp. 1–18 in *Feminism/Postmodernism*, London/New York: Routledge.

Nicholson, L. J. (ed.) (1990) *Feminism/Postmodernism*, London/New York: Routledge.

Nowotny, H. (1985) 'From the Future to the Extended Present – Time in Social Systems', pp. 1–21 in G. Kirsch, P. Nijkamp and K. Zimmermann (eds.), *Time Preference: An Interdisciplinary Theoretical and Empirical Approach*, Berlin: Wissenschaftszentrum.

Nowotny, H. (1986/1989) 'The Public and Private Uses of Time', pp. 29–36 in *In Search of Usable Knowledge*, Frankfurt a. M.: Campus Westview. First published (1986) in L. Balbo, and H. Nowotny, (eds.), *Time to Care in Tomorrow's Welfare System*, Vienna: Eurosocial.

Nowotny, H. (1989) *Eigenzeit*, Frankfurt a. M.: Suhrkamp; transl. (1994) *Time*, Cambridge: Polity.

Nowotny, H. (1992) 'Time and Social Theory: Towards a Social Theory of Time', *Time and Society*, 1: 421–54.

O'Brien, M. (1981) *The Politics of Reproduction*, London: Routledge & Kegan Paul.

O'Brien, M. (1989a) 'Periods', pp. 11–19 in F. J. Forman and C. Sowton (eds.), *Taking Our Time. Feminist Perspectives on Temporality*, Oxford: Pergamon.

O'Brien, M. (1989b) 'Resolute Anticipation: Heidegger and Beckett', pp. 83–101 in *Reproducing the World: Essays in Feminist Theory*, Boulder: Westview Press.

O'Malley, M. (1990) *Keeping Watch: A History of American Time*, New York: Viking/Penguin.

O'Malley, M. (1992a) 'Standard Time, Narrative Film and American Progressive Politics', *Time and Society*, 1: 193–206.

O'Malley, M. (1992b) 'Time, Work and Task Orientation: A Critique of American Histiography, *Time and Society*, 1: 341–58.

Ortner, S. B. (1984) 'Theory in Anthropology Since the Sixties', *Comparative Studies in Society and History*, 1: 126–66.

Palmer, J. A. (1992) 'Towards a Sustainable Future', pp. 181–6 in D. E. Cooper and J. A. Palmer (eds.), *The Environment in Question. Ethics and Global Issues*, London: Routledge.

Pasero, U. (1994) 'Social Time Patterns, Contingency and Gender Relations', *Time and Society*, 3: 179–92.

Pearce, D., A. Markandya and E. B. Barbier (1989) *Blueprint for a Green Economy*, London: Earthscan.

Pfeufer Kahn R. (1989) 'Women and Time in Childbirth and During Lactation', pp. 20–36 in F. J. Forman and C. Sowton (eds.), *Taking Our Time. Feminist Perspectives on Temporality*, Oxford: Pergamon.

Pirsig, R. (1979) *Zen and the Art of Motorcycle Maintenance*, London: Corgi.

Pizzini, F. (1992) 'Women's Time, Institutional Time', pp. 68–74 in R. Frankenberg (ed.), *Time, Health and Medicine*, London: Sage.

Pollard, S. (1963) 'Factory Discipline in the Industrial Revolution', *Economic Historical Review*, 16: 254–71.

Porritt, J. (1984) *Seeing Green. The Politics of Ecology Explained*, Oxford: Blackwell.

Poster, M. (1990) *The Mode of Information. Poststructuralism and Social Context*, Cambridge: Polity.

Prigogine, I. (1980) *From Being to Becoming. Time and Complexity in the Physical Sciences*, San Francisco: W. H. Freemann.

Prigogine, I. and I. Stengers (1984) *Order Out of Chaos: Man's New Dialogue with Nature*, London: Heinemann.

Pugh, D. (1989) 'Getting into Deep Water', *Guardian*, 10 November: 29.

Redclift, M. (1987/1991) *Sustainable Development. Exploring the Contradictions*, London: Routledge.

Reinberg, A. and J. Ghata (1965) *Biological Rhythms*, New York: Walker and Son.

Reinberg A., P. Ardlouer, J. De Prims, W. Malbeq, N. Vieux and P. Bourdelau (1984) 'Desynchronization of the Oral Temperature, Circadian Rhythm and Intolerance to Shift Work', *Nature*, 308(5956): 272–4.

Renner, M. (1991) 'Assessing the Military's War on the Environment', pp. 132–52 in L. R. Brown (ed.), *The State of the World 1991*, London: Earthscan.

Rifkin, J. (1987) *Time Wars*, New York: Henry Holt.

Rinderspacher, J. P. (1985) *Gesellschaft ohne Zeit. Individuelle Zeitverwendung und soziale Organisation der Arbeit*, Frankfurt a. M.: Campus Verlag.

Rinderspacher, J. P. (1989) 'Mit der Zeit arbeiten. Uber einige grundlegende Zusammenhange von Zeit und Okonomie', pp. 91–104 in R. Wendorff (ed.), *Im Netz der Zeit*, Stuttgart: Universitas, Hirzel.

Robertson, R. (1990) 'Mapping the Global Condition: Globalization as the Central Concept', pp. 15–30 in M. Featherstone (ed.), *Global Culture. Nationalism, Globalization and Modernity*, London: Sage.

Robertson, R. (1991) 'Social Theory, Cultural Relativity and the Problem of Globality', pp. 69–90 in A. King (ed.), *Culture, Globalization and the World-System*, Basingstoke: Macmillan.

Romanyshyn, R. D. (1989) *Technology as Symptom and Dream*, London: Routledge.

Rose, K. J. (1989) *The Body in Time*, New York: John Wiley & Sons.

Rossum, G. D. van (1989) 'Schlaguhr und Zeitorganisation', pp. 49–60 in R. Wendorff (ed.), *Im Netz der Zeit*, Stuttgart: Universitas, Hirzel.

Roszak, T. (1992) 'The Voice of the Earth', *Resurgence*, 150: 4–6.

Roth, J. A. (1976) *Timetables. Structuring the Passage of Time in Hospital Treatment and Other Careers*, Indianapolis: Bobbs-Merrill.

Sachs, W. (1992) 'Development. A Guide to the Ruins', *The New Internationalist*, 223: 4–27.

Schuller, T. (1990) 'It All Depends on the Timing', *Adults Learning*, 2: 51–2.

Schutz, A. (1971) *Collected Papers*. vol. 1, *The Problem of Social Reality*, M. Natanson (ed.), The Hague: Martinus Nijhoff.

Schutz, A. and T. Luckmann, (1973) *The Structures of the Life-World*, transl. R. M. Zaner and H. T. Engelhardt Jr, London: Heinemann.

Schutz, R. (1984) *Ökologische Aspekte einer naturphilosophischen Ethik*. Unpublished ms, Bamberg.

Schwartz, B. (1979) 'Waiting, Exchange and Power: The Distribution of Time in Social Systems', *American Journal of Sociology*, 79: 841–70.

Shallis, M. (1983) *On Time. An Investigation into Scientific Knowledge and Human Experience*, Harmondsworth: Penguin.

Sharp, C. (1981) *The Economics of Time*, Oxford: Martin Robertson.

Sheldrake, R. (1983) *A New Science of Life*, London: Paladin.

Shiva, V. (1989) 'Development, Ecology and Women', pp. 80–90 in J. Plant (ed.), *Healing the Wounds. The Promise of Eco-Feminism*, Philadelphia: New Society Publishers.

Shiva, V. (1992) 'Recovering the Real Meaning of Sustainability', pp. 187–93 in D. E. Cooper and J. A. Palmer (eds.), *The Environment in Question. Ethics and Global Issues*, London: Routledge.

Sklair, L. (1991) *The Sociology of the Global System*, New York/London: Harvester, Wheatsheaf.

Solovyov, L. (1962) 'The Reduction of Employees' Working Hours in the Soviet Union', *International Labour Review*, 86: 31–41.

Sorokin, P. A. and R. K. Merton (1937) 'Social Time: A Methodological and Functional Analysis', *American Journal of Sociology*, 42: 615–29.

Spengler, O. (1918) *Der Untergang des Abendlandes: Umriss einer Morphologie der Weltgeschichte*, Munich: Piper.

Spretnak, C. (1991) *States of Grace. The Recovery of Meaning in the Postmodern Age*, New York: Harper Collins.

Stanley, L. and S. Wise (1983) *Breaking Out*, London: Routledge & Kegan Paul.

Stanley, L. and S. Wise (1993) *Breaking Out Again. Feminist Ontology and Epistemology*, London: Routledge.

Starkey, K. (1988) 'Time and Work Organization: A Theoretical and Empirical

Analysis', pp. 95–117 in M. Young and T. Schuller (eds.), *The Rhythms of Society*, London: Routledge.

Starkey, K. (1989) 'Time and Work: a Psychological Perspective', pp. 35–56 in P. Blyton, J. Hassard, S. Hill and K. Starkey (eds.), *Time, Work and Organization*, London: Routledge.

Stegmüller, W. (1969) *Hauptströmungen der Gegenwart*, Stuttgart: Alfred Körner.

Thomas, H. (1992) 'Time and the Cervix', pp. 56–67 in R. Frankenberg (ed.), *Time, Health and Medicine*, London: Sage.

Thompson, E. P. (1967) 'Time, Work-discipline, and Industrial Capitalism', *Past and Present*, 36: 52–97.

Thrift, N. (1981) 'Owners' Time and Own Time: The Making of a Capitalist Time Consciousness, 1300–1800', pp. 56–84 in A. R. Pred (ed.), *Space and Time in Geography*, Lund: Gleerup.

Thrift, N. (1988) 'Vicos Voco. Ringing the Changes in Historical Geography of Time Consciousness', pp. 53–94 in M. Young and T. Schuller (eds.), *The Rhythms of Society*, London: Routledge & Kegan Paul.

Time and Society (1992–)

Wajcman, J. (1991) *Feminism Confronts Technology*, Cambridge: Polity.

Wallerstein, I. (1974) *The Modern World-System*, New York: Academic Press.

Wallerstein, I. (1990) 'Culture as the Ideological Battleground of the Modern World-System', pp. 31–56 in M. Featherstone (ed.), *Global Culture. Nationalism, Globalization and Modernity*, London: Sage.

Wallerstein, I. (1991) 'The National and the Universal: Can there be such a Thing as World Culture?', pp. 91–106 in A. King (ed.), *Culture, Globalization and the World-System*, Basingstoke: Macmillan.

Warren, L. (1991) 'Conservation – a Secondary Environmental Consideration', *Journal of Law and Society*, Special Issue: Law Polity and the Environment, 18: 64–81.

Weade, G. (1992) 'Locating Learning in the Times and Spaces of Teaching', pp. 87–118 in H. Marshall (ed.), *Redefining Student Learning: Roots of Educational Change*, Norwood, NJ: Ablex.

Weber, M. (1904–5/1989) *The Protestant Ethic and the Spirit of Capitalism*, London: Unwin Hyman.

Weber, M. (1904/1969) ' "Objectivity" in Social Science and Social Policy', pp. 50–112 in E. A. Shils (ed. and transl.), *The Methodology of the Social Sciences. Max Weber*, New York: Free Press, Macmillan.

Weber, M. (1917/1969) 'The Meaning of "Ethical Neutrality" in Sociology and Economics', pp. 1–49 in E. A. Shils (ed. and transl.), *The Methodology of the Social Sciences. Max Weber*, New York: Free Press, Macmillan.

Weber, M. (1919/1985) 'Science as a Vocation', pp. 129–58 in H. H. Gerth and C. Wright Mills (eds.), *From Max Weber: Essays in Sociology*, London: Routledge & Kegan Paul.

Westergaard, J. and A. Walker, (1989) *After Redundancy: the Experience of Economic Insecurity*, Cambridge: Polity Press.

Whipp, R. (1994) 'A Time to be Concerned: A Position Paper on Time and

Management', *Time and Society*, 3: 99–116.

Whorf, B. L. (1956) *Language, Thought and Reality*, Cambridge, Mass.: MIT Press.

Wood, D. (1989) *The Deconstruction of Time*, Atlantic Highlands, NJ: Humanities.

Wright, L. (1968) *Clockwork Man*, London: Elek.

Wynne, B. and S. Mayer (1993) 'How Science Fails the Environment', *New Scientist*, 5 June: 33.

Yaker, H., H. Osmond and F. Cheek, (eds.) (1972) *The Future of Time*, London: Hogarth Press.

Yearley, S. (1991) *The Green Case. A Sociology of Environmental Issues, Arguments and Politics*, London: Harper Collins.

Young, J. E. (1991) 'Reducing Waste, Saving Materials', pp. 39–56 in L. R. Brown (ed.), *The State of the World 1991*, London: Earthscan.

Young, M. (1988) *The Metronomic Society. Natural Rhythms and Human Timetables*, London: Thames and Hudson.

Young, M. and T. Schuller (1991) *Life after Work: The Arrival of the Ageless Society*, London: Harper Collins.

Zerubavel, E. (1979) *Patterns in Hospital Life*, Chicago: Chicago UP.

Zerubavel, E. (1981) *Hidden Rhythms. Schedules and Calendars in Social Life*, Chicago: Chicago UP.

Zerubavel, E. (1985) *The Seven Day Cycle. The History and Meaning of The Week*, New York: Free Press, Macmillan.

Contemporary key books on time

Adam, B. (1990) *Time and Social Theory*, Cambridge: Polity; Philadelphia: Temple UP.

Blyton, P., J. Hassard, S. Hill and K. Starkey (eds.) (1989) *Time, Work and Organization*, London: Routledge.

Davies, K. (1990) *Women and Time. The Weaving of the Strands of Everyday Life*, Aldershot: Avebury.

Dossey, L. (1982) *Space, Time and Medicine*, London: Shambala.

Dunne, J. S. (1973) *Time and Myth. A Meditation on Storytelling as an Exploration of Life and Death*, London: SCM Press Ltd.

Elias, N. (1992) *Time: An Essay*, transl. E. Jephcott, Oxford: Blackwell.

Ermarth, E. D. (1992) *Sequel to History. Postmodernism and the Crisis of Representational Time*, Princeton: Princeton UP.

Fabian, J. (1983) *Time and the Other. How Anthropology Makes its Object*, New York: Columbia UP.

Forman, F. J. and C. Sowton (eds.) (1989) *Taking Our Time. Feminist Perspectives on Temporality*, Oxford: Pergamon.

Frankenberg, R. (ed.) (1992) *Time, Health and Medicine*, London: Sage.

Fraser, J. T. (1987) *Time, the Familiar Stranger*, Amherst: University of

Massachusetts Press.

Graham, H. (1990) *Time, Energy and the Psychology of Healing*, London: Jessica Kingsley.

Kern, S. (1983) *The Culture of Time and Space 1880–1919*, London: Weidenfeld and Nicolson.

Landes, D. S. (1983) *Revolution in Time. Clocks and the Making of the Modern World*. Cambridge, Mass.: Harvard UP.

LeGoff, J. (1980) *Time, Work and Culture in the Middle Ages*, Chicago: Chicago UP.

Luce, G. G. (1973) *Body Time. The Natural Rhythms of the Body*, St Albans: Paladin.

Mead, G. H. (1932/1980) *The Philosophy of the Present*, A. E. Murphy (ed.), Preface John Dewey, Chicago: Chicago UP.

Moore, W. E. (1963) *Man, Time and Society*, New York: John Wiley & Sons.

Nowotny, H. (1989) *Eigenzeit*. Frankfurt a. M.: Suhrkamp; transl. (1994) *Time*, Cambridge: Polity.

O'Malley, M. (1990) *Keeping Watch: A History of American Time*, New York: Viking/Penguin.

Prigogine, I. and I. Stengers (1984) *Order Out of Chaos: Man's New Dialogue with Nature*, London: Heinemann.

Rifkin, J. (1987) *Time Wars*, New York: Henry Holt.

Shallis, M. (1983) *On Time. An Investigation into Scientific Knowledge and Human Experience*, Harmondsworth: Penguin.

Sharp, C. (1981) *The Economics of Time*, Oxford: Martin Robertson.

Time and Society (1992–)

Wood, D. (1989) *The Deconstruction of Time*. Atlantic Highlands, NJ: Humanities Press.

Young, M. (1988) *The Metronomic Society. Natural Rhythms and Human Time-tables*, London: Thames and Hudson.

Zerubavel, E. (1981) *Hidden Rhythms. Schedules and Calendars in Social Life*, Chicago: Chicago UP.

Index